The Shadows Within:
Houghton Mansion

"Until the Day Break and the Shadows Flee Away"

-Inscription on Houghton Family Monument

The Shadows Within: Houghton Mansion
David A. Raby

First Printing: 2014

ISBN: 978-1495976001

Ordering Information:

Special discounts are available on quantity purchases by corporations, associations, educators, and others. For details, contact the author at the listed email address below.

U.S. trade bookstores and wholesalers: Please contact David Raby at david@theshadowswithin.com

www.TheShadowsWithin.com

Dedication

This book is dedicated to the restless spirits at Houghton Mansion – may they finally find the comfort and eternal peace that they truly deserve! This is for you Mary, Albert and John.

Contents

Introduction

The morning of Saturday, August 1, 1914 was typical of midsummer in New England. That idyllic morning turned tragic in one community nestled in the Berkshires of Massachusetts. The reverberations of this tragic event can still be felt to this very day. While a century has passed, some say the spirits involved have not. If you are lucky enough to step into Houghton Mansion in North Adams, it is almost as if you can step back into time. The impacts of that morning are still evident. The walls do talk at the old and venerable house.

Much is written about the paranormal activity at the mansion – after all, everyone loves a spooky ghost story, but within these walls is a history that begs to be told. There are personal stories that have been lost in the passage of time. This book will inevitably get into those spooky campfire stories that you crave. The focus, however, will be on the people and families who made this mansion into the attraction it is today.

On that fateful day in 1914, who can imagine that a leisurely joy ride could result in tremendous personal loss? Several families experienced the greatest loss a human being can suffer – the untimely death of a loved one. Most tragic of all, a two year old lost his mother; a doctor could not save his young wife. One family lost their youngest daughter – a daughter who sacrificed everything to look after her ailing father. Days later, that father succumbed, having witnessed so much in his final days on Earth. A man, who was so distraught, decided he could not live with the guilt, so he chose to end his own life. All that tragedy took place in a span of ten days. The start of an idyllic midsummer's day turned into a nightmare – a dark and gloomy period of grief that continues to this day.

But the tragedy did not begin, nor did it end there. The Houghtons, a prominent and wealthy family had their share of personal tragedy. Behind the elegant walls and fanciful gardens was continual heartbreak and loss. Even while the mansion was being constructed, tragedy struck. An Irish immigrant lost his life in a freak construction accident. The mansion was the symbol of a family's prominence and wealth, but at night, when the shadows come out, it is their pain and heartbreak that is on display. Some believe that the family was cursed, for tragedy never seemed too far away. While I do not necessarily believe in curses, one thing is evident; the family did see far too much grief.

For the trusted chauffeur, a history that he worked so hard to hide and to run from was exposed for all to see. A family which had a strong core value regarding the importance of loved ones, buried far too many too early. A young family was torn apart in a blink of an eye. Collectively, a community was shocked over the losses that piled up to a man who did more to build it up than perhaps any other. All these stories, all these tragedies, all this raw human emotion has left an imprint on Houghton Mansion and will come to light in this book.

The walls of Houghton Mansion do talk. The spirits have a story to tell – this is their story. The walls are alive; however, these are not just ghosts that go bump in the night. These are spirits. That is, they are like you and me. Like us, they have thought, emotion, hopes and dreams, fears, and believe it or not, they even have the need to socialize. We have a physical vessel that all of our thoughts and emotions are attached to. The walls of Houghton Mansion contain residents whose physical vessels have long since died; however, their thoughts and emotions live on. This book is dedicated to them, may this book give these people an identity – they are not just a carnival attraction. My intent is to tell their story since many of us cannot hear them.

A Brief Word from the Author

Call it a bit of a guilty conscious or part of the maturation process of a paranormal investigator – and more importantly, as a human being – I felt the need to broadcast that the spirits that many people attempt to encounter within Houghton Mansion are people with a rich tapestry of history. These spirits have thought and more importantly, emotions. I know it may sound odd, but I felt a personal connection, a drive, to bring their stories to light.

I had a deeply profound epiphany one day, one that told me that I need to honor the memory of these individuals and to provide their story to you, so they are not considered as just ghosts. I felt the strong urge to honor these lives and to bring a sense of understanding to those that intend to visit. I was always intrigued by history, especially the stories of our fellow human beings. Being a paranormal investigator gives me the rare chance to be able to connect to people who lived before my time. While researching for this book, I was taken on a journey through a family's history and the ramifications of personal tragedy on prominent members of a community.

While looking through the history of the families in this book, I was touched on so many occasions. As I went deeper and deeper on this journey, my instincts grew stronger that this was a project that I had to do. Ironically, the original epiphany occurred when I was at the mansion. I woke up with a thought; I believe that the little seed that blossomed into this effort was planted by a member of the family that I sought to talk to.

I attempted to make this book similar to a handy reference guide than a book that told one story in chronological order. With so many people and so many stories, it could quickly become cumbersome to read. You may even notice that I also treat the old mansion as a living organism as well. That is because the walls are indeed alive – with history. The mansion, to me, is not just an inanimate object – it contains the memories of happy times as well as the imprints of numerous heartbreaking tragedies. Sadly the walls of the mansion contain the energy of its former occupants and I truly believe that each and every one should pass to where they belong.

In this book you will learn about the people who most influenced Houghton Mansion. You will learn about Albert C. Houghton and his family. A deeply devoted family man, his parents, wife, children, grandchildren, nieces and nephews, brothers and sisters shaped him as a man. It is through these stories where a clear picture will emerge as to why he may still be walking the halls of his beloved home. Of course for those that love a great "ghost story", you will learn about the things that went "bump in the night" when we visited the mansion.

When I began this project I had quite the internal struggle as to where I should place the details of the car accident that has provided so much of the interest that is seen today. Part of me wanted to place it first and take the narrative from there. I also wanted to place it at the very end, so that the accident account is not an antiseptic retelling of events. I wanted you to really know these people. Ultimately, you will find that I was pragmatic and placed it first. After you meet all the people involved in the tragedy, I will take you back to that horrible day and discuss what they may have seen, heard or felt from their perspective.

This book took several years of research, and every time I thought I answered one question, four or five more questions appeared. Does this book answer every question? I will be honest and say 'no', as any book to do so would be a tome of one-thousand pages. I will also be honest and say that historical records were also missing on several members, so this story is not as complete as I would have wished.

I also had to remove a great deal of information to keep this book at a reasonable length and price. Since the information was completed, I have included the information on my website. If you wish to browse some of the interesting stories and detailed look into siblings and nieces and nephews, please visit www.theshadowswithin.com.

My hope is that you will gain an appreciation for the families and the struggles they endured. Ultimately, I want people to think of them as people and not ghosts.

This is not only their story, this was their lives.

1. Saturday, August 1, 1914

The mansion's walls and roof could no longer protect them when they pulled away.

This story begins much earlier than this fateful day, but I realize that this day is what drives most of the interest into the families involved. I understand that the lure of a haunted mansion makes it easy to overlook the fact that the particular location has a story to tell. In order to get to know the people involved, we need to examine much more than just this snapshot of time. To most people, the only thing known about the individuals is the largely clinical account of the car accident and suicide. Just like everything else, there is much more than just this snapshot of time. We will first examine that fateful day before you are properly introduced to the people involved.

On a global scale, August 1, 1914 is important in the world's history as that is the day that World War I escalated. Four days earlier, Austria-Hungary declared war on Serbia one month after Archduke Franz Ferdinand was assassinated along with his wife by a Serbian national in Sarajevo. On August 1, Germany led by Kaiser Wilhelm II declared war against Tsar Nicholas II of Russia. Fearful of Germany's intentions, France mobilized their troops as well. The powder keg in Europe exploded resulting in the deaths of more than twenty million people as well as causing the widespread devastation in Europe. This war laid the foundation of future wars and conflicts that killed many more people and caused more strife that lasted throughout the century.

The Pleasure Ride Turned Tragic

While Europe was plunging into a war unlike any seen at that point, half the world away, the day started off as a typical summer day in North Adams. The news of impending war was likely not known as the sun rose over the horizon and bathed the valleys in daylight. The Houghton family awoke excited about the chance to take a daytrip in the family's first automobile, a seven-passenger Pierce Arrow touring car. The automobile was purchased three months prior from the Sisson Automobile Company, which was located in Pittsfield, Massachusetts.

To you and me, driving an automobile is a familiar enterprise, but to John Widders, who was very experienced with horse and carriages, the change was radical. Mr. Widders spent considerable time practicing driving the car to learn how to operate something with horsepower not provided by horses. He was still very uncomfortable driving a car, and he drove a bit cautiously making sure that he did not exceed a speed of over twelve miles per hour. Widders' experience practicing and driving the automobile consisted of approximately two thousand miles.

The plan was to take a scenic drive from North Adams, Massachusetts to Bennington, Vermont. In addition of John Widders, the chauffeur, Albert C. Houghton was to be joined by his youngest daughter, Mary Houghton. Along for the ride were Mary's close friend Sybil Hutton and her husband Dr. Robert Hutton. Sybil was Mary's childhood friend and was also a member of a very prominent North Adams family. Sybil was already in North Adams for several weeks visiting her mother, while her husband Robert, arrived the night before the accident for a long weekend. The bright and peaceful nature of that beautiful summer morning turned rather ugly and traumatic shortly thereafter.

The story of the accident is well-known and has been rehashed many times throughout the years. The following accident account is a compilation of details gathered from the initial news reports which included recounts from the witnesses as well as those involved in the accident and the first responders. As with any chaotic accident scene, some recounts by witnesses and reporting can be a bit contradicting.

Saturday, August 1, 1914 was supposed to be a happy day for the Hutton family. This day represented the first day of their vacation together. Sybil and her two-year old son were in North Adams for several weeks visiting Sybil's mother. Her husband, Robert, could not get away from his medical practice for that length of time, so he planned to reunite with his wife and son for the weekend.

The trip already started out on a bad note for Dr. Robert Hutton. As Dr. Hutton was travelling from New York City to North Adams in the afternoon of July 31, 1914, the train on which he was a passenger was involved in a derailment. While he suffered no injuries, his nerves were shot and he had reservations about going on an automobile ride. Understandably, he would have rather spent some time winding down from his experience. He did decide to go on the trip after all. It is impossible to know if Sybil would have stayed behind to be with her husband if he decided against going on the trip, and it is not possible to discover if Sybil convinced him to go against his own reservations.

If the possibility existed that Sybil would have stayed had Robert needed quiet time to collect himself, I am positive that this decision haunted Robert for the rest of his life. That moment in time would have replayed itself over and over again. It is amazing how one decision; one we sometimes do not think about can have the biggest of implications in our lives. These seemingly mundane life choices are ones that we see as paranormal investigators as the most fateful moments in life. As a paranormal investigator, one should have a renewed zest for life, because we know it can change in an instant. What would happen if Robert relented to that nagging voice in his head? Unfortunately, that was a decision he could not have back.

Sybil and Robert were the proud parents of a two year old son, Robert LeRoy Hutton, Jr. Their son was in the care of Mary Cady, Sybil's aunt, while Sybil and Robert accompanied the Houghtons for the pleasure ride. Unbeknownst to the two year old, when Sybil kissed him goodbye, that would be for the last time his mother would place her lips and arms on him.

While I am certain she was with him in spirit when he was alive, a little boy was unable to see his mother in physical form from that moment on.

Robert and Sybil Hutton made the short walk from the Cady home to the Houghton Mansion. The Pierce Arrow left the mansion at approximately nine in the morning. Albert C. Houghton was seated in the front passenger seat next to John Widders. Within the tonneau, the covered area in which passengers can sit, were Robert and Sybil Hutton with Mary in the rear seat. When the automobile pulled away from the carport, the mansion's walls and roof could no longer protect the passengers on that day.

The covered carport at Houghton Mansion. On August 1, 1914 a Pierce Arrow automobile left Houghton Mansion carrying the driver and four passengers. As they drove from under this covered carport, history was changed forever. This was the spot where their final journey

At approximately 9:30, the car was located on Pownal Center Hill in Pownal, Vermont. As the car ascended the steep roadway, they came across a work crew in the roadway that was repairing the road. There is also some thought that the construction team stirred up a cloud of dust that would have impaired Mr. Widders' visibility as he was steering to avoid the work crew. The car left the pavement and rolled down a steep embankment.

The roadway at the scene of the accident was considered a dangerous stretch of roadway. The accident occurred at the crest of a steep hill in which the roadway was heavily bordered by trees and shrubs, further reducing visibility. The closest homes were approximately one-quarter of a mile away. Many townspeople were expecting an accident of this magnitude sooner rather than later as this section of roadway was called an accident waiting to happen. This is a section of roadway the Houghtons were familiar with as they would regularly travel this stretch of roadway. After the accident Mrs. Houghton admitted that this particular stretch of the route caused a sense of dread in both her and her husband. According to Mrs. Houghton, this stretch of roadway was one of the more dangerous in the region.

On the southern embankment, the edge of the roadway overhung a very steep hill near the Boston & Maine railroad tracks that were located about two hundred feet below the grade of the roadway. The northern embankment was even steeper in grade. Even with these dangerous conditions, there was not much in place in the way of safety. Protecting the car from the embankment was only a flimsy wire fence on the side of the roadway. This wire fence would be no match for any automobile. A railing which was once at the location was taken down as a result of the ongoing construction. I cannot definitively state as fact if that railing would have prevented the car from leaving the roadway. The railing was going to be replaced when the work was finished.

The workers who were repairing the road at this time were employed by Mr. Frank Davis of Pownal, Vermont. The work was authorized by Pownal, Vermont Selectman A.J. Merchant. What is more tragic is that this work was part of a larger scope of work in which the roadway was being made safer. This roadway in this area was being widened, which involved blasting of rock in the area in order to accommodate a larger roadway width. As Widders and the Pierce Arrow came upon the work crew, he came across dump carts that were being loaded with soil where the repairs were ongoing. The roadway team consisted of at least twenty men.

Mr. Widders came upon the work site and turned left to avoid the work team. At the time, he claimed the vehicle was traveling at twelve miles an hour, the speed at which he had comfort. Mr. Widders claimed that the engine began to race before he lost control of the vehicle. Regardless of whether the engine was racing or not, when the car's direction was altered, he turned too close to the edge of the roadway and the car rolled over the embankment.

Some of the workmen who witnessed the accident had a different view of what occurred. Some witnesses stated that the car appeared to gain speed as it approached the work crew. This is alleging that Widders may have mistaken the accelerator for the brake pedal. It was said that Widders health had been in a bit of a decline over the spring and summer of 1914. If any of this is true, his illness could have certainly contributed to the accident. Widders did claim however that the engine raced before he lost control, it is entirely possible that the engine racing could have been the result of stepping on the gas pedal. Some of the workmen who stated the car sped up also stated that the car drove off the road at a greater angle than just slipping down an embankment as Widders stated.

The car rolled over three times while falling approximately fifty feet down the steep embankment where it came to rest upright in a field. Both Mr. Widders and Mr. Houghton were ejected from the car during the first revolution allowing them to escape serious injuries.

Sybil was thrown from the vehicle and crushed when the car rolled over her. Her husband Robert was also thrown from the car. When the automobile came to a rest, Mary remained in the car, the only passenger not thrown from the vehicle.

Robert Hutton, injured with a serious cut on his head, immediately thought of his wife's well-being and looked for her. When he found her, he discovered that she was crushed and her death was considered almost instantaneous, her final breath just mere seconds to a minute after the accident. It was said that her body was moved under the shade of a tree and covered with a robe that was provided by a nearby resident. As can be expected, her husband Dr. Robert Hutton was in shock over the loss of his wife and could not make a statement regarding the accident when investigators arrived. Even though Dr. Hutton needed medical attention, he refused to leave behind the body of his wife and stayed with her until her body was removed from the scene.

Mary, who remained in the automobile, was slumped over in the back seat. Her condition was very grave. Mary slipped in and out of consciousness, but spent most of her remaining time unconscious. When Mary was conscious and able to speak, she spoke of incredible pain regarding her spine. At the time, severe head trauma was also evident. Mary was kept as comfortable as one can under her conditions until doctors came to aid her.

Mr. Widders only suffered cuts and bruises, while Mr. Houghton suffered moderate injuries consisting of a fracture of his right shoulder and arm. Mr. Houghton also experienced shock as a result of the accident and when the seriousness of the accident was evident. While Dr. Hutton was a doctor, I am sure he was unable to help the others seeing that his wife had been killed.

Some of the men from the work team that was located on the roadway immediately went to retrieve help for the accident victims by rushing to the closest telephone. One of the first people on the scene was a reporter for the North Adams Transcript. The reporter's name was O. H. Ramsdell, who also summoned for some medical help to care for the wounded. Within a short duration of time there was a large gathering of curious townsfolk and those who were trying to help and comfort the wounded until medical professionals arrived. At one point it was estimated that there were thirty automobiles with curious onlookers at the scene, no doubt adding chaos to an already chaotic scene of carnage.

Within a half-hour of the accident, eight doctors arrived at the scene. From North Adams, Doctors Stafford, Crawford, M. M. Brown, George Curran and Arthur Curran arrived. On scene from Pownal, Vermont were Doctors Barber and Niles. From Williamstown, Massachusetts, Doctor Hull arrived to help.

At the scene it was obvious that Mary Houghton was most in need of medical treatment and she was the first to be removed from the scene. She was carefully removed from the back seat of the car and transported to North Adams Hospital in the car of attending physician Dr. Stafford. Keep in mind that modern medical practices and modern ambulatory vehicles were absent at this time, so the trip back must have been an ordeal for Mary who was in critical condition. The car carrying Mary arrived at North Adams Hospital at eleven in the morning, approximately ninety minutes after the accident.

Mary's face was described as being crushed, resulting in several severe fractures of her skull. She also suffered severe internal injuries and may have experienced a broken spine. Her condition was listed as grave and she was given a very slim chance at recovery. Doctor Stafford wished to operate on her in an attempt to spare her life, but her condition was such that an immediate operation would have been fatal. The doctor was attempting to stabilize her condition in order for a slight improvement so life-saving surgery can be attempted. Unfortunately Mary's condition never improved, but deteriorated rather quickly.

Mary Houghton passed away from her injuries shortly after three in the afternoon on August 1, 1914 despite several physicians that worked frantically to save her life. Her injuries were far too severe and the medical practices were unable to adequately handle the trauma she suffered. After Mary's death, her body was brought to the Houghton Mansion, her home and the site of her funeral.

Dr. Niles from Pownal, Vermont attended to Albert C. Houghton. Mr. Houghton was not admitted to the hospital, but was taken home to recover from fractures in his right arm and shoulder and to rest from his moderate case of shock.

Sybil's body was transported to North Adams by the automobile of Mrs. E. C. Gale from Williamstown, Massachusetts. Her husband then sought medical treatment for his injuries after accompanying his wife's body. Her remains were immediately placed under the authority of the undertaker Mr. Simmons.

While this was happening, the news of the accident spread quickly and reached North Adams. Immediately after the accident and after medical personnel were summoned, a call was placed to the Houghton residence. At the time Cordelia Houghton was entertaining her brother-in-law Albert W. Willmarth. Cordelia was notified that there was a terrible accident but the information was scarce. Mrs. Houghton was filled with anxiety as she did not know the details of the accident until her husband was brought home hours after the accident. For hours, Cordelia was unaware of the condition of her daughter or husband.

Main Street in North Adams began to fill with residents who heard about the accident. The people that gathered were both filled by sorrow as news began to trickle in and were waiting for more updates. Slowly the devastation became apparent. The first official word was given to Mr. W. R. Pritchard of North Adams Savings Bank. Shortly after that, W.F. Dinneen, the Police Chief of North Adams was notified. Immediately after both were notified, Mr. Pritchard, Chief Dinneen and several other prominent citizens including W.E. Whitaker headed towards the accident scene.

The caravan from North Adams happened to meet up with the automobile of Dr. Niles that was carrying the injured Mr. Houghton. This rendezvous occurred in what was known as Markham's Corner in Williamstown, Massachusetts. Mr. Whittaker left his car behind and hopped in the car that was bringing Mr. Houghton back to North Adams. It was on this ride where Albert Houghton notified him of Sybil's death and Mary's grave injuries. Mr. Houghton also told Mr. Whittaker that the automobile was travelling at a low rate of speed, but he could not explain why the car lost control.

Albert Houghton also notified Mr. Pritchard that Sybil Hutton was killed. Mr. Pritchard noticed a very bad cut on Mr. Houghton's face near his nose in addition to the serious discomfort he experienced with the broken shoulder and arm. As soon as he could Mr. Pritchard called Mary Cady, who was Sybil's aunt to inform her of the news. At this point, Mary asked her neighbors to take care of Sybil's child. When Robert Hutton Jr. was in the care of neighbors, Mary Cady rushed to the Houghton residence and the seriousness of the accident started to come into focus for Cordelia Houghton. At this point Mrs. Houghton and Mary Cady began to contact as many relatives they could reach to inform them of the accident.

Houghton's surviving daughters were not in North Adams at the time of the accident. Florence Houghton Gallup and her husband William A. Gallup were in Boston with her family because the family was planning to sail for Germany on a ship on the Hamburg American Line called America. While in Boston, it was discovered that the ship's departure was cancelled because of the declaration of war. When notified of the departure cancellation, the family began their trip back to North Adams. Because they were in transit, they could not be notified of the accident. They arrived in North Adams at six in the evening on August 1. At this point Mary Houghton had died. The Gallup family was understandably overcome with grief at the news of the accident and the death of Mary.

The Houghton's other surviving daughter, Susan McKean, was living in Lansingburgh, New York at the time. Susan, her husband Andrew and their two daughters were originally planning to visit North Adams in the afternoon of August 1. They were originally going to drive their family car, but when they were notified of the accident, they instead opted to take a train to North Adams. Upon arrival, the severity of the accident and Mary's death also hit Susan and her family hard.

Edward S. Wilkinson Jr., the widower of another daughter to the Houghtons, was also notified of the accident shortly after it happened and immediately left for the scene of the accident so he could bring updates to the worried families. It is not clear if he found any information or the level of detail he reported back to the Houghton or Cady families.

The accident was investigated by the police shortly after the wounded were receiving the care they needed. No charges were filed against John Widders. The State's Attorney for Bennington County, Vermont, arrived on scene around noon and took a look at the accident scene and talked to witnesses. He did not explain his reasons for the visit. Several of the workmen that were on the road at the time of the accident and who witnessed the auto's plunge were also in a state of shock. Some of the workers had no explanation except for human error on the part of John Widders.

When Mr. Widders was questioned by authorities, he told them that the shoulder of the roadway was soft or loose causing the car to skid sideways and down the steep embankment. Mr. Widders also told investigators that he found the car difficult to shift and he felt this was a contributing factor as to why the car veered off the roadway. When investigators looked at the side of the road, they concluded that the embankment did not cave under the weight of the car nor was it soft. They concluded that the tires came too close to the edge of the roadway, and slid off causing it to fall and roll over.

Even with the impending war in Europe, the news of the accident was the talk of the town. The tragedy touched the community immensely. As mentioned earlier, throngs of people visited the scene of the accident that day. By some estimates, over four hundred cars passed the scene to catch a glimpse of the site where the tragedy occurred. The scene became so chaotic that town of Pownal stationed officers to warn visitors of the danger of the roadway. Signs were posted as well cautioning motorists, but that did not stop the flow of visitors.

In the afternoon of August 1, the wrecked Pierce Arrow was removed from its resting place and brought closer to the roadway. The arduous process was undertaken by Homer Harvie of Pownal, Vermont. The car remained near the roadway until the evening of August 2, when the car was loaded onto a truck and removed from the scene. As early as the afternoon of August 1, several officials of Pownal met to discuss the overall safety of the road and the steps necessary to make the roadway safer in an attempt to prevent a similar tragedy.

The Suicide of John Widders

As darkness set, the tremendous sense of guilt consumed John Widders very quickly. Some people have claimed that Mr. Widders lived in

Houghton Mansion, on the third floor where servant's quarters were located. However, the local press at the time contradicts this belief as it was said that Widders lived in the upper floor of the stables. His living arrangements within the stable reportedly included his bedroom, a private bathroom and a parlor.

Since John lived on the Houghton residence property, he may have heard or seen some or all the grieving from the family members who gathered there. He assuredly was seen by family members concerned regarding his welfare. He felt responsible for the accident, and since the accident claimed two young women, his guilt was magnified. As a long-time employee of the Houghton family, Mr. Widders saw both Mary and to an extent, Sybil mature from babies to young women. Their deaths to this very day haunts Widders' soul, his immense grief can still be felt within the walls of the mansion.

Mr. Widders was visibly upset and unstable after the accident, understandable considering the circumstances. His friends who were trying to console him thought it was in his best interests to stay with him through the night in order to prevent him from doing something irrational. Widders could not be consoled and refused to go to bed. His friends sensed he was suicidal. James Hynes, the Houghton family's gardener and Mr. Widders' best friend, spent the entire night and tried anything and everything to settle his friend down. Frank Hacking, who was the chauffeur of Edward Wilkinson, Albert's son-in-law, was another close friend of Mr. Widders and tried to comfort Mr. Widders. Mr. Hacking stayed until one in the morning leaving Mr. Widders and Mr. Hynes together.

Around four in the morning on August 2, John Widders told James Hynes that he wanted to go look after the horses. Hynes thought it was a splendid idea as it may have taken Widders' mind off of the tragedy. John Widders and James Hynes went to the stables together. At one point, Widders tells Hynes that he was going to go outside to have a smoke. Both men walked outside of the stable. As the two men were outside, John told Hynes that he will go inside the stable momentarily and be right back. Hynes failed to follow John Widders as he seemed a bit more at ease.

When Widders failed to return after a period of time, Hynes became concerned and entered the stables to look for him. Unable to find John Widders, Hynes notified the police. Officer Cavannaugh was the first policeman to arrive and within a few minutes Officer Gilman also arrived on scene. When they checked the basement of the stable, they found the body of John Widders with a revolver lying by his side. John Widders shot himself, with the bullet entering his right temple and exiting in front of his left ear. His death was thought to be instantaneous. Hynes told investigators that he did not hear any gunfire.

Two doctors by the names of Crawford and McGrath were soon on the scene, but there was nothing they could do as John Widders was already dead. The Medical Examiner, O.J. Brown was notified and arrived in short order. When it was apparent Widders' death was a suicide, his remains were quickly turned over to Mr. L.A. Simmons, the undertaker.

The suicide of his long-time employee added to the grief of Albert C. Houghton. Mr. Houghton felt so strongly about John Widders that his remains were laid to rest within the Houghton family plot.

Albert Charles Houghton Dies

Mr. Houghton's injuries were described as minor, and his recovery was expected. For the first several days after the accident, physically he was improving. However, the loss of his beloved Mary, the death of Sybil, and the suicide of John Widders weighed greatly on his mind and heart. All of this tragedy was a shock to his already frail body. For years, various illnesses taxed his body, and it was shock that was preventing his improvement. Those that knew him and visited him saw firsthand the shock and agony and how it impacted him. In the afternoon of August 6, 1914, his condition deteriorated so much that the hopes of his recovery was thought to be slim and he was expected to pass away at any given moment.

The last death attributed to the automobile accident occurred on August 11, 1914, when Albert Charles Houghton passed away at three in the afternoon within his residence. It was also at three in the afternoon when his daughter died several days before. Many reported that he died of a broken heart as a result of the accident. This can be partially true as he suffered major illnesses the final years of his life, but fought the battle to live. When his daughter passed away, it seems the fight to live left his spirit. The stress of the accident as well as the injuries he suffered combined with his chronic health issues was simply too much for his frail condition. Although many knew his death was a certainty and only a matter of time, when he slipped out of consciousness for the final time, his doctor tried repeatedly to revive him. Albert C. Houghton was seventy years old at the time of his death.

A Town Pauses and Grieves

To understand what Albert C. Houghton meant to the community and its residents, all one has to do is to know how North Adams reacted on the day of his funeral. If one was to magically transport back in time and appear on a street during this event, it would be evident just how highly Mr. Houghton was regarded by most of the residents. His funeral was held in the afternoon of August 13, 1914 – North Adams as a community paused to reflect and remember.

The day after Mr. Houghton passed away, many of the prominent business leaders and manufacturers gathered together for several hours so they could discuss how the town could honor Houghton's legacy. The Mayor at the time, Wallace E. Brown called a special town council meeting so the community's leaders could also discuss and plan for the funeral.

As a result of the meeting of the merchants, they thought it would be best that they close at two in the afternoon and remain closed for the rest of the day. The banks, as well, were to close at two and remain closed. Arnold Print Works was to suspend operations at noon and remain shuttered until the next day. All other manufacturers were to cease operations for five minutes at four in the afternoon, when Mr. Houghton's casket was scheduled to be interred.

On the day of the funeral, members of the North Adams Merchants Association met at the Wellington Hotel at two in the afternoon and marched as one to the Methodist church where the funeral was held. North Adams City Hall, the public library and many of the stores and businesses were draped in black. The town council also met and walked as a group to the church. From Arnold Print Works, managers, foremen and laborers also walked as one in perhaps the most dramatic of sights.

The private memorial for Mr. Houghton began at 1:30 in the afternoon at the Houghton residence. This service was held for the members of the family only. Reverend James F. Bisgrove, the pastor of the Methodist Church officiated the private rites.

After the private service at his home, Mr. Houghton's body was placed in a hearse and moved from the mansion to the church at around two in the afternoon. Mr. Houghton's coffin was a replica of the coffin that the assassinated President McKinley was buried in. It was fitting as Mr. Houghton met with the sitting President twice. It was solid mahogany and covered by a royal black broadcloth. The handles were made of gun metal. The inside was lined with white silk.

At two in the afternoon the church doors were opened and for approximately thirty minutes his body was viewed by hundreds, if not thousands, that took the opportunity to solemnly walk past and pay their respects. The church filled up quickly. Even though the church had a rather large seating capacity, it was unable to hold all those who wished to pay their respects. A large crowd stood outside of the church while the funeral took place. It was estimated that there were more people outside of the church than inside the church.

The doors to the church were shut at 2:30. At this point, the casket was closed and moved to the front of the church. Many people ignored the family's request that no flowers were to be sent. His casket was surrounded by many beautiful arrangements.

Shortly before three in the afternoon, the members of Mr. Houghton's family as well as his closest friends arrived at the church in a caravan of eleven carriages. They were seated in the front and center reserved section of the church.

The Reverend Bisgrove again officiated the funeral at the Methodist Church. The eulogy was delivered by the Reverend J. Franklin Carter who was the former President of Williams College. The funeral of Mr. Houghton brought North Adams together as one. Wealthy merchants, bankers and manufacturers stood next to laborers. People from all walks of life joined together to memorialize a man born in neighboring Stamford, Vermont but considered North Adams his home. Mr. Houghton was responsible for a large portion of paying jobs and was vital in the establishment of civil services that many of us take for granted in this day and age.

The pallbearers were six men with whom Mr. Houghton was connected to in the day to day operations of Arnold Print Works. These men included: the Manager R. L. Chase, the Assistant Manager Arnold Bossi, Head of the Printing Department Albert H. Haslam, Head of Engraving John Dick, Office Manager Edward M. Meekins, and Willard S. Gallup.

The Eulogy of Albert Charles Houghton

Perhaps to understand the standing of Albert Charles Houghton all one needs is to reflect upon the eulogy delivered at his funeral. The eulogy was delivered by Dr. Franklin Carter who was the former President of Williams College.

> "Life is full of mysteries. When a railroad president is killed in a wreck of one of his trains; when a great inventor is crushed in his own commodious and comfortable car; when a cautious but daring aviator, soaring upward, falls to the earth to rise no more; when, in a twinkling of an eye, a beloved father sees a devoted daughter snatched from his loving care in a vehicle provided for family pleasure, we are startled, asking why such things can be, wondering anew at the tragedies and mysteries of human life. Nature is governed by immutable laws, and in spite of all these tragedies we must know that the laws help rather than hinder, promote rather than retard the development of character and the increase of human happiness. It is a mystery that fire is and burns, that water is and drowns, and steam is and defies, but the laws of all the elements and forces, blinding a crushing as they are at times, make this a stable world and teach us how to plant and reap, to conquer earth and sea and air. God never breaks through the laws to destroy. He has broken them once, and we believe more than once, to save, but He is not the author of confusion, nor, except in a remote sense, of the tragedies of human life.
>
> Rarely in the history of our region has a more appalling tragedy called mourners together than the one that has summoned us. We do not easily, even for a little, escape the bewilderment caused by such a combination of disasters, but I think that we may feel that the final loss, the death of this eminent citizen, was caused, not by blows to the body, but by wounds that pierced his spirit. Once a commanding figure – a king, if we accept Carlyle's definition of a king as one who can, the measure of far-reaching forces, who that

knew him then fails to get, even in this final scene, a glimpse of the greatness of his spirit.

Of late years his superb endurance by physical vitality has been impaired and he has lived quietly in his beautiful home, ministered to by the gracious devotion of his own. His career was a measure, typical of the progress of our country. Born in the year in which, as I well remember, Henry Clay was defeated for the presidency, he had seen and helped the great movements which have made this country the miracle of modern history. Nowhere has the progress been more interesting than right here in the city where he found his opportunity, an opportunity which he nobly improved and for which he repaid the city a hundred fold. There are many present who can well remember the influence, wide and fine, which this man once exerted in all this region and in this commonwealth.

There was no great movement which did not know his touch; there was no worthy human cause around him which did not have his support. In all circles of gracious sympathy his mind and heart were active. The Armenian massacres were not so far away as to fail to move his indignation and deep pity. The poor boys at the Berkshire farm elicited his interest and friendliness. The establishment of the Normal school in your city was catered and mightily helped, really secured by his cooperation. The Young Men's Christian Association and the Salvation Army found in him a friend. The college, the particular glory of Berkshire is what it is today in no small degree because of his loyalty and devotion to its welfare. He scattered his wealth in one continuous fortifying shower over all this region.

I saw much of him in those days of physical and mental vigor. I never went into his presence without feeling the breadth of his vision, the keen penetration of his intellect, and his masterly ability to comprehend and control a situation. I have never left him without a new conviction that he was a man of power, a man of broad sympathies and noble purposes. He had in his very presence the strength and the breezy atmosphere of these Berkshire hills. A native of these hills, he stamped them with his lofty personality and greatly helped to make this city, and to make it the mighty center of educational and commercial activity, of comfortable and beautiful homes which it is come to be.

But the reach of his influence was not confined within the boundaries of these hills. His political sagacity and independence no less than his business success and enterprise were potent factors throughout the commonwealth and even in national relations. He was educated, not in academic halls but, like Lincoln and many a great American statesmen, in the schools of poverty and conflict. Few were better trained. Thousands of college graduates have far less education than he attained.

In these later years of retirement and comparative physical weakness has not been a model of dignity and cheerfulness has he not borne domestic sorrow, disappointment, physical infirmity, and the consignment to inactivity which, to a nature like his must have been oppressive and strangely bitter, with calmness and sweetness? And if the last awful tragedy proved too overwhelming for his physical power, did he not still play the man in its blinding and desolating avalanche? May we not call upon all who knew him, and especially upon those who knew him before the first bitter losses and have known his existence, to stand up and say 'This was a man!'. But he was more. He was THE man of this prosperous city.

When the writer of the future shall record the history of this city, the name of Albert Charles Houghton will be invested with a praise far surpassing that due to any other of its early citizens for fair sightedness in planning, for devotion to the welfare of all in executing, for the discovery of new conditions and wise adaptations to meet them, for the promotion of business prosperity and the advancement of education and for responsiveness to every good appeal. When this city shall have 100,000 inhabitants; when the comfortable houses upon these hills and in the fertile valley shall have been greatly multiplied, when the schools shall have kept pace with this enlarged population, both in number and power, largely owing to his foresight, and the churches shall manifest even more effectively than today the blessed truth that this is a God-fearing city there may or may not be a statue erected to the memory of this great citizen. If there be, upon its face might well be inscribed these words:

'To Albert Charles Houghton, actual founder of the City of North Adams, its first mayor, originator of its excellent charter, ardent promoter of religion, education and enterprise in all this region, large minded and large hearted, friend of humanity, this statue is erected by a grateful posterity.

My friends, these words may not be written in marble as republics are ungrateful, cities sometimes forgetful, but they should be written on the tablets of our hearts as we bury him today, not to be erased while memory lasts.

May I close by repeating a few lines from Coleridge which I was taught to love by a great teacher in the neighborhood college:

> 'It seems a story from a world of spirits,
> When any man obtains that which he merits,
> Or any merits that which he obtains.
> Goodness and greatness are not means but ends.
> Hath he not always treasures, always friends.
> A good, great man? Three treasures – love and light
> And calm thoughts, equable as infant's breath;
> And three fast friends, more sure than day or night.
> Himself his Maker and the angel Death'."[1]

Those were words from a dear friend and a colleague.

Following the church service, the casket bearing the remains of A.C. Houghton was carried down the steps of the church. The crowd of thousands watched the solemn procession. The hearse then carried Mr. Houghton to Southview Cemetery where there was a brief and private internment. Mr. Houghton was buried alongside his beloved daughter Mary, and not far away from his trusted employee, John Widders.

The accident account is well-known and well recited. When reading of such an account it is too easy to lose focus that these were not just names and a familiar accident. Unfortunately as a society we have become sensitized to tragedy, undoubtedly the result of constant barrage of news of death, murder, and war. A story of human tragedy that spawned paranormal activity is looked to as a good campfire tale – but we'll get into the story of those involved with the goal of you having the feeling that you met this family. Hopefully the spirits will find peace knowing that their lives, their stories, are being told.

One often feels deep sadness at the mansion, it can be said that the story of A.C. Houghton could explain some of this feeling. But the collective experience of all those individuals is more than likely the cause for the energy and may be a reason why the spirits have an anchor tying them to this realm.

---

[1] "City's Activities Cease as a Final Tribute to A.C. Houghton's Memory." *The North Adams Transcript* 13 Aug 1914: 1, 5.

2. Albert C. Houghton – His Story

> The legend of Albert Charles Houghton should be as a man, not as a "ghost".

To history books, Albert Charles Houghton is known as the first mayor of North Adams, Massachusetts. He is also known as a highly successful businessman, who helped take Arnold Print Works from a struggling business to an important icon in the economy of the region. In North Adams, he is still regarded as someone who left his mark on the community. To paranormal investigators, he is a target of paranormal communication. It is my hope that through this project, you will get to know him for much more than that.

It is difficult, if not impossible to miss the impacts he has had in North Adams. Even to those that are not at all familiar with him, all one has to do is to look on a map and see a section of North Adams that was once referred to as "Houghtonville". If you find yourself in town, you may end up driving on Houghton Street. Take a drive on historic Church Street and you will find yourself in front of Houghton Mansion.

However, if you search his name online, most accounts you will see gives the familiar story of the car accident and many reports stating emphatically that his spirit is reportedly haunting his former mansion. Many accounts assume that his spirit is restless as the result of the car accident; which I concede can be a contributor to his spirit being restless. But by looking at his entire lifetime, the car accident was merely one more event in a constant lineage of personal tragedy – one which I admit still haunts him to this day, but in my opinion is not the driving factor in preventing him from moving on.

His life, while extremely successful, was full of heartbreak. It is easy to forget that no matter how wealthy or successful one becomes, tragedy is not any easier to handle. My theory is that he is not at peace because of all the heartbreak that he endured in his life. That automobile accident may have been the final straw that has prolonged his journey into his eternal peace and comfort. The results of that accident may have led him down the path of reliving his decisions, his personal hardships, his hopes and dreams. These events may have created an anchor that is holding him back from fulfilling his final fate.

Albert C. Houghton refused to sit still. He always pushed himself to do more, to be better and to help shape the region to his high ideals and visions. He never sat idly by as the world passed him. He had to have a hand in many of the things that occurred around him. This is perhaps the strongest anchor for him which combined with his personal tragedies is the true reason he remains pacing the familiar hallways of his home. To understand why he may be present, it is important to first learn who he was exactly and what shaped him as a human being.

The Early Years

Albert Charles Houghton was born in Stamford, Vermont on April 13, 1844. He was the seventh of nine children born to James and Chloe (Carpenter) Houghton. His siblings, in the order of their birth, were: Julia, Andrew, James, Hudson, Emeline, Annis, Chloe and Harriet. His father was originally a farmer who would later open up a general store in Stamford. James Houghton would then practice law and became a politician who would help shape the political climate in Vermont.

The Houghton family lived in a residence that was once known as the Willmarth House. His father James' life began modestly; there was little private education that was afforded to his own children. There was no vast wealth, no business empire that he was born into. Simply put, this was a family of a small-time farmer who worked tirelessly to support his large family.

The story of Albert Charles Houghton is the quintessential American success story – from humble beginnings to riches. In the land of opportunity, Mr. Houghton saw his chance, took continual risks and was rewarded for his hard work and determination by accumulating wealth and respect. Unfortunately for Albert, with each success, tragedy always seemed to be around the corner.

The son of a farmer built himself into a business and civic leader of a thriving industrial city in the Berkshires. While Albert was young, his father saved enough money from farming to open a general store in Stamford, Vermont. His father's entrepreneurial spirit influenced young Albert as well as his other family members.

Albert attended the local school in the district. He was described as someone who took his study seriously. He decided at an early age that he wanted a professional career versus a laborer or a farmer. Albert sought a future practicing law. As a young boy, Albert had an interest in the arts; however, the economic status prevented him from realizing his dream until he had earned the resources to partake in the finer things. He was later enrolled at the Bernardston Academy in Bernardston, Massachusetts. The family then experienced some financial difficulties due to his father's declining health and the family could no longer afford the tuition.

While the financial situation prevented him from getting the education he desired, the experience provided young Albert an invaluable lesson that stuck with him for the rest of his life. He would later attribute his removal from the academy as a watershed moment in this life. He later told others that he learned that his dreams to accomplish large things would only be possible through two avenues – education or wealth. Since one avenue was removed, he decided the other avenue was the only chance he had. His drive to do great things veered him towards building a vast business empire so that he could accomplish his dreams.

Albert's personality made him a natural to build a business empire and to become a political heavyweight. He dreamed big, but he had the drive to see his dreams come to fruition. He was skilled in negotiations. He paid attention to the finer details, but had the vision to see how every minutia fit into the larger plan. His strong presence made him able to take charge of any situation, but his executive ability was top-notch. He was confident, not only in himself, but confident in his visions. One could be confident, but if you do not have charisma or charm, no one would buy in. Not Albert Houghton, he was known to be charming and highly enthusiastic. Between his charm and his confident nature, he would often make others confident in his own dreams.

One can often be arrogant with a healthy sense of confidence, but Albert did not exude any arrogance. A wealthy tycoon is often vilified as being harsh and uncompassionate, but for Mr. Houghton, that is furthest from the truth. He was described as being incredibly calm, never losing his cool or his temper. He was courteous to those who approached him. If you did not agree with his point, he would listen to you and then discuss the matter with you in his gracious and convincing manner. It was said that after a few moments, one would not only change their tune, but become enthusiastic to Mr. Houghton's point of view.

Because he came from a humble background, he always strove for bigger and better. He worked hard; in fact, he would not take a vacation because there was too much to do. He would not let outside interests cloud up any of his visions. He was described as having no hobby removing himself from his earlier interests in the arts. The only spectator sport that held his interest was business. He did not, however, neglect his family. Family was very important to Albert, and whatever time outside of work and business interests he had was devoted to his family.

While Albert was in school, his older siblings began to start their own families. The month of August, 1849 was a happy time in the Houghton household, at the time Albert was just five years old. On August 15, 1849 Albert's sister Julia Ann Houghton married William S. Brooks. On the very next day, August 16, Albert's brother Andrew Jackson Houghton married Elizabeth Stroud. For the Houghton family, two children were married in two days; unfortunately, the similarities did not end there as both marriages were cut short by tragedy.

Albert Houghton was just six years old when he experienced his first dose of tragedy. Elizabeth Stroud Houghton, the wife of his brother Andrew Jackson Houghton passed away on May 18, 1850. Andrew and Elizabeth were only married for eight months and two days when she died. Elizabeth was two months shy of celebrating her eighteenth birthday. Her widower was only twenty years old when he had to bury his newlywed wife.

A year later, when Albert Houghton was seven years old, he became an uncle for the first time, when Julia and William Brooks welcomed Hattie L. Brooks into the world. Albert would have many nieces and nephews, but this was important to note as this was when Albert

Albert Houghton was just a small boy when he witnessed just how cruel life could be. A teenage bride passes away just eight months into marriage.

became an uncle for the first time. My original draft contained the details of all of Houghton's siblings, nieces and nephews, but the details created a very large book. Information on the extended family is found on the website referenced in the Appendix of this book.

Albert's brother Andrew Jackson Houghton would marry his second wife, Harriet Newell on May 12, 1852. Their marriage occurred just days prior to the second anniversary of the death of Elizabeth Stroud Houghton. Andrew and his new bride would move to Boston where he would operate a bakery and later a very successful brewery.

Another brother, James Royal Houghton married Lestina Maria Hicks on January 1, 1855. Albert was almost eleven years old at this point in time. James Royal Houghton would later play a very prominent role in the development of Albert Houghton's business empire. James' wife Lestina has an interesting connection to Albert's future wife Cordelia. When Lestina's mother passed away, she lived with her uncle, who happened to be Cordelia's grandfather.

Annis Houghton, the sister of Albert, married Calvin Benjamin Cook on July 2, 1857. At the time of their wedding Annis was sixteen-and-a-half years old and Calvin was twenty-three years old. After their wedding, the bride and groom moved to Charlestown, Massachusetts where Calvin got involved in the dairy business. Annis was pregnant by the winter and her first child, Ada, was born on August 18, 1858.

Albert's brother Hudson Houghton married Caroline F. Goodrich on December 7, 1858. After their marriage, Hudson and his newlywed wife moved to Boston where he found employment in the dairy business and later as a baker and as a clerk.

Sadly, on November 12, 1861, Albert lost a niece as Laura A. Cook passed away just past her eighteenth month. Laura developed a medical condition in which she developed inflammation of her bowels. Laura was the second child born to Albert's sister Annis and her husband Calvin Cook. Annis was pregnant with her third child, Warren, when Laura passed away. The young mother had to overcome the tremendous grief of burying a child. For Albert, he lost a niece.

Annis was again pregnant in 1863, this time with her fourth child. Unfortunately when she was pregnant, she developed Typhoid Fever. She had the illness for five weeks and as a result of the illness, she suffered a

In less than eighteen months, Albert Houghton witnessed the burial of both his niece and her mother. Laura Cook's tombtone is on the left and Annis Houghton Cook's tombstone is on the right. A young mother left behind two young children and a grieving husband.

miscarriage that would ultimately claim her life. On April 30, 1863, Annis passed away at the age of just twenty-two years old. At this time Albert Houghton was nineteen years old. Albert Houghton had to deal with the heartbreak over the loss of his sister Annis. Since they were so close in age I would assume that they were extremely close growing up. Annis' widower would move back into the area, and served as a Private with the 8th Regiment in the Vermont Infantry during the United States Civil War.

Albert Houghton's first business experience was within a country store owned by his uncle. Within a short period of time, Albert became the owner and manager shortly after his eighteenth birthday. The business diversified by becoming specialized in buying and selling lumber. This was a profitable market as many of the local mills operated by burning wood. Later on, young Albert became involved in the buying and selling of wood lots, beginning his experience in real estate that would help build his large wealth.

The Start of an Empire and a Family

In 1865, at the age of twenty-one years old, Albert and his older brother James Royal Houghton formed a partnership under the name of A.C. Houghton & Company. In the autumn of 1865, the Houghton Chemical Works was opened in Stamford, Vermont. This operation is significant because it has been described as Stamford's first large-scale industry. Before the opening of the chemical factory, employment in Stamford was based in agriculture, forestry and mining. Although Stamford already left its mark on the history books as reportedly charcoal that was produced in Stamford was used in smelters in North Adams that turned the iron ore from Mount Greylock's mines into the sheets of iron that were used to manufacture the Civil War ship Monitor.

The USS Monitor was the first ironclad warship commissioned by the United States Navy. The ship is famous for its battle versus the confederate ship CSS Virginia which used to be known as the USS Merrimack. This famous battle took place on March 9, 1862 during the Battle of Hampton Roads. This is considered the first naval battle between two armored ships.

The products that were manufactured at Houghton Chemical Works included charcoal, wood alcohol, wood tar and acetate. This business was highly successful for sixty years before it ceased operations on April 3, 1925. The Houghton Chemical Works also had an impact on the business venture Albert C. Houghton focused on later in life. The acids and dye materials that were developed by the Houghton Chemical Works were sold to and used by the developing calico printing industry throughout the country.

While Albert and his brother were beginning their successful business, family tragedy would again hit the Houghton siblings. Julia Ann Houghton Brooks, the oldest sibling, was diagnosed with cancer. She was the mother of a teenage daughter, Hattie L. Brooks and wife of William S. Brooks. The cancer slowly consumed Julia and she passed away on September 1, 1866 at the age of thirty-eight years old. Julia was buried in Houghton Cemetery in Stamford, Vermont. Julia's death occurred a little more than two weeks before Albert and Cordelia were to marry. I cannot help to feel that what should have been Albert's happy day was muted by the death of his sister. Albert Houghton was only twenty-two years old when his sister passed away. Inevitably he witnessed his once vibrant sister become ravaged by cancer – an impact that in no doubt troubled him deeply.

Unfortunately, Julia's family would experience unfathomable losses just a short time later. Her widower passed away from consumption on September 6, 1870 at the age of forty-eight. Julia's only child Hattie would later pass away from consumption at the age of twenty-two on July 8, 1873. Hattie was married for a little over two years when she passed away. Her grieving husband, left for Central America where he was never heard from again. So for Albert Houghton, the loss of his sister Julia was only the beginning, as her entire family died tragically in a very short amount of time.

The death of his oldest sister Julia overshadowed what should have been Albert and Cordelia's happiest day. Even more tragic, in less than seven years, her entire family would join her in burial in Houghton Cemetery.

On September 17, 1866, Albert C. Houghton married Cordelia Jeannette Smith in Stamford. At the time of their wedding, Albert was twenty-two years old and his new bride was twenty-one years old. For both the bride and groom, this was the first and only marriage. Cordelia was also from Stamford, Vermont and we will examine Cordelia in greater detail later in this book. Albert and Cordelia began their life together in Stamford. A little more than one year after their marriage, Albert and Cordelia would welcome their first child Laura into the world on September 30, 1867.

Albert's younger sister Chloe Marie Houghton married John Edwin Warner on November 14, 1867. After their wedding, the bride and groom moved into the home of the groom's parents in Newton, Massachusetts. Warner worked as a grocer in his father's business J. Warner & Son.

In 1868, Albert Houghton entered politics as he was elected to serve in the House of the Vermont State Legislature. At the time he was only twenty-four years old, one of two members of that age. Albert was one of the fifteen Democrats to serve in the House chamber. At this time, the Republicans had a supermajority, with two hundred and twenty-four members in the House chamber.[2]

Albert C. Houghton's business interests regarding the chemical works brought him regularly to North Adams. It was during these regular visits that he saw the potential which would shape not only his future, but the future of North Adams. During his visits to North Adams, Albert pictured moving his family to the community. While Stamford, Vermont was his birth city, Albert saw an untapped potential in North Adams.

In 1868, Albert Houghton purchased Brooklyn – yes Brooklyn. Not the borough of New York City, but the area of North Adams that would later become known as Houghtonville. The area known as Brooklyn was also known as the Fuller Farm. This vast tract of land was originally a very dense forest consisting of oak and pine trees. Around 1833, two local brothers with the last name of Cada purchased this densely wooded land that is situated north of the current River Street. The valuable timber was harvested and when the Cada brothers cleared the land and the property was sold and became the Fuller Farm.

Albert Houghton saw the potential of this property to expand his business dealings, and purchased the entire property. He bankrolled the cost of building the streets and building the residential and store-front properties on the lots and sold them at a considerable profit. He did not sell all of the

---

[2] "Legislative Statistics." *Vermont Daily Transcript* 28 Oct 1868: 2.

lots as he saved a few parcels for his family and at one point had a considerable farm and a number of houses. This real estate venture turned into a large windfall for Albert Houghton. One interesting tidbit of information, Albert had entered horses in local races. One such horse in which Houghton saw success was a horse named General Grant. Houghton shared this interest with his brother-in-law Calvin B. Cook, the widower of Annis Houghton Cook.

The chemicals brought Albert and his brother considerable wealth relatively quickly. In fact, in 1869 it was reported that the Houghton Chemical Works produced over three hundred thousand gallons of acid which sold for twenty-five cents per gallon. This equals approximately seventy-five thousand dollars for that one product[3], which in that era was a substantial amount of money. This was the foundation for the business empire that Albert C. Houghton was able to build.

Harriet Houghton, Albert's youngest sister, married Albert W. Willmarth on May 19, 1869. Albert Willmarth would succeed his father in running the Willmarth Hotel in Stamford, Vermont for a number of years. Willmarth and the Houghton family were quite fond of each other, and in fact, Albert Willmarth was visiting with Cordelia Houghton when the terrible car accident occurred on August 1, 1914. Willmarth also purchased Albert Houghton's share in the Houghton Chemical Works when Albert Houghton decided to leave the venture.

Albert and Cordelia's family grew as on November 3, 1869, Florence Louisa Houghton was born. The Houghton family now consisted of two daughters. Florence was the last child born to Albert and Cordelia while they lived in Stamford, Vermont.

It was also in the autumn of 1869 when Albert Houghton attempted to operate his very first manufacturing business in North Adams. This first firm was established in the Houghtonville property that he still controlled. According to one account, this business was a grain mill called the Parker Mill which was located on Brooklyn Street in North Adams. The business however was not as successful as he would have liked and he was forced to shut down its operations. One of the very few times that Mr. Houghton

---

[3] "New England News Items – Vermont." *The Springfield Daily Republican* 5 Feb 1869: 2.

tasted the bitter pill of defeat in the business world. It would be two years later when manufacturing success found Mr. Houghton in North Adams.

After the failure of the manufacturing endeavor in North Adams, Albert and his family were still living in the household of his father James and mother Chloe in Stamford. At this time, Albert and Cordelia had a growing family with two children, Laura and Florence. Also living in the home was Albert's older sister Emeline, who was thirty-one years old. The household also employed two domestic servants to help with the chores around the home.

Tragedy struck as on October 22, 1870, Albert Houghton's niece Josephine Houghton passed away from pneumonia. The daughter of Hudson and Caroline Houghton was only nine months old when she passed away. Tragically, much darker days were ahead for Albert and Cordelia Houghton.

Sadly on January 13, 1871 Albert and Cordelia experienced the greatest loss a parent can endure. Three-year old Laura passed away from what was termed brain fever. Since the Houghtons knew they were going to settle in North Adams, the body of Laura was buried in Southview Cemetery in North Adams instead of the Houghton Cemetery in Stamford. Obviously this time was of great turmoil for the young family. I would venture to guess that the care of Florence, who was under two years old, required the Houghtons to keep it together during this difficult time.

It was a little more than one month later when Hattie Vining, the daughter of Julia Houghton Brooks, passed away tragically at the age of twenty-two years old. These were dark days indeed for the entire Houghton family.

The Dream and Pull of North Adams

Albert Houghton again sought to expand his business interests and again looked to the south to North Adams. Shortly after the death of their first child, the Houghton family moved into a home on Eagle Street in North Adams.

When Albert saw North Adams, he saw an opportunity for a thriving town to develop into a regional economic powerhouse. He saw the untapped potential and the resources that had all the makings of a successful manufacturing community. He would later come to witness his vision first-hand. He spent considerable time and energy thinking how to develop North Adams. His vision included an economically vibrant community in which its success would trickle into the neighboring communities. Whenever Albert developed his own projects, he would ensure that they meshed with his grand vision for the community.

The rise of Albert C. Houghton and the rise of North Adams were intimately linked. This is not to say that Mr. Houghton was the only manufacturer in town, as others before built a strong foundation. Albert Houghton also looked into North Adam's own government seeing the need for improvement. Mr. Houghton was very interested in modernizing the municipal government. In the course of many years, Albert reached out to many experts in this field including those with experience in developing modern government. Mr. Houghton became very passionate about this subject and often talked about his findings to his business associates, his family and to anyone else with an interest. In fact, if you warped back in time and ran into him on the street, he would likely start a conversation with you about the topic.

In particular, Albert saw the need to modernize the North Adams school system and public utilities as well as to efficiently tap into the vast resources that were underutilized in order to turn North Adams into a destination. Mr. Houghton wanted the growing town to become a thriving city.

As you can imagine, his ideas were not well-received by the established town leaders. To them, Albert C. Houghton was a radical and he was simply dismissed. In fact, to the old-timers, Mr. Houghton's ideas were so radical for them that they considered his ideas as some sort of insurgency movement. Simply put, the old-timers felt threatened by someone with energy and ideas.

But Albert was tenacious, especially when it was regarding something he truly believed in. He had a few political battles with a politician named Mr. E. R. Tinker that were well-known at the time. Albert stood up for what he felt was right and best for the people of North Adams and he would not back down. He helped plant the seed that would see the future growth of North Adams.

Some at that time credit Albert Houghton as a leading role in the incorporation of North Adams as a city. Whether that claim is true or not, what is true is that Albert spent a considerable time and gave freely of his effort to ensure that the North Adams city charter was the best it could be for the times. In fact, the North Adams city charter was considered so exemplary that other communities copied it as their own charter.

When Albert Houghton moved to North Adams, he began accumulating what would become a very large empire in North Adams. In 1871, the Beaver Mills property hit the market. The property included the mill, water privileges, and the ownership of the adjacent stores and tenements. Albert C. Houghton entered a partnership with Cordelia's relative William W. Gallup, Chester Baily and Arthur A. Smith in order to purchase the Beaver Mills property. The firm name was Gallup, Baily & Co. Shortly after this firm purchased the mill and surrounding buildings, Mr. Baily's shares were bought out by the other partners and the firm's name was changed to Gallup, Houghton and Smith.

The Beaver Mills was originally built in 1833 as a three-story stone mill constructed by Lorenzo Rice and George W. Bly doing business as Rice & Bly. They operated twenty looms at the location and they furnished raw material in the shape of linen to calico printing manufacturers. The original mill also consisted of tenements for the workers. In 1845, an additional partner was brought on board by the name of Thomas P. Goodrich. A rather large addition was constructed and the capacity of the mill was now around ninety operating looms. In December of 1850, the mill was completely destroyed by fire. The destruction was above and beyond what the insurance would have covered as such Rice & Bly were unable to rebuild.

In 1851, a new partnership was formed with Rodman H. Wells, Shubael Brayton and Henry Wells. Together they constructed a stone mill at the Beaver site that was four stories tall with the dimensions of 102 by 40 feet. The partnership was known as Wells, Brayton & Co. In 1862, the other two partners sold their interest to Shubael Brayton and S. Johnson with the name changing to S.W. Brayton & Co. In 1870, fire once again struck the site and gutted the interior of the mill. The fire was again financially devastating and Mr. Johnson sold his share to S.W. Brayton. The mill was rebuilt and enlarged immediately after the destructive fire. The rebuilt Beaver mill was placed on the market and Albert C. Houghton with his partners was able to purchase this mill.

Around the same time that Albert Houghton entered the partnership to purchase the Beaver Mill, he entered into another partnership with the Arnold brothers – Harvey, Oliver and John to purchase a mill in North Pownal, Vermont. The Arnold brothers owned and operated the Arnold Print Works in North Adams. While a partner with the Arnold brothers in the North Pownal mill, the business skill of Albert Houghton was quickly apparent to the brothers and is perhaps the cornerstone of what was the next large step in the business holding of Mr. Houghton.

While Albert was expanding his business reach, Cordelia Houghton was pregnant again in the autumn of 1871. The Houghtons' third daughter, Susan, was born on March 26, 1872 in North Adams. Inevitably, the birth of Susan helped the family heal from the loss of Laura, although a parent never gets over the loss of a child.

Arnold Print Works

Before I get into the involvement of Albert C. Houghton within the Arnold Print Works, I will provide a little background of the company that would help define Houghton and would help define a region's economy. As for Houghton's involvement of the print works, I will stick to brief summaries as a detailed look into the print works will easily be its own volume of information, I would rather stick with the personal stories rather than focus too heavily on one aspect of Houghton.

Arnold Print Works was at one time the largest employer in North Adams. Flash forward to the present day, if you happen to find yourself in North Adams, you will still see many large structures that are remnants of the Arnold Print Works empire. While Albert C. Houghton was not involved in the start-up of the company, under his control, the business blossomed to great heights. At its peak, the company was the largest cloth printing and dyeing manufacturer in the entire world.

The Arnold Print Works was a major economic engine in the region. Not only did the mills employ thousands, but the business attracted other mills to the region. With the large number of employees within Houghton's portfolio, other businesses and services popped up to cater to his employees. The workers he attracted into North Adams needed places to live and needed food, clothing and other essentials which increased the demand for more money making enterprises. When talking about the economy of the region, one simply cannot ignore the magnitude of Arnold Print Works on the region.

Arnold Print Works was originally known as Harvey Arnold & Company and was started in 1861 by three brothers: Oliver, Harvey and John Arnold. Over the next several years, the shares of the company were sold from brother to brother. If I were to discuss all the transactions, you would be comfortably asleep. At that time the company was of modest size. There were several cotton mills in the area and the company used location to its advantage.

In December of 1872 a large blaze destroyed the factory which was located on Marshall Street. This blaze put the future of the company in doubt. According to one report, the fire caused one hundred and fifty thousand dollars in damage, while the mill was insured for only one hundred thousand dollars.[4] In stepped Albert Houghton. Mr. Houghton had business dealings with Harvey Arnold & Company and was involved with the Arnold brothers in the ownership of a cotton mill in North Pownal, Vermont.

Reconstruction was started immediately and the mills with updated machinery began operations again in the spring of 1874. With Albert C. Houghton in the fold, the company was eyeing aggressive expansion in its near future. On July 1, 1874 Harvey Arnold sold to Albert C. Houghton one-third of his interest of three-quarters of the firm. The business was still being run under its original name at this point, but Houghton's influence was growing.

As Houghton was heavily involved in the reconstruction of the print works, his mother, Chloe's health began to deteriorate. She was battling a condition called pleurisy, which is the inflammation of the lining that surrounds the lungs. This medical condition makes it very difficult to breathe as a result of sharp pains in the chest. The inflammation can cause a buildup of fluid, which could cause the lungs to collapse. Chloe Houghton passed away on January 22, 1874 at the age of sixty-five years old. She was buried in Houghton Cemetery in Stamford, Vermont.

---

[4] "The Latest News." *The Wheeling Intelligencer* 30 Dec 1872: 1.

After the death of Chloe, her widower and Albert's father James moved into the home of his youngest child Harriet and her husband Albert Willmarth. The family once again experienced tragedy as almost one month to the day that Albert Houghton's mother passed away; he once again experienced the loss of a sibling. On February 21, 1874, Hudson Houghton passed away at the age of thirty-eight as the result of pneumonia. Even more tragic is the fact that Hudson left behind his wife and three children – his children's ages ranged from one to fifteen years old. Hudson's widow Caroline remained in Boston to raise her family.

Less than one month after the death of his mother, Albert's brother Hudson passed away. As was the pattern throughout his life, family tragedy and business troubles seemed to occur simultaneously.

As if the death of his mother and brother were not enough for Albert Houghton to bear, 1874 proved to be a challenging year. In the early morning of April 12, 1874, a destructive fire occurred at the chemical plant in Stamford, Vermont that was owned by Albert and his brother James. The fire began at approximately two in the morning and spread very quickly causing significant damage to the structure. While the building itself was insured, losses piled up as a result of the firm being unable to fulfill outstanding orders. On a local level, the fire at the chemical works caused a temporary loss of employment of those who depended on the plant to earn a living. The chemical works fire occurred shortly after a fire at Hall's Mills, another large employer in the small town. Together the two fires caused an economic hardship in Stamford as many were temporarily unemployed.

While the destructive fire at Houghton Chemical Works forced hardships as the plant needed to be rebuilt, Arnold Print Works financial footing also began to deteriorate. In the last quarter of 1874 and into 1875 the financial situation became very grim. The issue was that the mills were largely purchased and expanded on credit. When there was a lull in the market, the profits began to fall. The creditors shortened their credit and as a result the firm began to really push out product in an attempt to meet their obligations.

During this financially difficult time, Cordelia Houghton became pregnant for the fourth time. I have to assume that with the destruction of the chemical works as well as the dire financial situation of the print works, Albert Houghton had a few concerns about supporting an expanding family. On April 17, 1875, Cordelia gave birth to the family's fourth daughter, Alice. The Houghton family consisted of three living daughters at this time.

In May of 1876, the financial situation at Arnold Print Works reached a point where it failed. At the time of the failure, the mill employed 225 workers.[5] Since Arnold Print Works consumed a great deal of resources, other local mills were impacted heavily by the failure. The five other mills included those operated by Gallup, Houghton & Smith in North Adams (the Beaver), E. H. Arnold & Company's Union Mill in North Adams, the Williamstown Manufacturing Company in Williamstown, the Arnoldville Mill in Adams, and the North Pownal Manufacturing Company in North Pownal, Vermont.

These additional closures resulted in twelve hundred employees without a job.[6] Besides being a major partner in the Beaver Mill, Albert Houghton also had interest in the other mills as well, so the financial implication of this failure was significant. It was assumed that the men involved were going to lose everything as a result of this failure. At the time, the Houghton family's residence was listed under Cordelia Houghton, so losing their home was not a possibility.

On October 10, 1876 the firm was reorganized under the name Arnold Print Works Company with David A. Brayton, from Fall River, as President and Albert C. Houghton as Treasurer. It was in the company's darkest hours that Mr. Brayton saw the brilliance of a young Albert Houghton. In seeing his drive and his ideas, he saw a valuable asset that was underutilized.

During the uncertain future of the Arnold Print Works, the Houghton family continued to expand. In the autumn of 1876 Cordelia became pregnant again, and Mary Cordelia Houghton was born on July 25, 1877 in North Adams. Mary was the fifth and final child, all daughters, born to Albert and Cordelia Houghton.

---

[5] "Heavy Failure at North Adams, Mass." *The Vermont Phoenix* 12 May 1876: 2.
[6] Ibid.

Also in 1877, William Arthur Gallup purchased the interest of his father W.W. Gallup in the firm that purchased the Beaver Mill complex. Shortly thereafter, both Houghton and W.A. Gallup purchased the shares of Mr. Smith and renamed the firm Gallup & Houghton. William Arthur Gallup became an important man in A.C. Houghton's life, both professionally and personally – as Mr. Gallup later married into the Houghton family.

A dozen years earlier, Albert Houghton partnered with his brother to start the Houghton Chemical Works in Stamford. With his hands in many more enterprises, Albert could not devote enough time to the business he helped begin in his native town. In 1877, Albert C. Houghton sold his interest in the chemical works to his brother James Royal Houghton and his brother-in-law Albert Willmarth, who was married to Harriet Houghton. The firm's name was changed to J.R. Houghton & Co at that time. Houghton Chemical Works would later be known as Stamford Chemical Works until its closure in 1925.

On February 12, 1881, Albert Houghton lost his father as James Houghton passed away in the home of his daughter and son-in-law Harriet and Albert Willmarth. Less than six months later, Albert Houghton lost his sister. Harriet Houghton Willmarth, the youngest of the Houghton siblings, when she died on October 8, 1881 at the age of thirty-three, Harriet's death was the result of a stomach hemorrhage. In the span of less than six months, Houghton witnessed the burial of his father and his youngest sibling. This would be the second time that Houghton lost a sibling close to the death of a parent.

Arnold Print Works built the largest dyeing plant in the world at that time, in 1882. This structure was very expensive for the era and was responsible for revolutionizing the cotton dyeing industry. The building was nicknamed "Blue Dip" because it simply dyed fabric blue. The firm also opened an office in Paris to stay ahead in the fashion industry and opened an office in New York City where the designs were drawn.

On April 20, 1882, Albert C. Houghton and William A. Gallup purchased the former Union Woolen Company and sold the building to the town on June 1 that same year so that the existing building could be converted into the Union Street School. The original mill was constructed in 1826 by Salmon Burlingame. In 1869, an economic downturn caused the mill to fail and the structure would never return to the glory of its heyday.

So the question remains, why would Houghton and Gallup purchase a rundown mill and sell it off? Both men were extremely philanthropic and this endeavor could have been meant solely to benefit the community of North Adams with a sorely needed school site. Part of me wonders if the move could have been an opportunity to prevent competition from moving in and restarting an enterprise which could have siphoned from the profits that both men enjoyed. Of course, it could have been a combination of both giving back to the community and preventing competition. The Union Street School was opened in 1883.

On January 6, 1883, Mr. Houghton purchased Brayton's shares of the Arnold Print Works and became President with William Arthur Gallup named as Treasurer. Prior to being President, Albert Houghton was the firm's Treasurer. Under Mr. Houghton's watch, Arnold Print Works exploded into an economic juggernaut. When the company first started, they were auxiliary to the various cotton mills in the area. The position was reversed in that the print works was the primary industry with the cotton mills being an auxiliary industry that fed Arnold Print Works. In fact, by 1900, many of the cotton mills were bought by and operated by Arnold Print Works. These included the mills in Williamstown, Massachusetts and North Pownal, Vermont and the Beaver and Eclipse mill in North Adams.

One interesting aspect of Mr. Houghton's business acumen was the lack of worker animosity that plagued many of his counterparts. Mr. Houghton was seen as a very generous employer that there was unheard of labor peace between a very large manufacturer and its labor force. It was said that while under his control there were very few strikes at Arnold Print Works and that his company paid the highest wages of any business in his industry. While this is true, it is also true that Arnold Print Works in an attempt to keep costs down would hire child labor as was the practice in many industries at the time.

Nowadays when one thinks about a business magnate, you think of a miserly type whose interest is their pocket and no one else's. What type of businessman was Albert C. Houghton? His companies were highly regarded for their treatment of their employees. The wages were higher than companies in the same industry. With Mr. Gallup, Mr. Houghton encouraged, if not demanded, that the environment was one where faithfulness and ability were rewarded through raises and promotions.

Because of his treatment of workers, tenures were often long and employees were generally satisfied. Albert C. Houghton found out that happy employees were productive employees.

The Houghton family moved out of the Eagle Street home and moved into a residence at 31 Summer Street. Summer Street at the time was considered the best location in North Adams. The neighbors of the Houghton family included W. W. Freeman, who owned the Freeman Print Works, later known as the Windsor Print Works. Another neighbor was Edwin Barnard who partnered with William Arthur Gallup and purchased a clothing store that was located in the Wilson Hotel building in North Adams. Gallup will appear as a central figure in this history throughout this book and his life will be explored later in this book.

Albert's brother-in-law, and husband to Chloe, John Edwin Warner passed away on June 29, 1889 at just forty four years old. Albert's sister was a widow at forty-three years old. Chloe would remain in the household of her husband's parents. When John Edwin Warner Sr. died two months later, the two women in the household became widows in a short amount of time.

On May 28, 1890 Massachusetts's Governor Brackett nominated Albert Houghton as World's Fair Commissioner for Massachusetts for the 1893 World's Fair that was held in Chicago, Illinois. The nominations were sent to the President for action. While he was nominated to be a Commissioner, ultimately he did not serve the role. This is speculative, but an economic slowdown which peaked in 1893 might have made Houghton prioritize saving his businesses versus serving as a World Fair Commissioner.

Albert Houghton was not directly involved in the startup of the North Adams Regional Hospital, but Houghton and his family and close associates were instrumental in the fledgling institution thriving and being able to survive a rough patch so that it could serve the community. The idea of the hospital was born as a result of a terrible accident on October 21, 1882, in which thirty-five workmen were killed or suffered severe injuries as a result of a freak accident in a freight yard that was previously used during the construction of the Hoosac Tunnel. Without a sufficient medical institution in place, the scene was highly chaotic and some of the lives lost could have been saved.

As a result of the accident, in fact on the very same day, two men, W.L. Brown and W.S. Johnson started and circulated a subscription-based publication with all the proceeds being used for the construction of a hospital in North Adams. This newspaper raised the majority of the funding needed to construct the hospital with other funding coming from special fundraisers and loans. The hospital opened on March 2, 1885. When the hospital opened, nurses were recruited from New York since there were many nursing students in need of a job.

Before the turn of the century, several members of the Houghton family and their network of friends had considerable influence on the operation of the hospital. Harriet Gallup, who was the first wife of William Arthur Gallup, was a Vice-President. Cordelia Houghton was a Director. Hattie Cady, Sybil Hutton's mother, was Clerk.

The North Adams Hospital ran into some deep financial troubles. On September 11, 1890, Albert C. Houghton assumed the entire debt of this hospital so that it would be on more sound financial footing. The debt of the hospital at that time was about ten thousand dollars. On that very same day, Houghton's business partner and future son-in-law William Arthur Gallup announced that he would donate the funding necessary for the construction of a large wing as a memorial for his deceased wife who died six months earlier. Houghton would later donate the salary associated with being the Mayor of North Adams directly to the hospital's coffers instead of his own pockets.

Education remained a topic that held a special place in Houghton's heart. As mentioned earlier, Albert felt strongly that there were two avenues to take to change the world, the first education; the second, wealth. For Houghton, that first path, education, was his first choice. However, when his father became sick young Albert had to leave Bernardston Academy. Albert made sure that his own children were afforded the best educational opportunities that he could provide. Because of his interest in education he was named a member of the Board of Trustees of Boston University, also serving on the standing committee for the Graduate School of Arts and Sciences.

Houghton was also especially fond of Williams College, especially since it was located in nearby Williamstown, Massachusetts. He was named as a Trustee for Williams College and began his term on June 22, 1891. Albert was appointed as a Trustee for life. Albert was also very generous to Williams College, in one instance providing the funding necessary to endow a chair for German literature. He also donated a substantial sum of money for the construction of a new dormitory, which was opened in 1905.

Birth of a Political Figure

As mentioned earlier, Albert Houghton did serve one term in the Vermont State Legislature when he was younger. It is unclear why he did not pursue a second term. It could be that the lure of North Adams was so great that he decided to forgo a second term to concentrate on starting a business and personal life in North Adams. He could have placed more emphasis on starting his family and business that he did not have the time needed to continue to fulfill the duties in the Vermont government.

While Albert Houghton's political experience consisted of only one term as Vermont legislator and two terms as the Mayor of North Adams, that is not an indication of his political pull. He had more vested interests in the well-being of North Adams than to seek a more visible political office. He was a very prominent voice in government in the Commonwealth of Massachusetts. While he did not run for statewide offices, his pull was definitely felt on Beacon Hill.

Albert Houghton closely associated himself with William Russell who became the Governor of Massachusetts. In addition to Governor Russell, he had other strong political allies such as Boston Mayor and U.S. Congressman Patrick Collins. William Whitney, who served as the Secretary of the Navy under President Cleveland was another strong political ally of Houghton.

Albert C. Houghton also had a chance to meet and mingle with three U.S. Presidents – Cleveland, McKinley and Theodore Roosevelt. Houghton held President Cleveland in his highest regards and would help secure his nomination for the Presidency.

Albert C. Houghton was a loyal Democrat for most of his life. Up until the mid-1880's, Berkshire County was a reliable stronghold of the Republican Party. This is one of the reasons that Albert faced strong criticism when he first moved to North Adams and began his quest to see North Adams progress. In 1888, Albert Houghton began to publically endorse the candidacy of President Grover Cleveland especially with Cleveland's proposed bill that would help American mills compete globally.

While Houghton worked hard on the charter and trying to convince others to see his vision for North Adams, he generally stayed on the sidelines when it came to the brutal sport of politics. This changed during the 1892 Presidential election as Houghton was a staunch supporter of Grover Cleveland. Prior to this, he would support candidates, host them and network with very prominent people in government.

Grover Cleveland was the twenty-second President serving from 1885 through 1889. He lost his reelection campaign to Benjamin Harrison, although he garnered the majority of the popular vote. After sitting out of politics, President Cleveland decided to once again campaign for the office he held previously. The 1892 Presidential election would be a rematch against the incumbent President Harrison.

For that rematch to occur, Cleveland had to secure the nomination of the Democratic Party. Interestingly enough, Cleveland's largest obstacle to the Democratic nomination was New York Senator David B. Hill who served as Cleveland's Lieutenant Governor when Cleveland was the Governor of New York from 1883 through 1885. When Cleveland gave up the Governorship to become President of the United State, Hill assumed the role as Governor.

One of the main reasons Cleveland reentered politics was an attempt to prevent Senator Hill from obtaining the Democratic nomination. Cleveland was strongly opposed to free silver movement of that era and favored maintaining the gold standard. Cleveland also was in favor of reducing the high tariffs that were placed to protect American goods in the marketplace; he opposed imperialism and was against government subsidies. Cleveland was at best considered a moderate, and was considered pro-business, and anti-labor.

As his support for Cleveland was well-known and Houghton was connected to powerful people in government, there was a movement to have him become a delegate to represent the Commonwealth of Massachusetts in the national Democratic convention that was held in Chicago, Illinois. Since Houghton was considered a political force that helped Democrats gain strength in a traditional Republican stronghold, he was seen as someone who should have a prominent spot in the convention. The Republicans nominated a wealthy business owner from the Berkshires to be a delegate at their convention, so many pushed Houghton to represent the Democrats in a similar role from Western Massachusetts.

In an effort to ensure himself a seat, he openly campaigned for the chance to be a delegate. He opened a headquarters in a room of the Tremont House in Boston, where a steady stream of visitors visited Albert Houghton and were rewarded with fine delicacies. While the schmoozing was taking place at the Tremont House, in another room of the Parker House in Boston, a large group of workers were circulating flyers promoting Houghton as a delegate.

On April 8, 1892 Albert Houghton was nominated to serve as an at-large delegate for Massachusetts. The former Mayor Hubbard of Pittsfield, Massachusetts nominated Houghton and the Chairman of the Boston City Council, John H. McDonough seconded the nomination. His nomination was accepted.

The Democratic National Convention was held beginning on June 21, 1892. On June 18, 1892, the Massachusetts delegates, including Albert C. Houghton, left Boston at 10:30 in the morning on a Boston & Albany train. The trip from Boston to Chicago took twenty-eight hours by train. At the convention, Grover Cleveland narrowly won the first ballot and was nominated to be the Democratic nominee for the Presidency. In an effort to balance the ticket, the Democrats chose Adlai E. Stevenson as the nominee for Vice-President. Back home, Houghton worked tirelessly in an effort for Cleveland to carry the region.

The 1892 Presidential Campaign took on a somber tone because the First Lady Caroline Harrison was dying from tuberculosis. President Harrison avoided the campaign trail so he could be with his dying wife. Two weeks before Election Day, Caroline died, and all campaigning stopped altogether out of respect for the First Lady. Cleveland easily carried both the popular vote and Electoral College vote, becoming the only U.S. President to serve two non-consecutive terms, making him both the twenty-second and the twenty-fourth President of the United States.

In addition to his appointment as delegate and his tireless campaigning for Grover Cleveland, Albert C. Houghton was heavily involved in the North Adams charter. He was selected to be part of the committee that was responsible for drafting the charter as well as: Colonel John Bracewell, S. P. Thayer, Mark E. Couch, P.J. Ashe and C.J. Parkhurst.

Also in 1892, there were rumors of Albert Houghton serving in a greater office. In the 1892 gubernatorial race for Massachusetts, close Houghton friend and ally William Russell was seeking his third term in office. While the prospects of Governor Russell winning a third term were favorable, so was the election for Grover Cleveland for the Presidency. The thought was that Governor Russell would be rewarded with a spot in Cleveland's Cabinet and that the Lieutenant Governor would replace the outgoing Governor. With these rumors running rampant, the Democrats sought to fill out the ticket with a strong candidate who voters would be comfortable with assuming the office of Governor. Many thought that Albert C. Houghton would fill that need. Much to the dismay of many politicos in the region, this scenario did not play out as Mr. Houghton was not a candidate for Lieutenant Governor. In actuality, the Russell to the Cabinet rumor was just that, as Russell finished his third term as Governor and walked away from politics and resumed practicing law.

On September 24, 1892, Albert Houghton's oldest brother, Andrew Jackson Houghton, passed away from kidney disease at his home in Boston. Albert looked up to his brother Andrew and his astute business skill throughout his life. Andrew was a very successful bakery owner, grocer and would later establish one of the most successful breweries in New England in this era. At the time of his death, Andrew was a millionaire. After Andrew's death, Albert Houghton was named to run the A.J. Houghton and Company's Vienna Brewery and would retain a large interest in the business. It was his deep admiration of Andrew that led Albert to donate the city library to the town of North Adams in his memory years later.

The Houghton family moved out of their Summer Street home and into a residence a short distance away at 36 Church Street. Living near the Houghtons were close friends, the Wilkinsons and the Cadys. Both of these families have strong ties to the Houghton family and will be discussed throughout this book.

Houghton's old residence on Summer Street was torn down in 1921 to make way for an expanded Y.M.C.A. building. In 1961, the Y.M.C.A. again outgrew its building so it purchased more land on Morris Street to accommodate another expansion. In 1966, the North Adams Redevelopment Authority approached Y.M.C.A. with the understanding that the association would have to move in the interest of redevelopment. The Y.M.C.A was later demolished to make way for a shopping center.

In 1893, there was an economic slowdown which impacted Arnold Print Works. As a result, the Arnold Print Works and the associated mills shutdown on August 14, 1893. At this point in time, the print works was weeks behind in paying their employees because the banks could not supply the currency needed. Edward Wilkinson Sr. had an idea; he proposed that the Arnold Print Works issue their own currency to be paid to the employees. The currency was recognized by the local banking institutions as being valid. When merchants and other business owners deposited the Arnold Print Works currency into their accounts, the banks charged Arnold Print Works the amount of the company currency. The situation worked so well that other businesses in North Adams conducted the same practice.

The shutdown lasted until September 25, 1893, when the print works returned to operation but only at half-production capacity. The mills slowly increased production when the cash flow situation improved. For a quick infusion of much needed capital, on March 23, 1894, the Beaver Mills changed hands as W.A. Gallup and Houghton sold the mill to Clarence W. Gallup, the brother of William A. Gallup. The mills however would return to the control of Houghton & Gallup at a later point in time.

Also in 1893, Albert was elected a Director of the West End Railway in Boston. Prior to his election, he was heavily invested in the venture. This is significant to the regional history as the West End Street Railway Company would later change its name to the Boston Elevated Railway Company, which was a precursor to what is now known as the Massachusetts Bay Transportation Authority. The West End Street Railway was organized in 1887, originally intended to construct and operate a short trolley line between Boston and Brookline. Some of the original trolley lines turned into what we now know as the Green Line.

In 1894, the North Adams Normal School opened, while the school has changed names several times throughout the years, it was through the tireless efforts of Albert Houghton that the college was located in North Adams. The selection of a location of the school, which is now known as the Massachusetts College of Liberal Arts, became a fierce political battle in the region. The municipalities of Fitchburg, Pittsfield and North Adams were all angling for the opportunity to host the school.

Fitchburg dropped out because it could not compete politically against the two representatives of the other communities, Albert C. Houghton of North Adams and W. Murray Crane, who represented Pittsfield's interest. Crane would later become a United States Senator. Although Houghton was a registered and loyal Democrat and the bulk of the state government was Republican at the time, it was a testament to Houghton's influence that the school was placed within North Adams. Houghton had so much political influence that he was able to influence the politicians on the other side of the aisle.

The President of the State Senate at the time was a man named William M. Butler. Mr. Butler had an interesting position as President of the Hoosac Cotton Company. Remember that Houghton had a rather large business requiring the need for vast quantities of cotton products. I am not stating that there was some sort of pressure applied; I am just giving the facts. When North Adams was selected as the location of the school, it was because of the tireless effort of Albert Houghton. This is just one of the many ways Albert C. Houghton shaped the community of North Adams, his impacts still felt to this very day.

Since the development of rail in North Adams was extremely important in opening up the region for economic development, Houghton took a strong interest in the regional rail network. On September 25, 1895, Albert Houghton was elected to serve as a director of the Boston and Albany Railroad Company. He would later serve in that role on the Fitchburg Railroad as well as the Boston & Maine Railroad.

The Summer of Construction - The Mansion in Born

I understand that it is not possible for the "birth" of a mansion. However, the old walls are different than the typical structure. The walls and floors absorbed a bit of history and every now and then, this history comes alive! Albert Houghton felt it was important to build the grandest home in North

Adams. As such, he commissioned the design of a residence that was fit for his family and stature. That day came in 1895. I will discuss the mansion in greater detail later in this book.

1 – Houghton Mansion
2 – Gallup Residence
3 – Wilkinson Residence
4 – William G. Cady Residence
5 – H.T. Cady Residence
      A.C. Houghton Property

Based on 1904 Property Records

This illustration shows the size of the Houghton property as well as the proximity of other family and close associates discussed in this book.

The summer of 1895 was also important in the history of Houghton and North Adams as very important construction was started on both the Beaver and Eclipse Mills that significantly enlarged both mills – doubling their capacity. On July 5, 1895, a meeting was held at Arnold Print Works regarding the increased demand for goods and the lack of space at its burgeoning facilities. At the conclusion of the meeting it was decided that both mills would be significantly enlarged. In addition to the bigger structures, the employment at both mills was doubled and the machinery throughout both mills was upgraded. A new steam power plant was constructed at the Beaver mill. The work was completed by Porter and Hannum, also a contractor at the construction site of the Houghton Mansion.

Albert and Cordelia Houghton leased to the city of North Adams their former stable to their Summer Street home in 1896. The stable was built in 1878 for the Houghton family. Before Houghton owned the property it was used as administration offices for the Hoosac Tunnel construction project. When the tunnel was finally completed in 1875, the Tunnel Commission under authority of Commonwealth of Massachusetts sold the land to Cordelia Houghton on January 23, 1878. The Houghton lived across Morris Street in the building that would later become the North Adams Y.M.C.A. The tunnel administration offices were torn down and the brick stable was constructed that year.

There was a controversy in North Adams to whether the city should lease the stable from Houghton or to build a new city hall elsewhere. Houghton offered to renovate the stables so that it can be easily used as a city hall. As a result of the renovation offer, during a special town meeting on October 12, 1895, it was voted upon that Houghton's stable would be suitable for the city hall. North Adams, in order to lease the stable for use as the city hall had to secure a $30,000 loan. After the loan was received, the title of the building transferred from Cordelia J. Houghton to North Adams on June 29, 1896. In addition, North Adams purchased the property next door at 35 Summer Street where it was later annexed to the former stable property.

Houghton's old stable was used as the City Hall until July 1973, when North Adams dedicated the North Adams Municipal Center which was to replace the old town hall. In 1974, the old structure was still standing and there was some question as to what would become of the structure. The original plans were for the building to be demolished as soon as the new building was completed and functions were moved to the new site.

However the structure was the last structure from the nineteenth century still standing in that particular area of North Adams and a college professor from the history department at what was then called North Adams State College began an effort to preserve the structure. The building was not in its original state as several additions were built to the original structure. The issue was that the building was in the middle of a seven acre section of Main Street that was eyed for an urban renewal project. It was thought to be impossible to build a vibrant new commercial center around the structure. Most of the other seven acres was already cleared, except for City Hall.

Moreover, the Hoosac Community Resources Corp. conducted a comprehensive study of North Adams and the old City Hall was not included in their recommendations of buildings to preserve. At the time the library had fallen into a state of disrepair – the same library that A.C. Houghton donated to the city for a library in his brother's memory. The library's preservation was considered more critical than the old city hall. In March 1978, the old City Hall was demolished.

The Honorable Albert Charles Houghton

North Adams separated from Adams in 1878, and because of that the municipality was rather young. Prior to the split, a vast majority of residents lived in the northern half along with the bulk of the manufacturing. The southern half was sparsely populated and was dominated by agriculture. In 1896, North Adams incorporated as a city and because of the efforts of the charter, the new government was to take a mayor-council form.

Under the present political conditions, you cannot seem to get a Republican and Democrat in the same room without a healthy dose of vicious personal attacks and he said/she said nonsense. However, Albert C. Houghton was so widely respected by both political parties that both nominated him to be their candidate for mayor. Imagine that, both political parties tripping over each other to nominate the same person, makes me wish for simpler political times where politicians looked out for the overall good of the people and not their party.

But in North Adams, he was the political powerhouse. Elected easily by both Republicans and Democrats, he served two terms as Mayor. He was first elected in December of 1895. At that time he had no interest in becoming the Mayor, he had his plate full trying to run his business empire, being part of several boards and balancing whatever time was left to his family. His closest friends and business associates convinced Houghton to run. It was thought to be a tremendous personal sacrifice for Houghton to run for Mayor as he was already spread thin with all of his interests.

The attention must have been sweet vindication for Houghton, as when he was younger, he envisioned how North Adams can develop and modernize and spent countless hours being shredded and ridiculed by established politicians as being too radical. While he spent considerable time trying to convince others how the city should be run, he now had the opportunity to run for an office that could help shape the community. It was the chance to not only talk, but to do. Seeing the fanfare over his candidacy must have felt like a well-deserved redemption to him.

Since Albert Houghton was a loyal Democrat, it was very easy for him to earn the Democratic nomination for Mayor. But on November 30, 1895, the Republicans themselves nominated Houghton to be the Republican nominee as well. During a meeting of the city's Republicans Colonel A. Potter put forth Houghton's name as the nominee after he gave an impassioned speech regarding the importance of them selecting an individual with great character and ability. A fellow Republican by the name of A.M. Whipple then took his turn to speak. While Whipple was not speaking against the candidacy of Houghton, he explained his shock that the Republicans would fail to nominate on of their own. Whipple suggested that the nomination be made by ballot of those who attended the Republican town meeting. The motion passed and the resulting vote gave Albert Houghton the clear majority of the votes. Colonel Potter then reiterated his motion that Houghton be named as the Republican candidate and the motion passed unanimously and enthusiastically. It was then decided that a committee would meet with candidate Houghton and inform him that he was indeed the Republican nominee for the office of Mayor.

While Houghton was both the Democratic and Republican nominee for the election of Mayor, we cannot forget about the Independent Party. To throw a bit more love towards Mr. Houghton, the Independents also favored Houghton for Mayor. The Independent Party even went so far as to take credit that Houghton was running for the office. Now flash forward to this day and age – can you imagine a scenario like this occurring in today's political climate?

Election Day for the municipal election was Tuesday, December 16, 1895. Based on the fact that Houghton was endorsed by all the political parties, I would assume that there was a lack of late-night nail biting that can be seen in today's elections. As expected, Albert Houghton garnered the majority of the votes with 1,385[7]. There were eight individuals that received votes as write-ins. The most write-ins went to H.T. Cady who appeared on twenty-one ballots, and brother W.G. Cady, who garnered ten votes. Overall there were forty-two write-in votes, so H.T. Cady received one-half of those votes, and between the Cady brothers, they garnered approximately three-quarters of the write-ins.

Other names elected to the city council include names that you will be introduced to later in this book. Edgar A. Stroud, a Republican, and brother-in-law of Houghton was elected to the council as well as Edward Shepard Wilkinson. Wilkinson was also a Republican and the father of future Houghton son-in-law Edward S. Wilkinson, Jr. While Houghton was a Democrat, the Republicans held a majority of the seats on the council with thirteen to the Democrat's eight seats.

This was not the first foray into North Adam's government for Houghton, at some point before he was Mayor he served on the town's finance committee before the charter was revised and the mayor-council form of government was initiated. Part of Houghton's role on the finance committee was to oversee the town's coffers.

Shortly before Houghton was sworn in as the first mayor of North Adams, there was a Leap Year Festivity that was held at the Columbia Opera House in North Adams on Thursday, January 2, 1896. Part of the festivities involved young ladies filling up dance cards with gentlemen who attended. The ball lasted until three-thirty in the morning. During the ball, a two-step was introduced that was composed by I.S. Browne, the title of the composition was "Our Mayor", and was dedicated to Albert Houghton. Some of the single ladies who were available to dance were Albert's single daughters, Susan, Alice and Mary.

The salary of the Mayor was one thousand dollars per year at that time. Working as the Mayor was a long and largely thankless job, but Houghton did not financially benefit from the town's coffers. During his time as Mayor, he donated the salary of the Mayor to the North Adams Hospital.

---

[7] "Full Returns." The North Adams Transcript 18 Dec 1895: 1.

Albert Houghton created somewhat of a local buzz when he purchased the Blackinton Mansion in 1896. The structure was the second grandest home in North Adams, second only to Houghton's own residence. The mansion was constructed in 1865 for Sanford Blackinton, a very wealthy and prominent textile mill owner. While Sanford died in 1885, his widow Eliza lived in the mansion until her death in 1896. When the mansion became available, Houghton snatched it right up. Many wondered why Houghton would purchase such a grand home during the construction of his own grand mansion.

During the City Council meeting on Monday, April 6, 1896, Albert Houghton sold the Blackinton Mansion to North Adams for the price of one dollar. Along with the mansion, Houghton donated $10,000 to be used to convert the Blackinton Mansion into the North Adams Public Library. The population of North Adams was exploding and the library at that time could not meet the demand of the population. The struggles of the undersized library were occurring for some time and the availability of the Blackinton Mansion seemed all too perfect of an opportunity to pass up.

The North Adams Public Library, the lasting legacy Albert Houghton dedicated to his brother Andrew Jackson Houghton.

When Houghton donated the mansion and funds to North Adams, he did so in the memory of his brother Andrew Jackson Houghton, who died a few years prior. Albert thought that the library was the perfect way to honor his older brother. Instead of donating a slab of stone, a statue, or a plaque, he felt it was more important to give the community a valuable asset that can benefit the entire community.

The day after Albert Houghton donated the library to North Adams, he had to deal with another tragedy in his family. On April 7, 1896, Warren Houghton, the nephew of Albert passed away in Denver, Colorado. Warren was the son of Annis Houghton Cook, and he was in the womb when sister

Laura Cook died. Warren died as the result of Consumption. Warren was only thirty-three years old and he was the father of three small children. His widow moved the young family back to North Adams to be close to family.

As if losing a nephew at such a young age was not traumatic enough for Houghton, the family underwent another bout of tragedy as Caroline L. Houghton, his niece and the oldest daughter of James and Lestina Houghton had to be institutionalized again at the Brattleboro Retreat. Carrie was out of the facility in the summer of 1896, when she began another slow descent into illness. On Monday, July 27, 1896, her brother Charles D. Houghton and her uncle Albert W. Willmarth feared for her safety and returned her to the facility. Although I cannot speculate on what caused her health to slide, it is important to note that her father's own health was fading and he was very uncomfortable in his final year which undoubtedly added stress to her fragile state of mind. Sadly, she was institutionalized for the rest of her life and passed away less than six years later at the age of forty-eight.

Towards the end of Houghton's first term in office, he was largely undecided if he wanted to run for a second term as Mayor. As late as Sunday, November 8, 1896, Houghton was undecided if he would seek or even accept the nomination for a second term in office. By and large, the townsfolk were very happy at the progress North Adams made during his first term in office and were eager for Houghton to run again so the progress can continue. However, Houghton had trouble seeing how he could again sacrifice his time and effort away from Arnold Print Works to again devote to the thankless job of running city government. He did decide to run, and he again won his seat decisively.

Just prior to being elected for his second term as Mayor, Albert Houghton had to deal with the death of another sibling. On December 1, 1896, James Royal Houghton passed away at the age of sixty-four. For the final years of his life James was suffering from a condition called catarrh. Catarrh is an inflammation of the mucous membranes in one or several of the body's airways or cavities. As a result a thick mixture of mucus and white blood cells can cause a chronic blockage that makes breathing very uncomfortable. As James was suffering from catarrh, he also developed a polyp within his nose. This polyp was removed, but as a result of the surgery he experienced necrosis of his cheek bone – necrosis is the death of a bone.

James was in such great pain for much of his final year of life, that his family was relieved that his suffering was finally over. For Albert Houghton, his second oldest brother was important in his life because it was with James that he partnered and operated the A.C. Houghton & Co. chemical works. It was through the chemical works that Albert Houghton became familiar with the calico printing industry and it was through this venture that Albert Houghton made repeated visits to North Adams that made him lust after starting a life there.

A Political Shift

Albert C. Houghton was a staunch and loyal Democrat throughout most of his life, although his political leaning shifted a bit in the final two decades of his life. It was during the Presidential candidacy of William Jennings Bryan in 1896, with whom he sharply disagreed with many of the facets of the Democratic platform. It was at this point that he started to endorse a Republican. This is no small feat considering it was earlier that year where he was appointed as a member of the Executive Committee of the Massachusetts State Democratic Committee. Although he was supporting a Republican candidate for President, he did not leave the Democratic Party.

William Jennings Bryan ran as the Democratic nominee for the U.S. Presidency three separate times, 1896, 1900 and 1908. Bryan lost the general election to William McKinley twice, in 1896 and 1900. He was described as being against banks and railroads in general – two institutions that Albert C. Houghton was closely affiliated with. He was also a staunch pacifist, a prohibitionist, and fought against the idea of Darwinian principles being taught to public school students. He also fought against the gold standard and wished to instead restart the coinage of silver.

During the 1896 Democratic National Convention, it was through the hard work of Bryan that the free silver idea was silently added to the Democratic platform. It was done without fanfare as it was highly controversial. Many were offended that a topic so controversial could be silently added without discussion or debate. The incumbent President, Grover Cleveland, in which

Houghton was a staunch supporter of, went into the convention with his closest allies hoping he would seek a third term in office but declined to accept their nomination for a third term. Remember at this time there were no limits for how many terms a President could have. Cleveland's supporters were very concerned over the direction Bryan and his allies were bringing the Democratic Party.

The Democratic platform in 1896 was so distressing for Houghton that he promptly turned his back on the party he had been loyal to his entire life. This must have made family dinners a bit less awkward as his sons-in-laws were Republican as well as his brother-in-law Edgar Stroud. In fact, many close associates of Houghton were Republican, so they must have been relieved that he joined forces with them, albeit only because he was against Bryan.

Albert Houghton became a very vocal supporter of Republican presidential candidate William McKinley. Houghton's support for McKinley energized the local base of the Republican Party. True, the Republicans respected Mr. Houghton as a Democrat and even supported his election, but now he was actively stumping for their party's candidate at the same time he was serving within the National Democratic Party.

His "coming-out" party was a speech that he gave at the Odd Fellow's Hall in North Adams. When he appeared with the North Adams Republican party chairman, the crowd erupted. From there, Mr. Houghton delivered a stirring speech. He was interrupted many times by loud applause as he was speaking. Of course, being a huge supporter of President Cleveland, a Democrat, he started out with his view that President Cleveland's administration was the best in the history of the country. He then stated that he was now seeking what was the best interest of the country. To Mr. Houghton, defeating the Democrat Bryan was the most important issue.

In Albert Houghton's opinion, Bryan was in the pocket of the silver mine operators in the United States and was pushing for the silver standard as a payback for their financial backing. Sound familiar? Today, we think about politics and think it's a modern invention, but go back one hundred years plus and the game was the same. Bryan's critics also leveled charges that he was seeking to destroy the Supreme Court and that he was trying to destroy democracy, both very strong claims. Mr. Houghton as well as other

Democrats felt that Bryan hijacked the Democratic Party and caused it to veer off in a dangerous direction.

In particular, the issues that Albert Houghton found with Bryan were numerous. One of the biggest issues according to Houghton was that under President Cleveland, he inherited a law in which the country would be put on a silver standard versus gold. Through his leadership, he called on Congress to repeal the law. Of course, the silver industry did not go down quietly. Bryan took this issue as his campaign priority, so much so that Houghton questioned where his funding came from. In the Democratic Convention in 1896, Bryan was easily nominated upsetting many of the moderate Democrats.

Albert Houghton also disagreed in Bryan's dealings in the Cuban war. Briefly, the United States purchased the Philippines for twenty million dollars. This move was widely unpopular and it was Bryan who helped shape this decision. Bryan then turned around and used the unpopular move as a campaign battle cry. He would tour the country and would literally shout about imperialism and read the Declaration of Independence and the Constitution. Mr. Houghton believed that after the Spanish fleet was destroyed in Manila the United States should have left. When there was a rebellion, it was now the country's responsibility to quell it.

Albert Houghton then discussed the advances of the United States in the first four years of McKinley's Administration. At that time, there was a marked increase in exports to the point where the United States exported more goods than the entire continent of Europe. Bank deposits were exploding, indicating that the working class salary was rising over the rate of inflation. In the end, McKinley was elected twice over Bryan, satisfying Albert Houghton.

In the summer of Houghton's second term as Mayor, North Adams was the location of a violent double-murder that grabbed much of the headlines in Massachusetts for several years. On August 7, 1897 the bodies of Henry Reed and his sister Blanche were found in their home. These murders shook the community and because Houghton was Mayor, he had to calm the masses and use his natural leadership talent to handle the influx of media and investigators. The crime itself was never solved and it was a source of regret for Albert Houghton that two members of his community were slain and no justice was served.

My original intent was to include this story, but I had to remove in an attempt to keep the book at a reasonable length and affordable. For the Reed double murder story as well as some surprising suspects, please visit the website referenced in the Appendix.

Retirement from Politics

Retirement is a word that seemed like a four-letter curse word to Albert Houghton. However, the job of running the city took a toll on him. Towards the end of the Houghton administration, the rapidly growing community started to pave roads, it opened new schools, and a new sewage system was operational. Under Houghton's watch, the city's infrastructure was being quickly updated. This trend towards quick improvements started to stir up opposition. Some felt that the city was being run into debt and borrowing too much to achieve Houghton's grand plans for the city. At the end of Houghton's second term, the city's debt was slightly over one million dollars – mere pennies nowadays compared to modern-day deficits. By the end of his second term, the opposition was strong and vocal, but was only a minority.

In only two one-year terms in office, eight miles of sewers were constructed, three news schools were built and an existing school, Mark Hopkins was doubled in size. Nowadays it seems as if it takes communities two years just to respond to a letter.

In the fall of Houghton's second term as Mayor, the honeymoon period was over and the political game hit full speed. It was at this time that he decided that he would not seek a third term as Mayor. One of the improvement projects undertaken was the paving of the roadway near the Beaver mill complex. Since Houghton owned the complex, it was of course a political hot potato. Political opponents of Houghton had a field day and did what they could to generate a story just in time for Election Day. At this point it was the largest infrastructure contract given at that time. Because of foul weather, the project was taking longer than originally anticipated. Since the workers were being paid by day versus a contracted total, there was the thought the workers were bleeding the city coffers. Part of the project included laying sewer pipe. When the project began the workers encountered solid bedrock which required unexpected blasting, also increasing the duration of the project.

Opposition, led by Harry R. Hamer, who incidentally was also running for the Mayor's seat, claimed that the work was a violation of the newly approved city charter. Mr. Hamer also claimed that the job was benefiting, Albert C. Houghton, the businessman, at the taxpayer's expense. While these were serious charges, not many in the community took the allegations very seriously. On October 30, 1897, Harry R. Hamer, the member of the Town Council who became a bit of a thorn in Albert's side, announced his candidacy for the Mayor.

Even though there was growing angst over the direction of the developing city, there was a movement to convince Albert to run for a third term in office. H. Torrey Cady who was running for the Republican nominee for Mayor stepped out of the race in an attempt to convince Houghton to seek another term. H. Torrey Cady was the uncle of Sybil Hutton, the woman who was killed instantly in the car accident on August 1, 1914. H.T. Cady himself was a reluctant candidate to run for Mayor, hoping instead to focus on his own business. When it was originally apparent that Houghton was not going to run, many of Cady's friends and associates begged for him to run. Stepping aside to let Houghton seek a third term was a dream outcome for Cady.

Mr. Cady started a petition to convince Houghton that he had the support of the community. Several prominent business men were the first to sign the petition. When the petition was brought to the Adams Savings Bank, Houghton happened to be there on business and happened to get an idea of what was happening. Mr. Houghton requested that the petition drive be stopped because at that point he was certain he was stepping aside and there was no way that he would change his mind.

With Albert C. Houghton dashing all hopes that he would change his mind and seek a third term, there was an opportunity for his opposition to tame some of the improvements Houghton was seeking. The opposition, led by Hamer was highly organized and very vocal trying to convince the voters that the city was headed in the wrong direction. Those who wanted the town to keep its pace of infrastructure improvement were scrambling to keep their momentum. Because H.T. Cady and another candidate by the name of Kearn withdrew their consideration in the hopes that Houghton would reconsider, James E. Hunter announced his candidacy for the Republican nomination on November 17, 1897. Hunter immediately announced that he was in favor of continuing the public improvements started by the Houghton administration. He left no grey area; he wholeheartedly endorsed Houghton's administration and vowed to create a seamless transition and continuance of Houghton's priorities.

James Hunter, like Houghton before and Cady, was also a bit hesitant to run for the office of Mayor. It took considerable effort from his associates and leading Republicans to convince him to seek the office. Since both Cady and Kearns withdrew in an attempt to lure Houghton back into the race, Hunter was a logical successor since he was an ardent supporter of Houghton and his policies. H. T. Cady was aware how uneasy Hunter was in running for office, so he reentered the race to ensure the momentum carried forward. Cady feared the Hamer might win and undo the projects and visions that the Houghton administration began.

While the first two mayoral contests were extremely tame considering there was only one candidate, the campaign to succeed Houghton was a nasty affair. Both candidates had opposing views. Mr. Hamer believed in controlling the spending while H.T. Cady was a supporter of Albert Houghton and his policies and he wished to continue the rapid improvements North Adams had seen under Houghton. Since both views could not be further apart, the campaign was a bit spirited.

Hamer felt that North Adams should be run like a corporation with the ultimate goal of not running a debt. By all accounts Hamer was very passionate and compelling about the issue and he was able to sway some opinion. But his undoing may have been the fact that while he was adamant that he did not like the present systems of improvements, when given the chance he did not specify what he would change as Mayor. He stated several times that he must first have the Mayor's seat before he thought about any changes. As expected, this did not fly with the local media, but since Hamer was so passionate about the topic, the election was much closer than many thought possible.

While the campaign wore on Hamer was getting more aggressive in his attacks of the Houghton administration. Since Houghton was not running, he did not insert himself too much into the discussion. This reluctance on the part of Houghton gave his critics ammunition in which they claimed that he could not answer any question or criticism posed to him. It appeared Hamer's constant barrage was starting to turn the tables in the campaign.

Finally, Houghton did answer back – in a big way. As the election neared, a public meeting was scheduled at Odd Fellow's Hall in which Houghton would outline his administration and answer questions from the public. Hours before the night's proceedings were to begin and before the hall was even opened, a large crowd gathered so they can attend the meeting. As soon as the doors opened the room was filled to capacity and then some. People were actually packed in the hallways and a staircase and people were intently listening at the windows that lined Main Street.

Albert Houghton talked at length about what his administration has done. His speech was interrupted several times by loud applause. When he finished his speech an hour and a half later, he asked if anyone had any questions for him, an eerie silence broke. This is important to note because Houghton's opponents had once said of him that he never answered questions that were critical of him. But given the chance to ask questions, the crowd fell silent. Then a rowdy round of applause filled the hall and lasted for several minutes. Mr. Houghton again was waiting for the many questions that his opponents stated he would not answer. Not a peep from the crowd, until Reverend Tinney asked the crowd to show their thankfulness of the nonpartisan methods Mr. Houghton ruled the city. Again, pandemonium erupted again, and then the meeting ended with Mr. Houghton seemingly shaking every hand that wished to congratulate him. This meeting was important as Mr. Houghton sought to discredit all the attacks his administration had endured as part of the grueling campaign that was meant to find his successor.

People who supported Houghton were going to vote for Cady in an attempt to keep the city growing based on the administration of Houghton. Many citizens were grateful that Houghton provided a sweetheart deal to North Adams when he sold the building that would become the Union Street School to the city. He brought the college to North Adams, when many other communities were vying for the opportunity. Houghton was not only responsible for the donation of the library in his brother's memory but also the funding needed to transform a residence to a library. He worked tirelessly to support the North Adams Hospital. More importantly, people were enjoying the series of public works improvements that were undertaken during his administration. His countless acts of charity and the fact that he opened doors to a host of jobs in the community made him a popular and beloved figure.

On Election Day, the results were a victory for H. Torrey Cady with 180 more votes than Hamer. Cady garnered 1,685 votes while Hamer received 1,505. A recount of the election was requested and as a result of the recount, the lead for Cady was cut by three votes for a final total of a 177-vote victory. Fifty-three ballots were left blank as apparently those folks wanted to make a statement that neither was preferred. The final ballot count was 1,683 for Cady and 1,506 for Hamer.

On January 3, 1898, Mayor H.T. Cady took the oath of office as the second Mayor of North Adams. Before Cady was sworn in however, the Council President, the newly sworn-in Edward S. Wilkinson, called on the outgoing Mayor Houghton to make a farewell speech. After his speech, Albert C. Houghton received a polite round of applause and then the incoming mayor was sworn in and provided his inaugural address to the citizens of North Adams. At this, Houghton ended his political aspirations, even though they were largely thrust upon him and he was reluctant to serve.

A Betrayal of a Trusted Friend

Charles Ralston was a trusted associate of Albert Houghton, one who would throw away his future and one who would become important in the history of Albert Houghton. While Houghton placed his trust in him, Ralston would not only take advantage of that trust, but also ripped apart his own family. His selfish actions made it appear as if he thought nothing of his dying wife or his two young sons. I feel that this particular experience would impact Albert Houghton and remain an experience that is etched in his memory.

With all the business interests of Albert Houghton on top of the responsibility of being the Mayor of North Adams, he felt it was necessary to hire a personal secretary to help him keep the mayoral responsibilities in order. He hired the editor of the Hoosac Valley News, Charles T. Ralston to be his private secretary. While Mr. Ralston worked during business hours in the Mayor's office, he also retained his connection to the Hoosac Valley News for some time.

At the time, Charles was a well-known man with an untarnished reputation. However, Charles had a couple of issues that would later prove to cloud his thinking. Mr. Ralston was rumored to be an alcoholic and to make matters worse for him, his wife Sarah became ill with a chronic heart condition. Charles and Sarah were the parents of two young sons – Jackson Frederick Ralston was born April 11, 1892 and Richard Paul Ralston, born on July 26, 1897.

As Mr. Ralston was Mr. Houghton's secretary, he had become very familiar with Mr. Houghton's signature. In January, 1897, he was no longer serving as secretary as Houghton decided against a third term as Mayor. Serving as Mr. Houghton's secretary, he made $1,000 annually – quite a handsome salary, considering that was the same salary as Mayor. Mr. Ralston at this point was no longer associated with the newspaper either. He secured a bookkeeping job for Whitlaw & Smith, a local bottling company and he also performed some side work for New York publishing companies. He was known to be a poor handler of money and had debt.

Mr. Ralston became a very desperate man with his addiction and out of desperation he hatched a plan for a quick infusion of funds. Around 2:30 in the afternoon on October 12, 1898, he went to Hoosac Savings Bank with a promissory note attempting to withdraw $1,800 from the bank. The note had two forged signatures, Albert C. Houghton and Foster E. Swift, who was the proprietor of the Wilson House, a hotel in North Adams. What is worse is that Ralston considered Mr. Houghton and Mr. Swift two of his closest friends.

Mr. Ralston's descent into alcoholism was well-known, but no one would ever think he would stoop to break the law. The treasurer of the bank, W.W. Richmond, was suspicious of Mr. Ralston's behavior and knew that something was not right. Mr. Richmond asked Mr. Ralston to wait while directors approved the note. Mr. Richmond requested that W.W. Butler on the Board of Investment and associated with the Berkshire National Bank place his initials on the note.

Mr. Ralston was unhappy that his plan hit a snag and offered to visit the director with the note. As Mr. Ralston was heading towards the Berkshire

National Bank, Mr. Richmond called Mr. Butler on the telephone and notified him of his suspicions. When Mr. Ralston arrived, Mr. Butler looked at the note and noticed that Albert Houghton's signature was not quite right. The forgery of Mr. Swift was accurate however, including the use of blue ink, which Mr. Swift only used to sign official documents.

Mr. Butler was caught up on the appearance of Albert C. Houghton's signature and asked Mr. Ralston where Mr. Houghton was when he signed the promissory note. Mr. Ralston answered that he was in New York City, as was often the case during that time of the year – but not this particular day. Mr. Butler placed his initials on the note even though he had reservations. He had sent Mr. Ralston back to the Hoosac Savings Bank. While Mr. Ralston was on his way however, Mr. Butler called Mr. Richmond and told him not to give Mr. Ralston the money.

Mr. Ralston appeared at Hoosac Savings Bank with the promissory note that had the initials of Mr. Butler, expecting to receive the money. Mr. Richmond then told Mr. Ralston that he would need to get the initials of everyone on the board prior to receiving the money and would not receive it until the following morning at the earliest. At this point Charles Ralston became very anxious and told Mr. Richmond that he needed the money immediately as he needed to catch the three in the afternoon train to New York. When informed he could not get the money, Mr. Ralston left immediately, leaving behind the promissory note.

He then went to his duty as bookkeeper until his usual quitting time of four in the afternoon. After he left, he disappeared from North Adams. Mr. Richmond took the note and consulted with both Houghton and Mr. Swift, and both informed him that the signatures were forged. The North Adams police were then notified of this crime and issued a warrant for his arrest with the charge of forgery.

The police thought that this was not an act of impulse, but a well-planned scheme. It was discovered that in September, Mr. Ralston went to the Hoosac Savings Bank and notified them that he wanted to borrow approximately $1,500 to $1,800 in October and asked if he could get the money if Mr. Houghton and Mr. Swift signed for him. When told that he could, he asked for a blank note which was given to him. A week before he tried unsuccessfully to obtain the money, he reappeared at the bank and asked for another note. The bank asked what happened to the first note he was given. Mr. Ralston concocted a story that he took it to Houghton after Mr. Swift signed it and Houghton refused to sign it second. He was given a second note for signature. When Mr. Richmond saw the obvious Mr. Houghton forged signature, he then realized that the first note he was given was more than likely ruined on a first forgery attempt.

Mr. Ralston was in Troy on October 14, but the police in Troy were not able to locate him there that day. While in in Troy, he visited a dear friend, Mr. Potts, who was an editor of the Troy Times. Also during his day on the lam, he attempted to change his appearance as he shaved off his facial hair and had his hair cut much shorter. He had also written two letters, one to his wife and one to his young sons. The letter to his children warned them of dangers life will throw at them when they reached adulthood. These letters were meant to be mailed and had made reference that his body would not be found.

Charles later travelled to Bennington, Vermont where he attempted suicide. He purchased some chloral, also known as trichloroacetaldehyde, which at one point was widely used as a sedative. It was lethal in large quantities, and in fact, was used in preparing DDT, the chemical that is infamous for its impacts on the environment. Charles drank a large quantity of chloral, but his body rejected it or he had second thoughts and he vomited. He later tried to drink a lethal dose of morphine; again, his stomach betrayed him.

Despondent, he walked from Bennington to Pownal, Vermont and at 10 p.m., he arrived at a hotel and asked to stay for the night. The hotel's owner, Joseph Kedian, had known him from previous encounters and put him up for the night. Mr. Kedian was concerned because Charles was covered in mud and was visibly exhausted. Charles' demeanor also concerned the hotel's owner as he was in a very nervous and excitable condition. The local papers carried the news of Charles crime and warrant so the hotel owner knew he was a wanted man. He was also concerned that he would commit suicide at the hotel and in fact found a bottle of carbolic acid in Mr. Ralston's coat pocket.

Mr. Kedian showed Mr. Ralston a copy of the newspaper with the article written regarding his warrant. Mr. Ralston was said to have eagerly read the article. Mr. Kedian stayed with Mr. Ralston that night for fear of his desire to commit suicide. During the next morning, Mr. Ralston told of his desire to do the right thing and turn himself in to authorities. Mr. Kedian arranged for Mr. Ralston's travel to the North Adams Police headquarters.

On the very next day, Saturday, October 15, 1898, Charles walked into the police station at 6:30 a.m. and turned himself in. He was arraigned in the district court and pled guilty to the forgery charge. The judge placed him under $2,000 bail and he was taken to a jail in Pittsfield to await the grand jury. Charles wife, Sarah, already weakened because of her illness, had to be confined to bed with the need for nurses to attend to her as a result of the events.

After her husband was placed behind bars to await his sentencing, Sarah's health failed rapidly. On January 5, 1899, while in her home on Bracewell Avenue in North Adams, Sarah fell very ill and it appeared she was not going to survive the day. A special request was sent in order for Mr. Ralston to spend time with his wife before she passed. The court ordered that Charles may visit, but under the circumstance that he would be accompanied by an officer to prevent his flight. She made it through that day, but never fully recovered.

On January 9, 1899, Charles appeared before the grand jury and admitted he forged the signatures. He expressed his desire to plead guilty to save the community the expense of trial. His willingness to concede guilt was thought by some to be an attempt to gain favor of the court in order to achieve leniency. His wife, Sarah, after all was very ill and her survival chances were slight. They also had small children that needed care.

In January, 1899 Charles was sentenced to two years for the forgery charge. Several of Charles' acquaintances were pressing that he would be released on probation as he did not receive the money and they claimed his reputation was spotless besides making the grievous error in judgment under great emotional turmoil. The judge, however, was not buying the argument and saw no need to leniency. Charles stated several times that he was under such heavy influence of alcohol that he was not even aware that he committed forgery and tried to embezzle money until a few hours after he left North Adams.

In the morning of Sunday May 28, 1899, Sarah Ralston passed away in North Adams Hospital at the age of thirty-five. She was admitted to the hospital four weeks prior and spent her final month bedridden. Charles did not come to North Adams during his wife's final moments or after her death. The remains of Sarah were brought back to Cambridge, New York for her funeral and burial.

With Sarah's passing and Charles sitting in prison, the Ralston children needed a new home. At the time of Sarah's death, Jackson was seven years old while his younger brother Richard was less than two years old. Jackson was sent to live with relatives, Jackson M. and Sara Ralston who lived in Hyattsville, Maryland. Jackson and Sara did not have children of their own. After his father was released from prison Jackson remained in this household.

For the younger brother, Richard was placed in another household. His name was changed from Richard Paul Ralston to Paul Frederick Padden. He stayed in the North Adams area. He would later discover that his name was changed and he would legally change it to Paul Padden Ralston. Paul was a musician and ironically enough, was a member of the Lafayette Chapter of the Masons, and was a member when the temple was constructed onto Houghton Mansion. Paul would later move to Albany, California, where he would pass away in February 1969.

Charles received two months off from his sentence for being a model prisoner and was released on November 6, 1900. When he was released he had no immediate plans for his future. However, his crime was well-known in the region because of his position in the community, the media coverage of the crime and his suicide attempts. In the end, when Charles Ralston was released, he no longer had his wife as she died when he was in prison. Those days he was locked up could have been better spent with his wife in her final days. This is something Ralston had to deal with for the rest of his life. Another tragedy is that the Ralston brothers were split up as children and experienced the most broken of families.

The Writing on the Wall

In the spring of 1898, Albert C. Houghton was beginning to see trends that deeply troubled him in regards to the lucrative mill business in Massachusetts. Houghton was one of eighteen members of a group of mill owners that was warning politicians and citizens about the loss of employment because of the government's expanding regulations. This group of owners sent a letter to all the newspapers in the state.

The owners at the time began struggling with contraction. For many years, the mills saw unprecedented growth, but the owners began to see the writing on the wall. Part of the issue may have been a saturated market, as product prices were falling fast. Those values of the plants were dropping considerably, and for the owners, the all-important profits were beginning to contract.

The mill owners in Massachusetts were seeing stiff competition from other regions of the United States, most notably, the South. The southern states were less restrictive on the mills, and the mills took advantage of lax oversight. The mills were running longer per day, employee wages were lower, and most notably taxes were considerably less. This gave the southern mills a greater advantage and allowed them to flood the market with cheaper products forcing the hand of the northern mill owners.

Some of the mill owners were seeing the competitive advantages of folding their northern operations and transferring south. The mill owners were attempting to give the legislators in Massachusetts a wakeup call. To some, the choice was to move south or to become bankrupt. Some mills moved to take advantage of cheaper labor, although they would sacrifice the expertise of the experienced mill workers. Albert C. Houghton joined in the efforts of the other owners because he was concerned with legislation which he thought would hurt the overall business climate in Massachusetts. Albert was known at the time to be very fair to his employees, and they generally rewarded the company with their loyalty and dedication. For Mr. Houghton, a move out of North Adams was out of the question. It would go against his vision he had for North Adams. There was no way he was going to hurt the people of the community that adopted him as one of their own native sons.

The mill owners warned of the consequences of the loss of the cotton industry in Massachusetts. They warned of lower property values and of the harm to the rest of the economy. According to the data at the time one out of every twelve adults in Massachusetts were employed in a cotton mill.[8] They argued that this large percentage of the population will be harmed by

---

[8] "Loss to the State." Boston Daily Globe 8 Apr 1898: 9.

a total breakdown of the industry. In particular, the mill owners took issue with the labor laws that were being enacted. They argued that the laws, while good intentioned, were harming their businesses as it prevented them from investing in new machinery and they countered that the laws actually harmed employees as there were less opportunities for them.

With the passage of the labor laws that the owners so bitterly fought, there was a marked decrease if not cessation of mill expansion and upgrades, while other states saw the explosion that once graced Western Massachusetts. The mills also struggled as they were less likely to attract investments. The once promising opportunities in cotton were now seen as a risky venture in Massachusetts.

The mill owners argued that if business conditions were not improved and that business becomes unprofitable, everyone loses as either payroll would need to drop to return to profitability or the businesses would simply shut down as the glass and iron industries in the region had done previously. At the time Massachusetts had the strictest labor laws in the Northeast, and the mill owners were seeking to be comparable with all of its neighbors in New England, not the free-for-all that was seen in the South. They also asked for a lowering of the taxes that were quickly rising. They recommended removing the machinery from the property tax, but keeping the taxes on the land and the building themselves.

Also in 1898, Houghton's health began to deteriorate. With his interest in Arnold Print Works as well as all of his other interests, he rarely had time to rest. He was no longer Mayor of North Adams, but he was still pulled in too many directions. As a solution, he was determined to recuperate and on April 6, 1898, he boarded the ship Teutonic while at port in New York City for a month-long trip to England.

The SS Teutonic was a steamship on the White Star Line, the famed company known sadly because of the Titanic disaster. In an odd twist of fate, in October of 1913, just eighteen months after the sinking of the Titanic, the Teutonic almost met the same fate. The Teutonic was merely feet away from having the same tragic ending as the Titanic. The ship was just east of Belle Isle, Newfoundland. The fog was very thick that night, when an outline of an iceberg could be seen. The ship reversed its engines and changed its direction. The Teutonic passed within twenty feet of the iceberg. Immediately after the incident, the passengers on board were aware of what just happened. Seeing this event was so close to the sinking of the Titanic, let's just say that the passengers were very grateful to the quick thinking displayed by the captain and crew.

Albert Houghton was accompanied by two of his daughters, Susan and Alice Houghton. At this time Mary was in school, it is unclear why Cordelia did not accompany the rest of the family. Florence, his oldest surviving daughter was married and four months pregnant at the time, and it is assumed that her husband needed to stay behind to see to the day-to-day operations of Arnold Print Works while Albert was resting. Perhaps Cordelia stayed behind to tend to Florence. This trip was largely a relief to his family as they had tried so many times to convince Albert to take a break; this may have been the first vacation he ever took. Albert and his daughters returned to New York City on April 27, 1898 from their trip overseas. The first thing he did was telephoned his family and told them how refreshed he felt from the time off.

After his vacation, Houghton returned to his busy schedule. On October 5, 1899, the Boston & Albany Railroad offered to make a gentleman by the name of Chauncey M. Depew a Director. When he declined the position, the railroad called on Albert Houghton who accepted their offer. Shortly after that, he had purchased the rights to Rattlesnake Brook in Williamstown, Massachusetts. Why would Mr. Houghton purchase a brook? He was a large stockholder in the Williamstown Water Company and this water source would help the company meet the demand that it was unable to for several years. The town of Williamstown benefited from this sale as on this property was a local drinking establishment that the town tried unsuccessfully for years to eliminate as it was considered a nuisance. The problematic drinking hole was torn down and everyone was happy, except for those that wanted a drink.

Even though the positive impacts that Albert Houghton had on the city were well-known, his political opponents were still making noise about him even after his retirement from political office. Continued bickering occurred during the 1899 mayoral election between Edward S. Wilkinson Sr. and William Dobson. Dobson blasted some of the infrastructure improvements made during the previous years. Dobson considered North Adams government to be controlled by a group of allies that included families including Houghton, Wilkinson, Cady, and Gallup.

Dobson called those in power "the ring" and he floated the idea that if the power brokers once again regained control of government, Church Street would be paved at an expense of one hundred thousand dollars. This assertion met some initial criticism as the city's paving program operated for four years prior at twenty thousand dollars per year. Dobson threw further allegations against the wall stating that Houghton intended to unload Rattlesnake Brook to the city for his personal gain. Houghton years prior sold Broad Brook to North Adams when the city needed additional water supply. But Houghton sold the water rights for the amount he purchased it for, meaning no personal gain. Houghton also had the water rights to Rattlesnake Brook, but had no intended plans at that point.

Dobson continued to hurl accusations in an attempt to stir up the voters. He then questioned the logic of North Adams purchasing the land where three schools were erected. These schools were placed on land that was owned by Houghton and William Gallup. The truth is that two of the schools were built on land that was sold for the purchase price, meaning Houghton and Gallup did not benefit from a profit. The third property did not sell at cost, but was sold for below the property's value. File this under "no good deed goes unpunished". The result was more vindication for Albert Houghton as Wilkinson not only beat Dobson in the 1899 election, but he crushed Dobson during a rematch the next election cycle.

At this point in time Albert Houghton was still heavily involved in the A.J. Houghton & Co. Vienna Brewery. An interesting story occurred in August, 1900 when there was a bit of a dust-up between labor unions and Albert Houghton. When the Methodist church in North Adams was building a new parsonage, otherwise known as a rectory, he was part of the church committee that selected the contract of a firm that employed non-union labor. The unions saw this as a slap in the face and as retaliation, the labor unions proposed a boycott of A.J. Houghton & Company products.

Shortly after the turn of the century, Albert Houghton's business career perhaps reached the apex. In 1901, there were slightly more than thirty-eight hundred millionaires in all of the United States of America – Albert C. Houghton was one of the members of this elite class.[9]

---

[9] "America's 3828 Millionaires." *The Vermont Phoenix* 3 May 1901: 2.

While Albert Houghton previously spent considerable time working in New York City, in 1904 he moved his personal offices of Arnold Print Works to the city. He did this to concentrate his efforts on the textile market there in order to continue the explosive growth of the print works, and in turn, North Adams. At this point in time, he limited himself to strictly any business at hand in New York City and left the control of the North Adams operations in the hands of his son-in-law William Gallup. In addition to the office in New York, Arnold Print Works at this time had other offices in Boston, Chicago, St. Louis and Paris, France.

Also in 1904, the cotton mills in New England faced some economic hardship. Mills across the Northeast were suspending operations until conditions improved. Arnold Print Works was no exception. On June 3, 1904, Arnold Print Works suspended operations on Fridays and Saturdays and closed the mills in order to cut costs. This was considered good fortune, as other mills shut down completely during the entire summer. That writing on the wall that Houghton saw in 1898 had come true, Arnold Print Works was in trouble and the storm clouds were gathering.

In June of 1905, President Theodore Roosevelt visited the Berkshires. One of the stops on his tour included North Adams, but he also stopped at Williams College to receive an honorary degree and to speak. Because of his standing at Williams College and because of his political pull, Albert C. Houghton was one of seven individuals who personally welcomed President Roosevelt. While at Williams College, he was entertained by the President of Williams College, Henry Hopkins, then after that a grand reception was held to welcome the President. On the following day he received his honorary degree and then spoke on the steps of the Congregational Church in Williamstown.

Albert Houghton lost another nephew as John Edwin Warner Jr. passed away at the age of thirty on December 5, 1905. John had contracted and suffered from Consumption. John was the son of Chloe Houghton and her husband John Warner. While he was married at the time of his death, he did not have any children.

Friday, November 30, 1906 was a very dark day for the Houghton family, as Alice, Houghton's second youngest daughter died. Alice was in New York City visiting her family for the Thanksgiving holiday, which was the week prior. Alice was only thirty-one years old at the time and her death was unexpected. Again, Albert and Cordelia had to bury one of their children and sadly, this would not be the final time. The death of Alice was the beginning of a very difficult stretch for the Houghton family. Most parents who have lost a child would sacrifice anything to get their child back and I am positive that would apply to Houghton and his businesses as well. But for the grieving Houghtons, the business empire was also threatened. For Albert Houghton, this was the beginning of a very dark period.

Albert Houghton lost another nephew as Edward Hudson Houghton, the son of Hudson Houghton passed away on February 10, 1907 at the age of forty-seven years old. Like his father, Edward developed pneumonia and the illness proved too much to recover from. Edward had business dealings with Albert as he was named the Treasurer of the A.J. Houghton Company in Boston, the brewery in which Albert held interest.

The Panic of 1907

The business skill of Albert Charles Houghton was well-known and for the most part his risks paid off handsomely. This was not the case in 1907. In 1906, Albert had a rather large and risky idea that, coupled with an unexpected financial crash, could have had catastrophic results to both his empire as well as the well-being of the community of North Adams. At this point, Albert was spending the majority of his professional time in the New York City office of Arnold Print Works. Albert became keenly aware of the commodities market. The price of cotton fell sharply and was attractive enough that he thought it would be a wise investment to purchase an extremely large quantity of cotton. A large amount of the raw material was stored in vast warehouses in North Adams. Since the cotton was bought at a very low price, he thought the market price would rise drastically and Arnold Print Works would have been rewarded with a very large cash windfall. It was not a bad idea, but the problem was with the storm clouds on the horizon that no one could foresee.

The problem was that in 1907, a serious financial crisis hit the economy of the United States. It all began when a man by the name of F. Augustus Heinze and his brother Otto devised a stock manipulation scheme involving the United Cooper Company. The scheme blew up in their faces and created a dangerous situation where many large financial institutions were failing and as a result banks were refusing to loan money. The recession was called the Panic of 1907, but others have coined it the "1907 Bankers' Panic" or "the Knickerbocker Crisis".

Normally, Mr. Houghton's gamble would have paid off, but no one can predict when a risky banker in New York City can cause an entire economy to crash, so the poorly-timed financial crisis seriously impacted the financial standing of Arnold Print Works. At this point in time, Mr. Houghton's health began to deteriorate slightly – the stress of this economic downturn coupled with the untimely and tragic death of his daughter Alice must have been too much to bear. If this was a personal gamble, I am sure the stress would not have been that great. The fact that Arnold Print Works was a major player in the local economy and employed many of North Adams' residents, so his gamble was broadly impactful.

In a financial statement that was filed to the Massachusetts Commissioner of Corporations on June 30, 1907, the company's assets matched to the dollar the company's liabilities. The financial situation was precarious, but the firm's management towed the line that the company was solvent. Besides the mills in North Adams, there were the firm's offices in New York City, St. Louis, Boston and Paris.

Suddenly creditors of the Arnold Print Works were calling in their obligations which jeopardized the company. The company was not insolvent, but temporarily could not meet the creditors' obligations and the company could not secure renewal of loans. This issue threatened to place the print works on shaky ground. Together Mr. Houghton and Mr. Gallup met with other prominent business men seeking advice. Taking in the advice they received, they voluntarily placed the business in receivership to protect the company, its shareholders, and the creditors. At the time the company employed upwards of six thousand employees. In addition to Arnold Print Works, the ancillary mills were impacted. These mills included the Beaver and Eclipse mills in North Adams, the Williamstown Manufacturing Company mill, and the North Pownal Manufacturing Company mill.

Albert C. Houghton's nephew Charles D. Houghton, who was also a creditor of the companies, petitioned Judge Powell of the United States Circuit Court in Boston to name Henry Warner as a receiver of the Arnold Print Works. On November 6, 1907, Arnold Print Works was placed in a receivership of U.S. Senator Winthrop Murray Crane, James J. Storrow of Lee, Higginson & Company in Boston, and an attorney, Mr. Henry E. Warner, also of Boston for a period deemed to last five years. In November of 1907, the receivers of the company found that the bills receivable, the immense inventory of finished goods and raw materials would have covered any debt owed by the company.

In addition, the ancillary mills also fell under the hands of a receivership. The North Pownal Manufacturing Company was under the receivership of A. E. Cudworth of South Londonderry, with Mr. Warner a co-receiver. At the time, the North Pownal operations employed eight hundred workers while Arnold Print Works employed more than three thousand. The Williamstown Manufacturing Company, employing five hundred, was granted a similar fate as well as the firm Gallup & Houghton.

The financial difficulty caused by both the national economy and the Arnold Print Works caused similar shockwaves throughout North Adams and the region. The Windsor Print Works in North Adams shortened their work week as it was expected the immense stock of Arnold Print Works will flood the market causing a crash in the price of goods.

Houghton vowing to right the ship, while battling the onset of health issues, took the necessary steps to get the business in better financial standings. The numerous cotton mills were sold off and the company's operation became centralized in one plant. The liquidation of the obligations almost depleted the capital. However, with hard work the print works regained its solid footing. As a result, the receivership was reduced to three years and the company reemerged with Mr. Houghton still leading the company.

In what was considered rare, the Arnold Print Works was able to pay off its creditors one hundred percent plus an additional six percent interest. They could have taken the easy route and declared bankruptcy, however, Mr. Houghton was a man of character and felt it was imperative to honor their obligations and not take the easy way out. To Albert C. Houghton it was much larger than what was best for him; it was what was best for his vision of North Adams.

Also in 1907, the Stamford Chemical Works, the business that was formerly Houghton Chemical Company, and before that, the A.C. Houghton Company, was burned to the ground. While Albert Houghton sold his interest of the company, many years before, it is important to note as that is the foundation of the business empire that Albert Houghton was able to build. It is sort of ironic that as the business empire was teetering on bankruptcy, the foundation built many years ago was destroyed during the same year.

As if Houghton was not already troubled with the loss of his daughter Alice and the financial disaster that seemed lurking for his business empire, on Tuesday, May 26, 1908 another terrible personal tragedy struck that would test his limits as a human being. On that day, Alice's seven year old son, Edward Wilkinson III, passed away after battling a number of lengthy illnesses. The Houghtons witnessed the burial of their grandson next to their daughter. I cannot fathom the stress or the grief, it must have seemed like their world was crashing in around them.

On July 31, 1908, the receivers of the businesses which include Arnold Print Works, Gallup and Houghton, Williamstown Manufacturing Company, and the North Pownal Manufacturing Company filed with the judge a plan of reorganization. At this point a preliminary plan was devised to pay creditors fifty percent of their claims, with the remaining debt to be paid by the issuance of five year mortgage bonds with six percent interest. The receivers stated in this filing that the high value of assets would comfortably pay all creditors in full.

On October 15, 1908, the receivers of the Arnold Print Works filed their first report with Judge Lowell of the United States Circuit Court. The report formalized a plan in which the receivers intend to sell assets at a public auction pursuant to a plan of reorganization that was devised by creditors. Upon receiving this report, Judge Lowell ordered a deadline of October 26 of that year for anyone to show cause to the court why this plan should not be permitted.

The largest creditors included Deering, Miliken & Co., The National Bank of Commerce of New York, Gallup & Houghton, and the North Pownal Manufacturing Co. The receivers included in their filing the rationale that the best means of preserving the value of the company's assets is to allow the company to continue to proceed in business.

On October 20, 1908 the assets of Arnold Print Works were ordered for sale at a public auction by Judge Lowell of the U.S. Circuit Court. On

December 1, 1908, the receivers held an auction where the Williamstown Manufacturing Company, The Arnold Print Works, and Gallup & Houghton would be sold to the highest bidder at the Berkshire County Courthouse in Pittsfield. At the time of the auction, bidders had to present a check for $25,000 for the Williamstown mill, $100,000 for the Arnold Print Works, and $50,000 for Gallup & Houghton properties. During the auction Gallup and Houghton were able to retain their businesses.

Albert Houghton's sister Emeline Houghton Browne passed away in her home on November 3, 1909 in Boston at the age of seventy-two. Emeline was widowed for nine years before she reunited with her husband. Emeline developed a condition called apoplexy, a condition she would endure for two months before her death. Apoplexy is a condition in which one experiences bleeding from an internal organ, although it is not clear which organ was involved in Emeline's death.

Because of Albert's preoccupation in the effort to save Arnold Print Works and his own deteriorating health, Albert stepped down from his roles as Trustee for both Boston University and Williams College. The decision to step away from both educational institutions was a very difficult one for him to make. He felt that he could not devote the time he felt was necessary to either institution.

On October 21, 1910, the Beaver and Eclipse mills were sold off in order to infuse Arnold Print Works with more cash in the final stages of the financial crisis that began in 1907. Both of the mills were sold to a cotton syndicate headed by William M. Butler of New Bedford, Massachusetts. The sale was orchestrated by Senator W. M. Crane who was named one of the receivers during the financial crisis. While in the past, the product made at the mills was used directly at Arnold Print Works, during the crisis, the manufactured product was not being used by Arnold Print Works, but sold to the highest bidder. The sale of the mills insured a more consistent level of income for the mills. In addition to the actual mill buildings themselves, the sale included 224 tenement structures which consisted of an area from Union Street up to the Clarksburg town line, a distance of approximately one mile.

On October 24, 1910, the Williamstown and North Pownal, Vermont cotton mills doing business as Williamstown Manufacturing Company and North Pownal Manufacturing Company were sold to W.B. and C.T.

Plunkett of Adams, Massachusetts. Both mills were incorporated into the Greylock Mills Corporation, a division of the Greylock Manufacturing Company located in North Adams. After the sale of the final two mills, they were outfitted with new machinery.

With the sale of inventory and the sale of the ancillary cotton mills, Arnold Print Works was able to work out a deal with its creditors so that it can resume normal operations. On November 15, 1910, the print works and the creditors agreed with the payment of claims. At the beginning of the financial crisis, the debt was just shy of nine million dollars. Quick assets were listed at eleven million dollars and the plants themselves were valued at five million dollars. As part of the agreement, the creditors were offered fifty-five percent in cash with the remaining forty-five percent in mortgage bonds carrying a six percent interest. Once this was approved the receivership was disbanded and the company was returned to the former owners and stockholders. With the sale of the ancillary mills, Arnold Print Works would concentrate solely on the printing of cloth.

Health Issues Slow Down a Dynamo

As mentioned briefly, Albert C. Houghton's health suffered as a result of the 1907 Panic. I think that the great personal losses the family faced only hastened his decline in health. He had already decreased his workload in 1904 when he decided to move his offices to New York City and concentrate on those efforts. The financial difficulty in 1907 caused him to again pick up his workload. But to me, that was not the full story, while this was going on he had to deal with incredibly crushing tragedies of losing both a daughter and a grandson. His personal and business lives were crumbling, and he was not getting any younger. In 1909, Albert went abroad to recharge again, this time to Italy. He returned to the United States on the ship S.S. Canopic which left the port of Genoa on April 19, 1909. Shortly after the trip to Italy, Houghton's niece Emma Houghton Chain and her husband Elmer Chain buried their five-and-a-half year old son Winthrop. He was suffering from Diphtheria.

Around 1910 when the receivership was over and the company was reorganized, Mr. Houghton's title of President was merely a figurehead arrangement. That statement would have killed him if I said it to his face back then, but in reality there is truth in that statement. Gallup ran the day-to-day operations of the company at this time and Houghton was regrettably not the same powerhouse he once was.

Albert Houghton began ceding many of the duties and responsibilities of President onto William Gallup. Mr. Gallup was still acting as the Treasurer but also took on the additional roles associated with President. Splashed in the headlines in newspapers in New England on Saturday, March 18, 1911 were reports that Albert C. Houghton was close to death within his apartment at the Murray Hill Hotel in New York City. Murray Hill Hotel is the same location where Alice Houghton Wilkinson had perished years prior. Houghton was seriously ill for weeks at this point and his condition was not improving.

At this point in time, Houghton was diagnosed with and suffering from three different ailments. These include chronic myocarditis, arterio-sclerosis and parenchymatous nephritis.

Chronic myocarditis is an inflammation of heart muscle that is often the result of infection from viruses or as a reaction to medication. The inflammation will damage the heart muscle and may even kill a portion of the heart tissue. This is different than a heart attack as with this condition, there is no blockage of the coronary arteries that define a heart attack. As an autoimmune reaction to viruses, the immune system can attack cardiac myosin as the protein is similar to some viruses. During the infection or even after the virus has left the body, the immune system can attack the cardiac myosin.

As with any disease, the symptoms can greatly vary based on the individual and other factors. Myocarditis in mild cases can end up resolving itself causing no considerable damage to the heart. However, Albert C. Houghton was diagnosed with a chronic condition, meaning damage was being done to his heart. A person suffering from myocarditis will often feel chest pain, from slight to a stabbing sensation, a feeling of breathlessness, palpitations, and fever. Current medicinal practices can help those that have been impacted by this ailment, however, recall that medicine was primitive at this time, so bed rest was a common treatment for those suffering this condition.

Arteriosclerosis is quite simply the thickening and hardening of medium to large arteries. This condition was also called myoconditis in the era we are studying, but that term is no longer in use by the medical community at large. This condition is common in the elderly, part of the aging process. Hypertension can aggravate the condition. Since we know Albert's heart was getting damaged from myocarditis and he was facing intense stress from the financial troubles of 1907, it is not out of the question to suggest that this natural aging process was being sped up by those conditions.

Parenchymatous nephritis affects the parenchyma of the kidney. I know what you are thinking, 'Gee, I am glad you cleared that up, Dave'. Have no fear; I will explain. This condition can be caused by repeated attacks of nephritis due to an irritating toxin that is persistent in the body. This creates a situation where fibrous connective tissue in the kidney breaks down. The epithelium which is responsible for secretions degenerates.

Parenchymatous nephritis could be the result of infections such as diphtheria, scarlet fever and smallpox. However, it is more than likely caused by autoimmune disorders which will attack the tissue of major organs. Remember that Albert suffered from his autoimmune system attacking the tissues in his heart, so it is likely it was also attacking his kidneys.

The kidneys can become enlarged, soft and filled with fluid. The kidneys may bulge causing bloody fluids to escape the kidneys and enter the urine stream. The condition can also lower urine production and thus allow the body to retain waste products and toxins. Nephritis also is an issue as necessary proteins can be excreted into the urine stream. Our bodies need proteins and this loss of proteins can create several grave conditions, including the loss of protein needed to prevent blood from clotting leading to sudden strokes. This condition can also lead to mild hypertension which as we learned can speed up arteriosclerosis and with a damaged heart from myocarditis, can create substantial health issues.

With the three different ailments that were specified, Albert more than likely experienced chest pains and overall weakness that prevented him from keeping on top of his normally hectic schedule. The once unstoppable force of a man was clearly showing his age.

The local newspaper had almost daily updates on his condition. It was a rollercoaster ride, where he improved only to suffer setbacks. Mr. Houghton's condition did eventually improve and he returned to North Adams after his annual winter migration to New York City. He kept the title of President of Arnold Print Works, but effectively, he was retired.

As Houghton's health failed and he became weaker, the Houghton's youngest daughter Mary devoted her life to the care of her father. She put aside any aspirations of having her own family so that she could be there for her father. Mary was described as a very nurturing person and she did her best to take care of her father. The family had the resources that they could have hired nurses to take care of any whim and need of Albert, but Mary felt that a little TLC from a loved one could not be bought.

Christmas Eve of 1911 was a tragic time for the Houghton family. Albert Houghton's nephew, Charles, the son of James and Lestina, lost his wife as she was battling breast cancer. While she was weak from the devastating nature of the disease, she developed pneumonia and that was too much for her body to take.

With Albert Houghton's health deteriorating, he continued to act more like a figurehead as President of Arnold Print Works. Houghton spent more and more time convalescing at home, with his daughter Mary taking care of him. The man who refused to take vacations suddenly felt that his body was betraying him. August 1, 1914 was supposed to be a relaxing day. When he returned to the mansion that day history was written and his already fragile body was injured. Worst of all, his youngest daughter was dead. With his broken heart, recovery was not possible. He lost the will to fight on.

In the afternoon of August 6, 1914, Albert's condition took a turn for the worse and any hopes of his recovery were beginning to dim. From this point forward his death became expected. Around three in the afternoon on August 11, 1914, Albert Charles Houghton took his last breath and his heart beat for the final time. He died peacefully surrounded by family in the family home that witnessed so much tragedy in a span of ten days. The mansion would once again have a beloved family member waiting for burial.

Albert C. Houghton had a substantial life insurance policy. The beneficiary of that policy was his daughter Mary, who herself passed away. The estate was the beneficiary of $206,727[10]. For the life insurance companies, 1914 was the most expensive up until that point, with Albert Houghton figuring prominently into that distinction.

Through Albert's Eyes: August 1, 1914

I mentioned earlier in the book that it is best to understand the tragedy of August 1, 1914 when you get the chance to know the people involved rather than read a clinical retelling of the incidents. When you read the accident details, put yourself in Albert's shoes and think about the brief overview of his life that I was able to tell. Imagine what he went through, all the tragedy, and then add that to the chaos of the accident scene and its aftermath.

August 1, 1914 was supposed to be a wonderful day. Albert Houghton's health has been a bit problematic recently, but his health was such on that day that he was eager to get out of the house for a day trip. Anyone who had the misfortune of being bed-ridden knows what a relief it is to get out, see the sun and get some fresh air. His caretaker, his own daughter, who gave up everything so that she could be there to take care of him, was excited to take her friend Sybil Hutton and Sybil's husband on a trip. The group of people more than likely had no idea of the impending war across the ocean. Ironically enough, Florence Houghton Gallup was supposed to set sail for Germany that very day. If the news of the declaration of war had been known, there would have been some concern over Florence's departure.

What is unknown is if the Huttons had a chance to ride in an automobile before this tragic day. How tragic would this be if this was their very first automobile ride and this first adventure tore apart a young and loving family? If this was the Hutton's first automobile trip, Mr. Houghton must have been proud to show off something that was still uncommon at the time. This day, was supposed to be a happy day, it was not supposed to end the way it did.

---

[10] "Insurance Payments in 1914 Biggest Ever Made in U.S." El Paso Herald 12-13 Jun 1915: 3A.

Cordelia and Albert Houghton were always concerned about the safety of the road that the car was on. Was this the thought in his head when the car came upon the work crew? This work crew incidentally was working on making the roadway safer. When people get into traumatic accidents, they often report that it was all a blur. Imagine as Albert Houghton was laying on the ground, thrown from the automobile, the sights he must have seen, the sounds he must have heard. I hope and I pray that none of you reading this would ever experience such an event.

As Houghton realized what exactly happened, he must have felt the impacts of the accident on his aging body. But to him, his own health was secondary. Imagine being him for this exercise. Imagine seeing a doctor holding his dead or dying wife. Imagine looking around to find your own daughter, and then you realize that the daughter who gave up her future to take care of you was slumped over in the rear seat of the car. She was the only one not thrown from the automobile and her body took the brunt of the automobile overturning three times.

As you get closer to the car, you see John Widders looking dazed and confused as he placed all of this on his own shoulders. When you get to the car, you realize that your daughter is in very grave condition. She is vocal about very serious pain in her back and neck. Her face was badly crushed. She was slipping in and out of consciousness, probably suffering from shock. You see the workmen running down the hill and screaming for help. This was supposed to be a pleasure ride!

Imagine watching your daughter in such serious condition and waiting for help to arrive. We take rapid response for granted; the wait must have been traumatic. Finally doctors start to arrive. When they find that Sybil is dead, they focus on the other survivors. If a doctor checked in on Albert, I am sure he scolded him and sent him off to his daughter. You watch as they gingerly remove her from the wreckage and carry her up the embankment so that she could be taken to the closest hospital, which happened to be North Adams Hospital. You finally give in to be taken away from the scene, but before you go, you take one last look and you walk by Dr. Robert Hutton holding his wife's dead body, refusing to leave her.

This is a scene which haunted Albert Houghton for the rest of his life, and some say to this day.

After the accident, Houghton was brought to his mansion so he could recover. He delivered the news of Sybil's death and Mary's grave condition. His own body bruised and broken, his thoughts were on his dying daughter. When Mary died, I cannot imagine the grief that must have been felt. At some point during the evening of August 1, 1914, his eyes closed. When they opened next, there was another commotion. He learned that John Widders shot himself in the stable. His trusted and loyal employee – a man he treated like a member of his own family was dead, because of the events of the car ride.

He later buried his youngest daughter – his third child that he had to bury. As for John Widders, Houghton held no grudge; it was merely an accident, it only seemed right to bury him in the Houghton family plot. The immense grief took a toll on his already frail body. The lack of his devoted, loving daughter must have made his home feel like a raw, empty void.

Slowly, Albert C. Houghton slipped away and the physical vessel that contained his thoughts, his emotions, his hopes and dreams, fears and concerns died. Based on details from people who have had near-death experiences, this is what happened next. He saw his own lifeless body lying in bed. He then witnessed the doctors feverishly working to save him. He turned his attention to his wife and family who were crying hysterically.

What happened next is that he may not have seen the light he was supposed to go towards. He became so focused on his life, his experiences, his tragedies, his struggles, the work he needed to do that he failed to see his loved ones waiting to guide him into the next existence. He then became a legend. Not for his work, his commitment to his family or his community. Those three things meant the world to him. He became a legend because he supposedly haunts a building. A building that is supposed to be lifeless, a combination of stone, wood, plaster, pipes and wires. A building is supposed to be hard and cold and not have a voice or a pulse.

The legend of Albert Charles Houghton should be as a man, not as a "ghost".

3. Cordelia Houghton

That quiet pall of darkness migrated to her majestic home.

Cordelia Jeanette Houghton is a central figure in the history of the Houghton Mansion, but yet, not much is discussed regarding her life, albeit for a few brief mentions. I say that the terrible car accident impacted her more than her husband due to the simple fact that Cordelia had to live her life after one final death, that of Albert Houghton. Cordelia also lived for over three-and-a-half years with the grief and loneliness that accompanied the loss of her loved ones.

Cordelia Jeanette Smith was the second child born to Noble W. and Louisa (Sanford) Smith. Noble was a farmer and raised his growing family on a substantial farm. The Smith family could trace their lineage back to some of the oldest families in New England and back to Nathan Smith who fought in the American Revolution. Cordelia's father, Noble Smith was born in Adams, Massachusetts to Reuben and Olive (Wescott) Smith. Cordelia's mother Louisa was born in Readsboro, Vermont to William and Lucy (Rice) Sanford. Lucy, Cordelia's grandmother, was one of a family of twelve siblings.

Cordelia was born in Stamford, Vermont on January 28, 1845. Cordelia was one of several siblings which included Sedgwick, Laura, Walter, Albert and Corliss. As mentioned earlier, Noble Smith owned and operated a substantial farm in Stamford and the farm allowed for the family to live comfortably. As it was with many affluent families at the time, the Smith family was able to afford a servant to help with household chores.

When she was a child, Cordelia was raised within the Methodist Episcopal Church and retained her strong connection to it throughout her life. Before she had a family of her own, she was a very active member of her church community. Her faith never wavered throughout her life or through her many devastating losses.

When Cordelia's mother passed away, several small children were left without their mother. When her father passed away, Cordelia's brother took in the unwed siblings. Louisa's grave is on the left while Noble's is on the right.

As a young woman, Cordelia lost her mother when on October 18, 1864, Louisa passed away at the age of forty-three. At the time of her mother's death Cordelia was nineteen years old. The death of Louisa Smith was devastating to the Smith family. Corliss Smith, the youngest of the Smith's children was only four years old when he lost his mother. The ages of her other children were six, thirteen, fifteen and twenty-one years old. In fact Louisa passed away one day after the thirteenth birthday of her son, Walter Noble Smith. Cordelia's father was left to raise the family without his wife.

On September 17, 1866, Cordelia married Albert C. Houghton in Stamford. At the time of her wedding, she was twenty-one years old. For both the bride and groom, this was the first and only marriage. Albert and Cordelia began their life together in Stamford. A little more than one year after their marriage, Albert and Cordelia would welcome their first child, Laura, into the world on September 30, 1867.

Cordelia's oldest brother Sedgwick Lonvaine Smith married Cora A. Church on November 7, 1867. At this time Sedgwick was working the family farm and continued to do so after the wedding. Sedgwick would later open a general store in Stamford, Vermont and serve as a Selectman for the town after briefly living in North Adams.

Cordelia gave birth to her second daughter when Florence Louisa Houghton was born on November 3, 1869. It was only slightly more than six months later, when on May 23, 1870, Cordelia's father, Noble, passed away in Stamford, Vermont from kidney failure at the age of fifty-two years old. With the death of both the matriarch and patriarch in the Smith family, the younger members of the family needed to stay with Sedgwick since they were not of an age to be on their own. Sedgwick and Cora would move to North Adams sharing a home with his unwed siblings.

Laura Smith, Cordelia's sister, married Edgar Alonzo Stroud on October 25, 1870. The couple would settle in North Adams, where her family would enjoy a strong bond with Cordelia's family.

Cordelia felt strongly that home and family life trumped any other pursuits, except for only perhaps religion. She was a very devoted and loving mother and wife. While her husband was seeking an opportunity to move to North Adams and further his business experience, Cordelia was focusing on her young family. In January of 1867, Cordelia's first child Laura became sick with what was diagnosed as a brain fever. The medical community no longer uses the term and while this is speculative Laura's illness could have been the result of encephalitis, meningitis or cerebritis. On January 13, 1871, Laura passed away; she was only three years old.

I cannot begin to imagine the heartbreak that Cordelia experienced. The only saving grace is that she had to keep going as the family consisted of a fifteen-month old daughter, Florence. When it came time to bury their little child, they purchased a family plot in Southview Cemetery in North Adams. The family chose this site as they anticipated their move south to North Adams. Only Laura was buried in the family plot until the tragedy unfolded on August 1, 1914.

The Houghton family moved to North Adams and their family grew. On March 26, 1872, Cordelia gave birth to Susan Houghton, their third daughter. Alice Josephine Houghton was born on April 17, 1875. Finally, on July 25, 1877, Mary Cordelia Houghton was born, completing the Houghton family.

Cordelia had a very strong distaste for social prominence. As she considered her home and her family the most important part of her life, she generally avoided the social scene that so many in her position craved. Rather than showing off her wealth, she found it much more enjoyable to spend low-key time with family and friends. While most wives of wealthy manufacturers were in numerous societies, Cordelia would have none of that. While the spotlight was thrust upon her family, she was happier to be in the shadows instead of upfront in the glaring light. She was described as being quiet, even keeled, and as having a big heart. She was very selective in the organizations she was a member of.

Cordelia was very proud of her family's legacy in the early years of the United States, including the fact that she was a descendant of a soldier that served in the Revolutionary War. Cordelia was a charter member of the Fort Massachusetts Chapter of the Daughters of American Revolution. Cordelia's daughters Florence and Susan were also involved in the establishment of the chapter.

One organization that Cordelia was not a part of, but held in high regard was Kappa Phi Alpha. The organization was formed around 1885 by students of Drury Academy. Kappa Phi Alpha held several functions and Cordelia had a helping hand in several of their receptions. This small role in Cordelia's life is important to mention as a future son-in-law, Edward S. Wilkinson Jr. was a member of Kappa Phi Alpha. Cordelia, however, volunteered considerable time for the North Adams Hospital as she thought it was imperative to the community.

Cordelia's younger brother Walter Noble Smith married Jeanette Cook on November 12, 1882. After their marriage, Walter and his brother Albert Reuben Smith purchased an existing grocery store that was located as part of the Beaver Mill complex. The store's name was W.N. Smith & Company. Cordelia's brother, Albert Reuben Smith, would not marry, but remained a bachelor throughout his life.

The youngest Smith sibling, Corliss Smith married Ida Esther Bryant on July 21, 1886. On September 23, 1888, Corliss, lost his six-month old son to cholera, a disease that was prevalent in this era. This was the only child that was born to Corliss and his wife Ida. Sadly, Cordelia knew from experience the tragedy of losing a young child, so she felt it was important to be there for her baby brother.

It was only several years later that on March 15, 1892, Cordelia had to deal with the death of Corliss, who was only twenty-nine years old when he passed away. Not only was he Cordelia's brother, but Albert Houghton also felt the loss as Albert provided young Corliss with a job as a sketch maker in the Arnold Print Works. For Cordelia, the passing of Corliss was worse in that his brief life was marred by tragedy throughout. Corliss was only four years old when his mother passed away; his father's passing was several years later. Unlike Cordelia, he did not have the chance to grow up in the household of his mother and father, but he spent time living with his older sister and family. When it finally appeared that his life was turning a corner, fate once again stepped in, and the only child he had passed away around six months after his birth. The life of Cordelia's brother Corliss was definitely a tragic one.

Cordelia became a grandmother for the first time as her oldest surviving daughter, Florence, gave birth to a son, Houghton Gallup on June 18, 1895. Unfortunately, the joy faded quickly as the baby lost his life just fifty-two days later. Another little life lost, once again Cordelia mourned for a baby. In a little more than two years later, Florence delivered another child on June 27, 1897, this time a daughter named Ruth. Again tragedy struck as the baby lived only forty-nine days passing away on August 15 of that year. For Florence the death of two children under two-months old must have been so devastating. For Cordelia, the losses were not only painful because it was her grandchildren that died, but she witnessed the grief of her daughter.

Cordelia was particularly close to her sister Laura, who also lived in North Adams. Laura's children were also particularly close to the children of Albert and Cordelia. Laura's husband Edgar Stroud was also involved in the government of North Adams, being elected on the City Council when Albert C. Houghton was first elected Mayor. As such, an already strong bond between the brother-in-laws was strengthened with their ties to governing the city.

In 1896, Edgar Stroud's health began to fail. His illness baffled his medical caretakers and he received extensive medical attention with no real relief. His once robust nature and unusually strong physique, for which he was known, was ravaged by his illness. As his death became closer, he was a mere shell of his former self. This was particularly tough on not only Cordelia, but also for Albert. Cordelia would be there for Laura as her husband's health deteriorated. On Saturday, December 11, 1897, Edgar lost consciousness to which he never regained it. On Tuesday, December 14, 1897, at approximately one-thirty in the afternoon, Edgar passed away at the age of fifty-three. Based on his symptoms he was experiencing it was thought that he may have had pancreatic cancer – a truly devastating and painful cancer. At the time of Edgar's death, his youngest child was only ten years old.

Just a few months after the death of Ruth Gallup, Cordelia's daughter Florence was once again pregnant. At this point I could not guess if Cordelia was excited or dreading the loss of another little one and seeing her daughter grieve yet again. This time Florence was lucky as William Albert Gallup was born on September 5, 1898 and was healthy. This good fortune would not last however as Florence had to deal with more heartbreaking experiences.

The spring of 1899 however, was a happy time for the Houghton family. Cordelia's daughter Susan married Andrew McKean on March 22, 1899. It was just weeks later when Alice Houghton married Edward Wilkinson Jr. on April 19, 1899. Susan and Andrew McKean would move to Troy, New York, while Alice and Edward would stay in North Adams and lived in the residence next to Houghton Mansion until they moved to their own home about a year later. Within three months of marriage, Susan became pregnant with the couple's first child. For Cordelia, another grandchild was born, as Susan Houghton McKean gave birth to Cordelia McKean on March 15, 1900.

On July 12, 1900, Cordelia's niece Stella Spruill, who was a daughter of Laura Smith Stroud, lost her infant son William seven days after his birth when he experienced severe convulsions. At this point in time, Florence was again pregnant, and I would assume the pregnancy was a bit less stressful as her son was healthy and did not show any signs of illness that took the other children from her. On September 22, 1900, Florence gave birth again to her fourth child, a son named John Gallup.

Edward Shepard Wilkinson III was born on May 20, 1901; this was a blessed time in Cordelia's life as she welcomed another grandchild with open arms. Edward was the son of daughter Alice and her husband Edward Wilkinson Jr. The Wilkinson family was described as bubbly and joyful which must have been an extremely satisfying blessing for Cordelia.

It was not long after the birth of Edward Wilkinson III, when Florence was pregnant again. In the early stages of pregnancy with baby number five, John Gallup passed away on September 6, 1901 just a few weeks shy of his first birthday. With her daughter still mourning over the loss of her third child to pass away, Cordelia watched in agony as another tragedy occurred. This time on April 28, 1902, Florence went into labor. There was a complication during delivery, but regardless a daughter, Mary Houghton Gallup was born. Florence named the baby in honor of her youngest sister. Because of complications, Mary had severe medical issues. After holding on for several days, little Mary Gallup passed away on May 8, 1902. Cordelia had to live with the unpleasant experience of having to witness the burial of a fourth grandchild, all born to the same daughter. For Florence, she buried two small children in eight months.

The Houghton's final grandchild was born on January 6, 1903 as Susan Houghton McKean gave birth to a second daughter, Florence Porter McKean. I am not aware if Susan and Andrew experienced any of the heartbreak that her sister Florence endured as records for New York are difficult to obtain.

As was often the case after the construction of the Houghton Mansion, the Houghton family would relocate to New York City in the late autumn. This was done as Albert would often work in New York office of Arnold Print Works and by staying in New York City, Albert would avoid uncomfortable travel between North Adams and New York City. As the Thanksgiving Holiday of 1906 was approaching, the Houghton family was reunited in New York City to celebrate the holiday together. Unfortunately, a holiday in which we count our blessings would be one that was associated with tragedy.

While Alice Houghton Wilkinson was visiting her family for the holiday, she began to feel ill. When her condition deteriorated, she was diagnosed with appendicitis. She underwent an emergency surgery in the New York hotel in which the Houghtons stayed. She developed an infection that would kill her days later. Alice passed away on Friday, November 30, 1906 at the age of thirty-one. For the second time, Cordelia was forced to bury one of her children. After the death of Alice, her widower and child moved into his mother's home immediately next door.

Shortly after the death of her daughter Alice, the financial well-being of the family was in crisis. Still reeling over the loss of her daughter, she had to stand strong for her husband's sake as he battled hard to save everything that he worked so hard for. In a cruel twist of fate, while this was going on, their grandson, the son of Alice, got horribly ill. His father frantic to save his son's life whisked him out to a better climate, but it was too late as Edward S. Wilkinson III passed away on May 26, 1908.

Not only did Cordelia lose her daughter, but she lost a grandchild she was extremely close to. The Wilkinsons lived next door so Cordelia would her grandchild very frequently. As she lost both of a daughter and a grandson, one can wonder what she thought when she looked at the home next door and felt just how bleak that home now was without two rays of sunshine to brighten her day. The Wilkinson residence lost the laughter of a child, and I am sure that Cordelia would often look at the house and how quiet it must have seemed. For Cordelia, the once happy home next to her own was shrouded with a quiet pall of darkness.

The residence on the left is the former Wilkinson residence. The structure on the right is part of the Houghton Mansion. The reminder of the loss of a child's laughter was just mere yards from the Houghton residence.

As a result of Alice's death and the near collapse of the business empire, the health of Cordelia's husband was failing fast. Cordelia fretted as her husband deteriorated. Houghton would reluctantly lessen his workload in an attempt to give his body a fighting chance. At this point in time, Cordelia's youngest daughter Mary would forgo any thought of starting her own life and family so that she could look after her father. While it must have been nice to have her youngest daughter in the house, I cannot help to think that Cordelia would rather Mary start her own family.

Cordelia's younger brother Albert Reuben Smith passed away on May 8, 1913 at the age of fifty-four. His health was suffering for two years with the impacts of kidney disease ravaging his body. Albert was living in the home of his sister Laura Stroud and this was the location in which he died. Less than a month later, on June 6, 1913, Cordelia's niece Harriet Malcolm lost her first child, Laura, just one day after her birth. Laura was born prematurely and had serious medical conditions as a result.

On August 1, 1914, tragedy once again struck the Houghton household. The aftermath of the car accident that claimed the lives of her husband Albert and her youngest daughter Mary was particularly difficult on Cordelia, as you can imagine. That quiet pall of darkness that hung over the Wilkinson residence next door suddenly spread to her own residence, especially the bedroom of Mary. How could Cordelia not walk by Mary's old bedroom and not think how incredibly quiet it was? Gone was the vibrant energy that graced the room. The room was devoid of life and for Cordelia it was a source of infinite sadness especially with Mary's belongings acting as a strong reminder of a life stolen.

The loss of Mary meant that Cordelia had buried three of her five children, and mourned the loss of five out of eight grandchildren. Instead of Mary gracing the hallways with her presence, her lifeless body was placed in the parlor to await her funeral and burial. In the meanwhile, Cordelia's husband, the man she supported through all his ventures and the man who relied on her companionship, was slipping from her.

Just several days after Cordelia watched her daughter's burial, her husband passed away in the mansion. Unlike Mary, who died in a hospital, Albert died in his bedroom at the mansion. Through all the tragedy that the Houghtons faced, Cordelia could count of Albert being there for her; he was now gone himself.

Cordelia continued to live at the mansion. The residence must have felt empty without her husband and youngest daughter. I am sure that flashes of their lives in her memory presented themselves to her in each room. It used to be that the home next door was a source of grief and sorrow for Cordelia, now each room in her own home would have its own memory and each memory would haunt Cordelia. Cordelia was not alone though as hired help lived at the mansion. Cordelia also could count on her daughter Florence who lived nearly across Church Street. Cordelia's sister Laura also lived in North Adams and they would spend considerable time together.

Her daughter Susan would often visit with her family as well. While Cordelia grieved for her husband and daughter, she would not let her sadness distract her from her philanthropic tasks. She remained resolute to take a lead role in continuing efforts that were important to both her and her deceased husband. Cordelia and her surviving daughters continued to donate money to causes that were important to Albert. Cordelia lived her share of tragedy, but she did not allow it to rob her of her identity or steal her own faith from her.

Unfortunately, the end of tragedy did not occur as more relatives were dying far too young. Jesse Spruill passed away at just forty-four years old on February 2, 1915. Jesse was the husband of Cordelia's niece Stella. Jesse had been suffering from gall stones for three years and as a result underwent surgery on January 30, 1915. As a result of the surgery, Jesse experienced complications and died three days later. Stella was left to raise her family without her husband; their youngest child was only six years old. Stella was particularly close to the Houghton family especially Cordelia and Florence.

In 1917, Cordelia's nephew Eugene Levaine Smith passed away. His widow Maud was left to raise two small children without any source of income. Eugene was the son of Sedgwick and Cora Smith. Maud Smith would later remarry and move to Florida, but her marriage only lasted two years before she passed away herself, leaving her two children as orphans. Cordelia's younger brother Walter Noble Smith passed away on March 25, 1917 in North Adams at the age of sixty-five years old. His wife Jeanette had passed almost nine months earlier.

Cordelia's health began to falter and according to records, she was diagnosed as having paresis, which severely impacts the brain. She was diagnosed with this dreadful illness around April of 1917. Not only was her physical health starting to deteriorate, but if she did have paresis, her mental capabilities suffered as well. She suffered for ten months after her diagnosis. Cordelia would develop pneumonia in February of 1918 and suffered for eight days. The impacts of pneumonia proved too strong for her already declining health. On Tuesday, February 26, 1918, shortly before three in the afternoon, Cordelia passed away within the Houghton Mansion. One similarity that I find striking is that three deaths – Mary, Albert and Cordelia occurred around three in the afternoon.

It was said that she was peaceful when death arrived and the light passed from her body. Cordelia was seventy-three years old when she passed away. It was now Cordelia's turn to rest in a parlor waiting for her burial. Cordelia was buried in the family plot with Laura, Mary and Albert. Cordelia's burial would be the final one within the Houghton family plot.

The gravestone of the matriarch of the Houghton family. Her burial marked the final interment in the Houghton family plot in Southview Cemetery. Sadly, her entire family may not be reunited at this point in time.

The matriarch of the Houghton household passed into the light, but she is still the matriarch of her beloved home. Sadly, her whole family may not be reunited as of this date.

Through Cordelia's Eyes: August 1, 1914

As we did for Albert C. Houghton, we will revisit August 1, 1914 through the perspective of Cordelia Houghton since we had the chance to briefly examine her life and know her a bit better than before.

The morning of August 1, 1914 started off as a beautiful mid-summer morning for Cordelia. While her husband and daughter had plans to take the Huttons for a pleasure ride in the family's new automobile, Cordelia planned to meet with several family members that day. Cordelia preferred not to go with the family because she preferred small and intimate gatherings and must have felt that showing off an automobile was too ostentatious for her liking. Cordelia planned to meet with her brother-in-law Albert Willmarth in the morning. Later in the day, Cordelia's daughter Susan and her family would stop by and visit, and no doubt see Sybil and Robert Hutton.

A little before nine in the morning, Sybil and Robert Hutton were walking towards the Houghton Mansion. The Huttons just left their two year old son across the street where Sybil's aunt Mary Cady would babysit during their short trip. Cordelia had already had the chance to socialize with Sybil since she was in North Adams for a couple of weeks already. This was most likely the first chance Cordelia had to greet Robert Hutton since he just arrived in town in the afternoon of the previous day.

While this is speculative, I would assume that a conversation such as this must have taken place. After Cordelia and Robert exchanged pleasantries, Cordelia likely would have asked Robert about his trip to North Adams the day before. Since Robert's train was involved in a derailment in which there were injuries, Cordelia must have been shocked and offered Robert the comfort that at least he was fine and to use the trip to get his mind off of that event. The fact is that Robert was a bit shaken up as a result of the derailment and was not all too keen on a trip; he would have rather had the chance to calm his nerves.

Cordelia saw all the passengers get into the car and she may have waved them off wishing them a safe trip. Cordelia then waited for her brother-in-law to arrive. When Willmarth arrived, Florence entertained him in the formal gardens on the grounds of the mansion. I am sure they enjoyed some tea or coffee. The silence of that day was broken when the telephone rang. Since Cordelia was entertaining outside, I would assume one of the servants answered the phone; this servant would then rush off to retrieve Cordelia.

As Cordelia excused herself and walked into the home, the worst possible news was given to her. The automobile carrying her husband, her daughter and the Huttons was just involved in a terrible car accident. Cordelia was given very little information since the accident just occurred. She did not have an idea of the conditions of any of the passengers, just that it was serious in nature. The sad part is that Cordelia would not know the specifics until an injured Albert Houghton was brought back to the mansion. Cordelia had to wait nervously not knowing how her loved ones were.

Meanwhile a telephone call from W. Pritchard to Mary Cady brought her rushing over to the Houghton residence. While the impacts of the tragedy were unknown at this time, both Cordelia and Mary were frantically calling as many relatives as they could reach. Cordelia's oldest surviving daughter Florence and her husband William Arthur Gallup and their family were in Boston to set sail to Germany. The global events of August 1, 1914 caused the change of their plans as the declaration of war cancelled the ship's crossing of the Atlantic. The Gallups upon learning the news of their trip's cancellation were on route back to North Adams, and as such they could not be reached. The Gallups learned the awful news when they returned to North Adams.

Cordelia's other daughter, Susan McKean, who was supposed to travel to North Adams to visit later that day delayed their trip until they could take a train to North Adams. The family was originally going to drive in their car to North Adams. This is speculative, but I would assume that they delayed their trip because Cordelia did not want them to ride in a car over to North Adams.

Cordelia also called her son-in-law, Edward Wilkinson who was golfing at a country club. Edward was a widower and was still very close with his in-laws. When Wilkinson discovered that Cordelia did not have many details, he rushed to the accident scene to see what he could gather. For hours, Cordelia was wrought with anxiety and dread as the route they took always concerned her. Could this have been a bit of premonition on the part of Cordelia?

The chaotic scene in the Houghton Mansion must have been more chaotic when the entourage carrying an injured Albert Houghton arrived at the residence. Cordelia must have rushed to meet her husband. Upon seeing him, two things must have stood out. For one, Albert Houghton suffered injuries at an age where broken bones are more serious than if it were to occur to a strapping young person. Second, the look of despair in Houghton's face must have said it all. Albert Houghton knew that Sybil Hutton was dead, and Houghton saw the condition of Mary. I also think the absence of Mary would have raised a high level of concern. After the terrible news was relayed, I can imagine the household becoming eerily quiet except for sobbing.

While the group brought Albert Houghton to his room to rest, there was not much that could be done for Mary. She was in the hospital being tended to by Doctor Stafford. She was in and out of consciousness although she was slipping into longer bouts of unconsciousness. She was in such bad shape that her condition needed to be stabilized and improved before they could operate on her. Mary Houghton passed away around three in the afternoon. The car accident just claimed its second victim.

At some point John Widders arrived at the property. While he escaped serious injury, the concern was over his mental well-being. At some point Cordelia must have seen John Widders, what was said is something I will not speculate on. Place yourself in either's shoes in this situation; it is not a pretty picture. Cordelia was stricken by grief over the loss of her youngest daughter – her third child that passed away. Meanwhile the lifeless body of Mary brought back to the home. Her once vibrant daughter was devoid of life and her warmth was just a memory.

The evening stretched on into night. Cordelia must have dozed off from exhaustion. At the break of the next day, there was yet another commotion. Cordelia would then find out that John Widders committed suicide in the stable on the Houghton property. Cordelia acted as an informant for the death certificate. It is unclear if she saw his body. There are certain sights one cannot erase from their memories; I would assume that his was one sight that haunted Cordelia for the rest of her life if she did.

Cordelia would then bury her daughter Mary in the family plot. After the funeral, she returned home and had to witness her husband's life slowly extinguish. Suddenly, she was now alone in the mansion, save for the domestic help. Again, she witnessed another funeral and buried her husband in the family plot. While there, she saw the freshly disturbed burial sites of John Widders and her precious daughter Mary. Suddenly there was a third grave - her soul mate.

Cordelia would walk by the bedroom of her youngest daughter Mary and see a room devoid of life. Mary's possessions, a somber reminder of a life stolen. No amount of sunshine could filter through the darkness Cordelia saw in the bedroom. How many times did she pause outside of Mary's room and let out an exasperated sigh?

Cordelia would slowly deteriorate herself after the death of her husband. I would assume that her remaining family kept her going for as long as she did. Her daughter Florence and grandson William Albert Gallup would visit often, so too did her other daughter Susan McKean and her family. Cordelia also was very close to her sister Laura, who lived nearby. In a perfect world, when Cordelia was at death, her husband Albert and her deceased children were there to guide her into the light. There is some question to that with the thought that Albert and Mary may still be present at the mansion. That reunion may have to wait, it is one that I hope and pray will happen sooner rather than later.

Light and shadow dance in the main staircase of Houghton Mansion. It has been said that Cordelia's energy, while passed into the light, is aware of who visits her stately residence.

4. Laura Houghton

A little life lost. Her life story was left unfinished.

Laura Cordelia Houghton was the first child born to Albert and Cordelia. Laura was born on September 30, 1867 in Stamford, Vermont. Laura was just over two years old when she became a big sister when Florence was born. Laura's life was tragically cut short at the age of three years, three months and seventeen days when she developed a fever of the brain and died on January 13, 1871.

While her death certificate lists brain fever as the cause of her death, that term is not used as much today. In the past, many conditions were lumped under the term brain fever. Laura's condition was more likely caused by encephalitis, a viral infection which causes inflammation of the brain or meningitis, which causes the membranes surrounding the brain or the spinal cord to become inflamed. Because of Laura's age as well as the medical practices at that time, Laura's illness proved to be fatal.

It is true that in this era, many families had to bury their little ones. Even though it was more prominent than it is today – it was assuredly not any easier to handle burying a child. Unfortunately for the Houghtons this is not the last time they will bury one of their children. It is often said that a parent should never bury a child, this stress and tremendous grief played itself over and over again in this family.

While Laura Houghton passed away in Stamford, Vermont, the Houghton family decided against burying her in the Houghton Cemetery in Stamford. Instead the Houghton family purchased a plot in Southview Cemetery in North Adams and laid Laura to rest there, where she would later be joined by her father, her mother, and her youngest sister.

I believe Laura continued to play a role in the Houghtons' lives as a big sister. Laura would have passed into the light but continued to be with Albert and Cordelia and their growing family. Laura would have spent considerable time with her younger sisters, playing with them, even though they were not aware of

A heartbreaking reminder of a little life lost - the gravestone of Laura Houghton.

her presence. I also believe that Laura was present during all the family's struggles and many disheartening times. Laura would have also greeted Cordelia as she entered the light – mother and child reunited at last.

5. Florence Houghton Gallup: Her Life and Family

> Her own home was a scene of countless tragedies. Four babies that she held and nurtured were buried before their first birthday.

Florence Louisa Houghton was born in Stamford, Vermont on November 3, 1869. Florence was the second of five daughters born to Albert and Cordelia Houghton. Florence was fifteen months old when her older sister Laura tragically died. Inevitably, having to care for Florence must have helped the family carry on in light of the tragic death of Laura. Florence was not old enough to remember her older sister who was also her playmate as most children do not remember anything prior to their second to fourth birthdays.

As a young girl, Florence was very playful and with an absence of a sibling who can play with her, she would often recruit her family's elderly neighbors to be her playmates. She would soon get playmates as her sisters Susan, Alice and Mary were born. As she matured and with proper training, Florence would learn to become more refined and "ladylike" however, I would venture to guess that every once in a while that her playful, if not rambunctious, spirit would emerge.

She was a young child when her family moved to North Adams. Florence received her primary education in the North Adams school system. In addition to the public schooling, Florence was sent to Englewood, New Jersey to further her education in a private boarding school that was operated by a Miss Crighton. She was then enrolled at the Rye Academy in Rye, New York to further her education. She spent a combined three years in Englewood and Rye.

Florence then studied abroad in Europe for two years. She was accompanied by her younger sister Susan and chaperone Mary Cady. Mary Cady was the aunt of Sybil Hutton. Together, they travelled to many of the famous and historical spots in Europe spending most of their time in Germany. I included information on Mary Cady later in this book as I found her to be a fascinating person and she played a role in the family and on August 1, 1914. Mary Cady even has a strong connection to the land on which Houghton Mansion currently stands.

According to the information Florence provided on a passport application, she was five and a half feet tall, with an oval face with a high forehead, a Grecian nose, a small mouth, and a dimpled chin. Her eyes were brown with light hair and a fair complexion. With Florence's father and future husband being very prominent in the community, she was thrust into a spotlight that she was not all comfortable with. She was described as being shy and restrained to others, but to those who she felt close to she was described as being warm and charming.

Through his work with her father, Florence was acquainted with William Arthur Gallup, who became a widower. At the time, Gallup was the Treasurer of the Arnold Print Works and business partner in the firm Gallup & Houghton that operated several mills. They fell in love and became engaged to be married. Both Florence and William Arthur Gallup shared another common bond. Both Florence's mother and William Arthur Gallup shared Reuben Smith Jr. and Olive Wescott as grandparents. This makes the bride and groom first cousins, once removed. In other words, William Arthur Gallup was Cordelia Houghton's first cousin.

One thing we learn as paranormal investigators is that we should never judge someone's actions. The idea of cousins marrying makes us cringe in this day and age. It was actually more common back in that era than it is today. Now we know the risk of children developing serious health issues increases the closer the gene pools are, but this was not largely understood back in this era. Florence and William lost four out of the five children, was this because of healthcare of this era or a larger issue regarding genes?

Noble Smith, who is the father of Cordelia Smith Houghton, was the son of Reuben Smith Jr. and Olive Wescott. William W. Gallup, the father of William Arthur Gallup, married Eugenia Olive Smith, the daughter of Reuben Smith Jr. and Olive Wescott. In addition to being first cousins, once removed, William Arthur Gallup was also considerably older than Florence. On the day of their wedding, Gallup was forty-one years old while his blushing bride was only twenty-three years old.

The wedding of Florence and William Gallup took place on Wednesday, September 20, 1893 at approximately eleven in the morning. The wedding took place in the parlor of Houghton family home on Summer Street. The parlor was exquisitely decorated by Twombly, a firm in Boston which specialized in opulent decorations for special events. In fact, many of the flowers used for the wedding were actually grown in the Houghton's greenhouse. The wedding ceremony was performed by Reverend George W. Brown, the Pastor of the Methodist Episcopal Church.

The wedding was held in front of a very small audience consisting mainly of the bride and groom's closest relatives and friends. After the wedding nuptials, the assembled guests enjoyed a wedding breakfast that was cooked by a then-famous chef from Boston by the name of Weeber. Immediately after the reception, the bride and groom left for their honeymoon which lasted for two weeks.

Prior to the wedding, Gallup purchased land at 149 Church Street and a new house was being built for the Gallup family which included his two surviving daughters from his previous marriage. When the couple returned from their honeymoon the house was not yet complete. As a result, the newlyweds stayed in the home of Mr. and Mrs. Homer A. Smith while the new house was being finished. Living with Florence were her stepchildren Marion and Dorothy.

On June 18, 1895, a son, Houghton Gallup was born to Florence and William. Just fifty-two days later, the infant suffered from the ulceration and hemorrhage of the bowels and passed away on August 6, 1895. This was the first of several children that Florence lost.

Gallup residence located at 149 Church Street in North Adams. This stately home would also see numerous tragedies, most notably Florence Houghton Gallup losing four out of five babies.

However for William this was already his fifth child who died. The family had a private funeral for their son Houghton in their home on Sunday, August 11, 1895.

Florence obviously was grief-stricken over the loss of her first-born baby. She spent time at her father-in-law's farm to be able to gather her thoughts and emotions. Florence must have been relieved to become pregnant again in the fall of 1896.

On June 27, 1897, Florence delivered a baby girl, Ruth Gallup. Again, tragedy struck as only forty-nine days later the infant suffered a hemorrhage and passed away on Sunday, August 15, 1897. At the time, the Reverend J.C. Tebbetts was out of town on vacation, however, when he had discovered that Ruth had died, he immediately returned to North Adams so he could perform the funeral rites for the infant. The funeral for Ruth Gallup took place in the Gallup residence and was private, only attended by close relatives.

Just a few months after the death of their second child, Florence once again was pregnant. On September 5, 1898, a son, William Albert Gallup was born. Luckily, for Florence and her husband, this child made it past childhood. However, the good fortune would not last.

Florence gave birth again, this time to a son, John Gallup, on September 22, 1900. Just a few weeks shy of his first birthday, John developed enterocolitis and cerebrospinal meningitis. Enterocolitis is an ailment caused by bacteria, viruses, fungi or parasites. This infection from any of the preceding sources causes the digestive tract to become inflamed. The inflammation of the small intestine is called enteritis; the large intestine is called colitis. Enterocolitis involves frequent diarrhea, and can also include nausea, vomiting, fever, chills, and severe abdominal discomfort. The danger here is that the uncontrolled diarrhea and vomiting would deprive a small child of water and minerals.

In addition to the dangerous fluid loss caused by enterocolitis, John was also diagnosed with meningitis which is the inflammation of the meninges, the protective membranes covering the brain and spinal cord. Meningitis is very dangerous because of the inflammation is within close proximity to the brain. One of the many symptoms of meningitis is vomiting, so between both ailments, the loss of fluids was too much for a small child to withstand and sadly John passed away on September 6, 1901. When John passed away, Florence was in the early stages of her fifth pregnancy.

In the foreground, the graves of four of Florence's babies that died. From left to right: Mary, John, Ruth and Houghton Gallup. All four children died before their first birthday. Sadly, at the time of this project, their gravestones were tipping over. In the background are gravestones of her husband, his first wife and their four children who died very young.

On April 28, 1902, Mary Houghton Gallup was born. Unfortunately, there was a complication during delivery in which the umbilical cord was trapped between the baby and the wall of the birth canal which caused the baby to be deprived of much needed blood supply – this is called the occlusion of umbilical arteries and veins. Because the baby was deprived of much need oxygen in her blood supply, the baby was born with major health issues. After hanging on for nine days, Mary Houghton Gallup passed away. For Florence, the death of her baby daughter Mary was the fourth child to die, for William Arthur Gallup, the death of Mary was his eighth child to pass away. With the death of Mary Gallup, Florence had to bury two children in just eight months.

The deaths of four children were, as expected, very difficult on Florence. She would quite often get away and spend time to recover at quiet places such as her father-in-law's farm in Clarksburg or at local resorts such as Idlewild. Her younger sisters would also stop by to comfort the grieving mother. Luckily for Florence, she had a large support system of family within a very short distance that could comfort her in her time of need. Unfortunately, the death of four children also did not mark the end of tragedy for Florence as she also lost her sister Alice in 1906 and Mary in 1914. Florence lost three out of her four sisters while she was alive.

Religion was very important in the life of Florence. While in North Adams, the Gallups were members of Saint John's Episcopal Church and donated many gifts to the church. In fact, it was through the generosity of Florence and her husband by giving them a substantial donation the church was able to undergo considerable alterations. In addition of the donation to help expand the church, Florence donated the cost of a large stained-glass window to be placed in front of the church. The window was a memorial to her deceased sisters, Alice and Mary. At that point the value of the stained-glass window was valued at twenty-five hundred dollars, and was the largest donation to the church at that time.

Florence was also a charter member of the Fort Massachusetts Chapter of the Daughters of American Revolution. Florence was also heavily involved socially in her church. She was involved in a group called the Congregational Girls' Club. This group was involved in missionary work for the church. She would often attend meetings and conferences as well as perform general duties as part of this club. Also part of this club was Cordelia's cousin Stella Spruill and Stella's daughter Eleanor Spruill.

After the death of Cordelia Houghton, the Houghton Mansion sat empty. Florence and William Gallup had intentions to move to the now vacant mansion, but they had a stately home of their own, almost across the street from the mansion. When the idea first surfaced, Gallup's daughter Marion and her husband George Flood decided to place their Blackinton home on the market so they can move into the Gallup residence in North Adams. On May 16, 1919, the Floods sold their home and made their intention known that they would move into the Gallup residence. It was also announced that the Florence and William Gallup would move into Houghton Mansion.

In addition to the Houghton residence on Church Street, the old Houghton residence on Summer Street was still part of the Houghton estate. Florence Gallup and her sister Susan McKean donated the Summer Street property to the North Adams Y.M.C.A on January 19, 1920. Up until that time the Y.M.C.A. was previously headquartered in the Odd Fellows Hall since its incorporation. The demand for services would soon outgrow the existing building so an extensive addition was constructed onto the donated Summer Street property with the cornerstone being laid at a ceremony on October 20, 1922.

On Sunday, June 5, 1921, Florence's son William Albert Gallup married Lucy Pollard at the St. John's Episcopal Church in North Adams. Lucy Pollard was the daughter of Frederick and Lucy Pollard and was raised in North Adams. Lucy's parents were both born in England. The bride's dress, interestingly enough, was made from the bridal gown of Cordelia Smith Houghton, the wife of Albert C. Houghton. After the wedding the bride and groom left for their honeymoon in a new convertible, a gift of Florence Houghton. After their honeymoon, the newlywed couple moved to Cambridge where William attended Harvard.

William Albert Gallup also enrolled in the Massachusetts Institute of Technology and graduated in 1923. After graduating from MIT, he then went abroad and received a doctorate in social technology at the Federal Polytechnical School that was located in Zurich, Switzerland.

Florence became a grandmother on November 27, 1924 when Lucy Pollard Gallup was born while William Albert Gallup was a student in Zurich, Switzerland. At the time, both parents were twenty-six years old when they welcomed their first child. After William earned his post-graduate degree in Switzerland, his young family moved to Boston. In 1926, they welcomed their second daughter, Florence Louise Gallup, to the family. William Albert Gallup would become a lecturer at M.I.T and as a result the family purchased a home in Newton, Massachusetts.

When William A. Gallup retired from the Arnold Print Works, Florence and William moved to Boston to be closer to their son who by this time had started his own investment counseling firm. They then later moved into a stately home on Chestnut Street in West Newton. Their home was immediately next door to their son – you cannot get much closer than that.

In 1927, Florence and her husband sold Houghton Mansion to the Masonic fraternity for a sum that was considered very nominal.

Florence became a grandmother twice more as William Albert Gallup Jr. was born in 1929 and Jane W. Gallup was born in 1935. Florence was quite close to her grandchildren and spent considerable time with them. While she endured the loss of four children, she relished the fact that all of her grandchildren were healthy.

On October 27, 1928 Florence's son William lost his mother-in-law as a result of an automobile accident. For Florence, the news of this accident must have brought back painful memories of the accident that took the lives of her sister and ultimately led to the death of her father. The scenario was eerily similar. The Pollard family was returning from a football game in New Haven, Connecticut, when the man driving the automobile, Wesley Lazotte lost control of the vehicle. The car veered off the road, crashed through a fence and flipped over on the Pittsfield – North Adams Road in Lanesboro. Lucy B. Pollard, the mother of William Albert Gallup's wife was killed at the age of sixty. Lucy's son, William Pollard was seriously injured, but fully recovered. The driver was arrested as a result of the accident and was subsequently sued.

In March, 1929 Florence and her sister Susan donated to Stamford, Vermont eighty acres of land that was located in the watershed of Broad Brook. This land was originally purchased by Albert Houghton and remained part of his estate after his death. Florence and Susan offered the land to the community free of charge. While the land was not considered vital in watershed protection in that time, the town was more than happy to receive this gift as any development may have had impacts on the drinking water supply. The town would have rather the land be vacant and undeveloped. The deeds changed hands on March 18, 1929.

Florence and her husband William were on vacation in Paris in August of 1930, a vacation they had planned for several years. While in Paris, William was ill and passed away. Florence's only surviving sister; Susan was also abroad at the time. Susan was able to return stateside on August 28, 1930 on the ship Mauretania sailing from Southampton, England to New York City. It is not possible to know whether word got out to Susan that her sister's husband passed away. It is also quite possible that she did receive the news and cut her trip short to be with her sister.

After her husband's passing, Florence regularly took trips abroad with a very close friend and traveling companion, her cousin and fellow widow, Stella Spruill. Among the many places they visited, Florence and Stella visited France, Japan, and southern United States. She also took pleasure spending considerable time with her four grandchildren, Lucy, Florence, William Albert Jr., and Jane Gallup.

Florence was also working tirelessly to preserve her family's legacy. She worked with her only surviving sister to erect a new public library in North Adams to honor her father's and her husband's deep interest in the North Adams Public Library. Those plans were left unfulfilled for various reasons.

Her health started to deteriorate as she aged. On Friday, May 12, 1939 Florence felt well enough to go for a ride to get away from her house. Florence then experienced a cerebral hemorrhage and shock. At 1:30 in the morning on Saturday, May 13, 1939 Florence passed away in her home on Chestnut Street in West Newton at the age of sixty-nine. Her death shocked her friends as her spirits seemed lifted that day and she seemed better than she had been for some time. Is it possible that she was aware that the end was near and that she would soon rejoin her husband and deceased children in Heaven?

The ashes of Florence were interred not near her husband, but near the graves of her five children, daughter-in-law and grandson.

On Monday, May 15, 1939, the funeral services were held for Florence in her home in West Newton. The funeral was private and was limited to a few members of her family and her closest of friends. Her remains were cremated and buried in the Gallup family plot in Hillside Cemetery in North Adams. Like her funeral, the committal service for her ashes was also very private. Her ashes were interred close to her children's graves.

As for the Gallup's son, at some point, William Albert Gallup and his wife purchased a home on Chestnut Street in the Beacon Hill section of Boston. The home which was slightly smaller than fourteen hundred square feet was built in 1830 and contained thirteen rooms and three baths.

William Albert Gallup, the only child of Florence and William to survive childhood, made his career in the financial sector, even owning his own firm William Albert Gallup, Inc. which was located on Federal Street in Boston. In addition to his residence in Beacon Hill, he also maintained the family farm in Clarksburg that was used as a summer residence. The name of the Clarksburg estate was Mayunsook Farm. He battled illness for five years before he passed away on Monday, January 14, 1957 at his home on Chestnut Street at the age of fifty-eight.

At the time of his death, he left behind his wife, Lucy Gordon (Pollard) Gallup, a son William Albert Gallup Jr., and three daughters – Lucy Pollard Carter, Florence Louise Atkins, and Jane W. Menz. The funeral for William Albert Gallup was held on Wednesday, January 16, 1957 at the Church of the Advent in Boston. After the funeral his body was brought to North Adams and placed in the vault at Hillside Cemetery. In the spring his remains were buried in the Gallup family plot.

After his death, the Beacon Hill home was sold and his widow moved to Weston, Massachusetts. The estate in Clarksburg remained in the family at that time.

Through Florence's Eyes: August 1, 1914

For Florence Houghton Gallup, August 1, 1914 was the day her family, including her stepchildren, was to set sail across the Atlantic Ocean to Germany. Incidentally, that day was also the very same day that the conflict that we now know as World War I escalated in earnest as Germany declared war on Russia. On Friday, July 31, 1914, Florence with her husband William and their son Albert joined her stepdaughter Mrs. Samuel Jones on a trip to Boston so that the family can embark on the voyage to Germany. On the morning the ship was to set sail, the family learned that the voyage was cancelled.

I am sure that the news of the trip being canceled was very disappointing for the Gallup and Jones families. I would also assume that there was a bit of anxiety as Samuel Jones was currently living and working in Germany at that time. I assume that Mrs. Jones was heading back to Europe after visiting her family in North Adams. The reunion with her husband would have to wait. For the Gallup family, the trip was meant to spend time with the Jones family in Europe and to experience the German culture. Florence spent two years abroad in Europe, so I also assume she was looking forward to returning abroad, albeit for a shorter stay. Unfortunately, the disappointment of a cancelled trip would take a back seat to more tragic news several hours later.

After they learned that their trip was cancelled, the families took the next train back to North Adams. Since they were in transit when the news of the accident broke, there was no possible method available to notify Florence of the accident involving her father and sister. It is not possible to know if the family learned of the tragic events when they arrived at the station, but imagine yourself stepping off of a train feeling sorry for yourself that your trip was cancelled unaware that your sister was killed and your father was injured. Then imagine that moment when you are told. The train arrived in North Adams at six in the evening, Mary had already passed away. There was no chance to say "goodbye".

Florence and William A. Gallup endured a great deal of tragedy in their lives. First and foremost, Florence had four children die, while her husband lost eight children and a first wife. Stop back and think about that number for a second – eight children. I do not think that I need to elaborate further on that. Florence already lost two of the four sisters and she also lost a nephew. On this very day, Florence discovered that she just lost her third sister.

Obviously Florence and her husband went to the Houghton Mansion to be with the family during this great tragedy. As the sun set over the mountains of the Berkshires, the mourning continued. Of course on the very next day, the Houghton Mansion once again became the scene of chaos as John Widders committed suicide on the property. For Florence, she was very familiar with John Widders as he was a long-time employee of the family.

The body of Mary, her youngest sister was also in the mansion awaiting her funeral and burial. For Florence, as well as the rest of the family, there were far too many funerals and burials. When Albert Houghton, her father, declined in health, Florence once again had to experience the feelings of losing another beloved family member. When Albert Houghton breathed his last breath, there was yet another funeral and another burial.

For Florence, during Albert's funeral, the grieving was tremendous, for it was only days ago that her sister was buried. As Albert was buried, there were two other fresh graves, one very close to Albert belonging to Mary and one only yards away belonging to Widders. The sacred ground of the Southview Cemetery became the new home for the physical vessels for three souls that died eleven days apart. These three souls are all still reportedly present in the former home. One question I have in my mind is did Florence experience anything paranormal that could have possibly been associated with her father, her sister or John Widders?

William Arthur Gallup

Any comprehensive history of Houghton Mansion or Albert C. Houghton cannot skip a discussion of William Arthur Gallup. We cannot ignore him because like Houghton, Gallup was a prominent citizen of North Adams, and important to the history of Arnold Print Works. Also like Houghton, Gallup has called Houghton Mansion home. As learned when discussing his second-wife, Gallup like Albert C. Houghton experienced an extraordinary amount of loss and personal tragedy.

The Gallup family had very deep roots in America; in fact William was the eighth lineal descendant of John Gallup who settled at Nantucket in 1630, the year that the Massachusetts Bay Colony was established. The history of the Gallup family establishing itself in America is also a fascinating history.

John Gallup was born around the year 1591 in Mosterne, England. He married Christobel Bruschett and had several children. The lure of an establishing colony was too great for John as he considered uprooting his family and settling in the New World. On March 20, 1630 John set sail on a boat named Mary and John, part of a fleet of ships called the Winthrop Fleet. John's wife and children remained in England for the time being, the plan was for John to become established and then the rest of his family will join him.

When John arrived in Massachusetts, he settled in Boston where he was granted land and wharf rights. He built his house and the area in which he settled was known as Gallup's Point. He was able to purchase a vessel and became involved in coastal trade. For additional income, he served as a pilot for ships entering Boston Harbor.

By this time, John was trying to convince his wife and family that it was time for them to sail across the Atlantic and join him in Boston. His wife Christobel was nervous about taking a long and dangerous journey across the ocean. At the time, it took about eight weeks to sail across the Atlantic. John was so dismayed that he considered returning back to England to rejoin his family. Since Gallup had become a distinguished man in the new colony, the loss of John worried Governor Winthrop. Governor Winthrop wrote a letter to Reverend John White in England pleading for his assistance in the matter. John was very important to the colony because he was essential in the coastal trade between Massachusetts, Connecticut and Rhode Island.

Reverend White met with Christobel and it took some time, but he persuaded her to take the voyage across the Atlantic. John's family finally arrived in Boston on September 4, 1633 onboard the Griffin. To meet the ship was John who helped pilot the boat into Boston Harbor. The Gallup family also can claim some famous descendants. Within the descendants are poet Emily Dickinson and George Gallup, who invented the Gallup Poll. Also descended from John Gallup are two U.S. Presidents, George H. Bush and his son George W. Bush.

William Arthur Gallup was born on October 28, 1851 in Clarksburg, Massachusetts to William W. Gallup and Eugenia Olive (Smith) Gallup. William W. Gallup was at one point a modest storekeeper, who built up his finances to the point where he was a business partner of Albert C. Houghton. William W. Gallup was born on January 29, 1824 in Dalton, Massachusetts. Eugenia Olive Smith Gallup was the aunt of Cordelia Houghton and was born on February 1, 1830 in what is now North Adams. Together William W. Gallup and Eugenia had eight children, of which William Arthur Gallup was the oldest.

There was close to a twenty-four years age range from the oldest child, William Arthur Gallup and the youngest child, Albert Charles Lyman Gallup. William's siblings were, by order of birth: Emerson Gallup, Olive J. Gallup, Clarence W. Gallup, Willis Jackson Gallup, Louisa Eugenia Gallup, Harvey Alpheus Gallup, and Albert Charles Lyman Gallup.

William Arthur Gallup attended elementary school in North Adams before attending Drury Academy. While attending Drury Academy; he was introduced to the world of business when his father needed help at his store that was located at the corner of Holden and Main Streets. The young William would work at his father's store after school and during school vacations. When William Arthur Gallup was older, he did not consider this experience as his first job, but he considered this work experience as the duty of a man's son.

In 1867, at the age of sixteen, William Arthur Gallup was hired for what he considered to be his first job. He took a job at Briggs & Bolands, a local tailor. The teenager earned a salary of $12.50 per month. While he worked at this shop, he was also receiving instruction on how to become a tailor himself. After about a year on the job, he decided that being a tailor was not something he wished to do long-term.

In the fall of 1868, William Arthur Gallup was hired at a grist mill belonging to Albert C. Houghton, which was the first business enterprise in North Adams for Houghton. One thing to remember is that Gallup was Houghton's first cousin through marriage. The business relationship would only grow over time, and Gallup would be an integral part of the success Houghton achieved later on. A few months later, Gallup again grew bored and decided that working in a grist mill was not the niche for his skills. In January of 1869, he resigned from Houghton's mill to work as a clerk in Adams National Bank. Gallup finally found his niche in the financial world and thirty-three years later he ascended to the position of President of that very same institution. However, after only one year as a clerk at the bank, another opportunity presented itself.

On January 3, 1870, Gallup began his career at the Arnold Print Works, first as a junior clerk when the company was known as Harvey Arnold & Co. He was associated with the firm for fifty-six years and rose to the ranks to Treasurer, an executive, and ultimately, the owner after the passing of Albert Houghton. Two years after Gallup joined the print works, the factory was destroyed by fire. When the future of the company was in doubt, none other than Albert C. Houghton entered the fray and took on a significant role with the reconstruction of the factory. Since Gallup impressed Houghton several years earlier, he ascended to higher offices within a very short timeframe. With each step up, Houghton was impressed by Gallup's keen business sense and motivation to succeed.

Around the year 1874, Gallup was seriously considering entering into a partnership with Edwin Barnard in which they would open a clothing store in North Adams. Gallup was relying on his past apprenticeship at Briggs & Bolands that was necessary to run a clothing store. This idea did not launch immediately however.

In 1876, the print works was facing serious financial issues as a result of a recession. Since the business was in its infancy, the plant was in serious jeopardy. The firm was reorganized and Gallup was named a clerk and a Director. It was seven years later when Houghton bought out David Brayton and assumed the Presidency of the print works, that Gallup was promoted to Treasurer, a position he would hold for forty-three years.

The dream of opening a clothing store with Barnard as a partner was finally realized in 1876 as well. Gallup would maintain a role as partner in this enterprise for five years. He stepped away from the clothing store in 1881 as the interests of the rapidly expanding Arnold Print Works necessitated his entire attention.

In addition to opening the clothing store in 1876, Gallup also married in that year as well. On October 5, 1876, Gallup married Harriet Elizabeth Marsh. Harriet was born on October 27, 1858 in North Adams to parents Charles Webster and Mary Francis (Whitman) Marsh. The couple had six children; however, only two of their children survived childhood.

Harriet Gallup gave birth to the couple's first child when Harriet M. Gallup was born on August 6, 1877. It was also that year when William Gallup purchased his father's interest in the cotton manufacturing firm of Gallup, Houghton and Smith. This firm operated the Beaver Mill in North Adams. He would also be named as Treasurer of the North Pownal and Williamstown Manufacturing Companies that year as well. He would continue in this capacity until 1882 when he was named as one of the Directors. The next year, in 1878 Gallup and Houghton bought out their partner Mr. Smith and the firm's name was changed to Gallup & Houghton.

Gallup's wife, Harriet became pregnant again, giving birth to the couple's second child William Arthur Gallup, Jr. on April 1, 1879. A son, Francis W.

Gallup was born on October 2, 1881. The Gallup family was expanding rapidly and Gallup's business relationship with his cousin (through marriage) Houghton was an ideal arrangement. On January 6, 1883, Gallup was named to the rank of Treasurer in the Arnold Print Works. It was shortly thereafter that Arnold Print Works began an explosive growth to become the largest operation of its kind in the world by the turn of the century.

In the same year that Gallup was appointed the Treasurer of the Arnold Print Works, Harriet and William welcomed their fourth child into their family with the birth of Marion Eugenia Gallup on July 14, 1883. Everything was looking up for the Gallup family, until the tragedies began. On September 4, 1884, the couple's first child Harriet M. Gallup died as the result of croup. She was only seven years old when she passed away.

Croup is a respiratory ailment that it triggered by a viral infection in the upper airway. The viral infection leads to a swelling of the throat which makes breathing very labored. The typical symptom that is well-known is the barking cough that is produced. Since medical treatments were so archaic during this era, Harriet's croup got so severe that she passed away from the infliction. Typically when children perish because of croup, it is because of respiratory failure or cardiac arrest which results from severe croup that is left untreated.

Nine months to the day that Harriet passed away as the result of croup, the couple's third child, Francis also died as the result of croup. Francis was only three years, seven months, and two days old when he passed away on May 4, 1885. On April 7, 1886, the Gallups welcomed their fifth child, as Harold Webster Gallup was born. Their last child, the sixth, Frances Dorothy Gallup was born on August 20, 1888.

On June 6, 1889, William's mother Eugenia Olive Smith Gallup passed away at the age of fifty-nine after battling liver cancer. She passed away in her home. Gallup's father William W. Gallup became a widower, and tragically a few months later, his son, William Arthur Gallup would become one as well.

Quite often when researching genealogy in this era, tragic early deaths were common as medicine was not as advanced as it is now. Things we take for granted nowadays were unheard of back then. In fact, even into the early

1900's, early medicine could be considered downright barbaric when compared to today's life-saving medicine and operations. While a relatively young person dying was more common during this era, it did not lessen the emotional toll on those remaining.

While researching the immediate family of William Arthur Gallup, it seems tragedy came to the foreground much too frequently. One such example is the untimely death of Gallup's first wife, Harriet Gallup.

Harriet Elizabeth Marsh was born on October 27, 1858 in North Adams. Her parents were Charles Webster Marsh and Mary Francis Whitman Marsh. She spent most of her life in Albany, New York as her family moved there when she was very young. She married William Arthur Gallup on October 5, 1876 just shy of her eighteenth birthday. From all accounts she was social, and was very serious about her religion and giving back to the community. She had a special place in her heart for Saint John's Church and the North Adams Hospital. On August 26, 1878, her mother passed away in Albany at the age of only forty-one.

In the year 1889, Harriet's health began to fail. In fact her friends became so alarmed by her condition that they convinced her to go to the hospital in Albany, New York. Her illness of course had a tremendous impact on her husband, especially since her illness was largely mysterious in nature. She was soon under the care of a specialist who just happened to be a very close friend of Harriet. It is unknown what medical condition she dealt with as any research provided very little clue.

When Harriet first realized just how dire her condition was as the result of the illness, she refused to take pity on herself. She did whatever she could to learn about medicine. Her compassion to those in need grew even greater during the time of her illness. She was not fearful of dying as her faith was strong; she was inspirational to the other patients as she faced her battle with tremendous strength and courage.

On October 27, 1889 Harriet celebrated her thirty-first birthday in the hospital; unfortunately it would be her final one. But as was the case throughout her life, she thought of others first. In a purely touching move, Harriet sent a present to each sick child that was in the hospital at that time. Harriet also thought of the doctors and nurses who gave so selflessly of themselves. She made sure each and every one of them had a flower as she wanted to brighten their day as well. It was Harriet's birthday, but she wanted to bring joy to others on her special day. Harriet delighted in seeing the sick children's face light up when they received their gift. For Harriet, a mother of six, children warmed her heart.

Shortly after her birthday, Harriet underwent an operation that was thought to be the only method of treatment that would have prolonged her life. The operation was considered a success and the thought was that she was going to make a full recovery and live a long and healthy life. Unfortunately, she suffered an internal hemorrhage which took her life. Harriet died on October 31, 1889, just days after celebrating her thirty-first birthday. This amazing and kind woman who went out of her way to brighten the lives of others began her journey to reunite with her deceased children.

At the time of her death, Harriet left behind four children, the youngest being only fourteen months old. Unfortunately, as we have learned and mentioned earlier, only two out of her six children survived childhood. Within just a few years after Harriet's death, two more of her children joined her.

Even though Harriet did not have an impact on Houghton Mansion, her story is integral to understanding the life of William Arthur Gallup, who did live at the mansion and inevitably left his mark within the very foundation of the structure. Without the death of his first wife, William would not have married Albert Houghton's daughter and the mansion as we now know it might not have been sold to the Masons, so it was important to tell her tale.

Even with his wife's death, Gallup failed to slow down when in 1890, William A. Gallup became a trustee of the North Adams Savings Bank. Two years later, he was also elected as a Director of the North Adams National Bank, the financial institution he worked as a clerk for just one year in 1869. In 1900, he later ascended to the role of President of North Adams Bank, for which he served in that capacity for five years. Gallup performed all these duties with his heavy work load from the Arnold Print Works. I wonder if Gallup focused so hard on work to take his mind off of the numerous tragedies he endured in his lifetime.

Tragedy once again struck the Gallup family. On Friday, November 28, 1891, his oldest son, William Arthur Gallup Jr. was on his pony for a routine ride. When he returned home in the evening, he complained of not feeling well and went to bed early. On the following day, he was still not feeling well and claimed that his pain was worsening. William Gallup Sr. became concerned over the welfare of his son, so he called for a doctor. Doctor Matte examined William Jr. and began treatment. These treatments were not working as his health continued to deteriorate quickly.

On the evening of Tuesday, December 4, 1891, another doctor by the name of Dr. Rice was called in to see if he can improve the situation. He then called Dr. Vanderveer of Albany, New York, who arrived in North Adams the very next day. Despite all the doctors and treatments, it was too late. Peritonitis had set in and William Arthur Gallup Jr. passed away at twelve years old. Peritonitis is an inflammation of the thin tissue the lines the inner wall of the abdomen and covers many of the organs in one's abdomen. This condition could be caused by a type of trauma or from an appendix that has ruptured.

The death of his son, his namesake, was especially hard on Mr. Gallup. He lost his wife two years prior, and before that he lost two other children, daughter Hattie and his son Francis. William Sr. and his son William Jr. were particularly close, as the two shared many strong bonds. I would take

The death of Harold Gallup was the fourth child Gallup was forced to bury. Unfortunately with his second wife, Gallup buried four more babies far too early. Graves from left to right: Harold, Francis, Harriet, Harriet Marsh Gallup, William Arthur Gallup, and William Arthur Gallup Jr. Gallup's five other children are in the background close to his second wife, Florence.

it a bit further and say that not only was the death of William Jr. difficult because he was his child, but I also think that his death made William Sr. relive all the other painful deaths and stirred up all of that emotion from the past. I also think that William Jr. as well as the other children were a connection between William Sr. and his deceased wife. William Gallup Jr.'s funeral was held at the family home on Saturday, December

6, 1891.

William Arthur Gallup then suffered a serious accident on June 2, 1892. He was taking an early morning horseback ride when he was thrown from the horse. He was found around six in the morning by the roadside unconscious, face down in sand. He suffered a serious concussion and was listed in critical condition. He was able to fully recover from this accident.

As if the loss of three children and his wife was not enough, Harold Webster Gallup developed bronchitis and passed away on December 5, 1892. Harold was only 6 years 7 months and 21 days old at the time of his death. The death of Harold marked the fourth child of William Arthur Gallup and Harriet to die far too soon.

William Arthur Gallup would regroup and marry Florence Houghton, the daughter of Albert C. Houghton on September 20, 1893. As mentioned earlier, fate was not kind to the couple as they had five children, but only one survived past childhood. In total, William Arthur Gallup had eleven children, and he buried eight of them.

On April 10, 1894, William Gallup's father, William W. Gallup remarried. The widower married Cathrene M. Smith in North Adams. For both the bride and groom, it was their second marriage. The groom was seventy years old and the bride was sixty-five years old. Both father and son became widowers in a short amount of time, and both remarried around the same time as well.

On September 15, 1900, the father of William Arthur Gallup passed away as a result of heart disease. William W. Gallup was seventy-six years old. At the time of his death, he resided on Quincy Street in North Adams. Since William W. Gallup was highly revered, his body was placed within the parlors of the Congregational Church several hours before his funeral service for many mourners to have a moment, almost as if he were lying in state. The funeral itself also took place at the Congregational Church. His remains were buried within Hillside Cemetery in North Adams.

William Arthur Gallup maintained a great interest in the North Adams Public Library, the same library that Albert Houghton donated to the city in honor of his brother in 1896. In 1901, Gallup was elected to the board of trustees of the library and was reelected to that role until 1921, when he decided that his time of the board was up and that someone fresh should take over.

As is seen throughout this book with various people, politics played a major role in William Arthur Gallup's life. Gallup was a loyal Republican; however, he had no desire to run for political office. His brother, however, Harvey Alpheus Gallup was on the North Adams City Council, became the twelfth Mayor of North Adams, and would serve within the Massachusetts State Senate. William Arthur Gallup did have the opportunity to meet and greet at least two sitting United States Presidents in McKinley and Theodore Roosevelt. I cannot confirm if Gallup met Grover Cleveland as Houghton had.

When Albert C. Houghton moved his office to New York City in 1904 so he can closely monitor the all-important textile market and to better position Arnold Print Works, William Arthur Gallup was put in charge of the day-to-day operations in North Adams.

When the financial difficulty hit in 1907, Gallup resigned all of his banking responsibilities when the Arnold Print Works was facing serious financial difficulties. He intended to spend all his efforts in the reconstruction of the print works to avoid a collapse of the firm. The financial troubles at Arnold Print Works were embarrassing for William and he also did not want the financial institutions he served to face that embarrassment as well.

During the financial crisis of 1907, Albert C. Houghton trusted William to help the company remain solvent. Mr. Gallup worked long hours, working days, nights and weekends to muddle through the complex financial issues and to get the company back on solid footing. In fact, after the financial crisis was over, Mr. Houghton's health had suffered greatly due to the turmoil; Gallup was given more and more responsibility of Arnold Print Works. He not only performed the duties of the Treasurer, but also of the President. While A.C. Houghton still held the title of President until his death, it was William Gallup who performed many of the duties of that office during that time.

While Albert Houghton was more of a dreamer, William Gallup ran Arnold Print Works in a more conservative manner. He avoided expansion unless absolutely necessary and was hesitant in experimenting with untested new technology. Gallup also continued Mr. Houghton's idea of how to treat their employees and took steps to improve the social and economic welfare of their employees. Under Gallup's leadership the Arnold Print Works Mutual Benefit Association was developed and insurance benefits were improved. More importantly, hard work was appreciated and recognized and Mr. Gallup continued to encourage the best and brightest to be promoted from within the company.

While Mr. Houghton's health suffered as a result of the financial crisis in 1907, William Gallup's health did not. He attributed his strength and stamina to his lifestyle. Mr. Gallup was very conscientious in how he treated himself. He never smoked or drank alcohol, was very careful in what he ate and stayed physically active. He would start each day with a brisk walk throughout the hills of the community on his way to and from the office. He was so serious in his duties, that he rarely attended social affairs. With whatever time he had to spare, he would spend it with his family or in church. William was also described as a very modest person who felt he was no more important than the person on the bottom of the organization. He was often the first to arrive and often the last to leave the print works.

In 1909 he was elected to the Board of Trustees of the North Adams Hospital and retained his membership on the board until his death. William constantly gave to the hospital oftentimes covering the operating deficit. He made a significant donation towards the cost of a new maternity wing dedicating it to his deceased first wife.

As mentioned previously in this book, as Albert Houghton's health started to deteriorate during the financial crisis of 1907, Gallup served as the de facto head of Arnold Print Works while Houghton was more of a figure head. The impact of Houghton's risky move to procure an extremely large quantity of raw cotton immediately before an unexpected economic recession, hit Arnold Print Works extremely hard. Prior to this, the print works had an excellent relationship with North Adams. This relationship began to sour, however, because of the financial crisis. For a period of three years, the print works was fighting the North Adams Board of Assessors regarding the property tax assessed on the company.

In 1911, this property tax battle came to a head. William A. Gallup was representing the print works during negotiations with the city. It was Gallup's position that the 1910 tax, which was not paid due to the disagreement, should be lowered to the point it was prior to the 1907 financial situation. In the two years prior, the disagreement between the two parties was settled in court. The courts lowered the valuation for 1908 and 1909 by a million dollars combined, although this figure still represented an increase from 1907. As part of the 1910 tax battle, Arnold Print Works agreed to present their books to the North Adam's Board of Assessors so that a more accurate figure could be derived.

William was also a trustee of the North Adams Young Men's Christian Association (YMCA) for many years including up to the time of his death. William was very religious, not only a regular attendee of Saint John's Episcopal Church, but he served a number of roles for that parish as well. He served as vestryman, clerk, and treasurer of the parish. In 1891 he was selected a junior warden – a position he held for fifteen years until he became senior warden for ten years. He also represented the parish at several diocesan conventions. William was also a lifetime member of the Brotherhood of Saint Andrew.

William was also involved in many professional organizations. In 1916, he was named a member of the executive committee of the Associated Industries of Massachusetts and was a prominent member and officer of the Berkshire County Manufacturer's Association. He was also a trustee to his alma mater, Drury Academy.

On July 28, 1919, William Arthur Gallup was appointed by the Massachusetts Forestry Association as Chairman of the local committee that was tasked to gather signatures to request the reclamation of lands in Massachusetts that were idle or considered wasteland. The goal was for the purchase of 250,000 acres of land suitable for the production of timber. The land would be replanted to either produce timber or to protect watershed areas of public drinking reservoirs.

William celebrated his fiftieth year with Arnold Print Works in 1920. As part of the event a special publication of *The Arnold Print* was developed and distributed on Christmas Eve prior to the anniversary. *The Arnold Print* was a publication developed through what would now be called the Human Resources division of the company. The edition highlighted William's career from an office boy to the eventual President and owner of the company.

In February, 1926 William Gallup sold the controlling interest of Arnold Print Works to Dr. Samuel M. Jones of North Adams. Dr. Jones was Gallup's son-in-law (married to Dorothy) and operated as plant manager prior to purchasing the controlling interest. When Dr. Jones ascended to President of Arnold Print Works, George B. Flood, another son-in-law with ties to the company became Treasurer. With this, Mr. Gallup retired and closed out his financial interest in the plant.

After retirement, William and Florence moved to an apartment on Beacon Street in Boston to be closer to their son. As mentioned previously, the Gallups sold the Houghton Mansion and it was converted into a Masonic temple. William was not completely retired however. He maintained an office from his new residence and spent several hours daily to attend to his extensive financial interests and personal business. Even in Boston, William Gallup took an interest in the affairs of North Adams and continued to provide support to the city he had called home for most of his life.

In 1929, Mr. and Mrs. Gallup donated a valuable piece of property at the corner of Ashland and Porter Streets to Massachusetts for use as a state armory. This land was originally owned by Gallup's father, William W. Gallup. William Arthur Gallup purchased the house and large plot of land in January, 1896 from his father for sixteen thousand dollars.

The North Adams Library was an important cause for not only the Houghton family, but the Gallup family as well. When the library's need was greater than the original building could handle, it was recommended that an addition be added onto the library. While Mr. and Mrs. Gallup lived in Boston, they stayed close to the news from North Adams.

Mr. and Mrs. Gallup also offered to pay for the refurnishing of the entire library if the town would build a much needed addition to the building. He then paid for a well-known Boston architectural firm, Coolidge & Carlson to design the plans and present to the city for consideration. In a letter to the town, Mr. Gallup asked for an estimate for the entire renovation and the Gallups would pay for those costs. Previously both Mr. and Mrs. Gallup donated the costs to completely furnish the children's room on the second floor in the library. They made this generous gift in memory of the couple's numerous deceased children.

But most of the contributions William Gallup and his wife Florence Houghton Gallup made towards the betterment of North Adams will never be known. Both William and Florence were private and for the most part did not like the spotlight. Many of the charitable gifts the family gave to the community were done so anonymously. Most times when the Gallups donated vast resources they did so with the request that the gifts were to be announced as anonymous or that the gift would go unannounced. The only ones who truly knew what was given were limited to the immediate family. With the passing of those who truly knew, the true level of generosity has been lost in history. One of the last things William Arthur Gallup involved himself with was the Boston Tercentenary celebration where he served on the committee planning the event.

Since William was very serious in the matters of business, he rarely took time for himself throughout his life. For many years, Florence and William dreamed of a lengthy vacation together when Mr. Gallup retired. By 1929, their long-time dream became a reality. On September 2, 1929 they left Boston on a boat to France. After a few weeks in Paris, they were joined there by their niece, Elizabeth Gallup. They stayed in Paris until January, 1930 when they spent time in southern France and Italy, where the weather was considerably warmer. In the spring, they returned to Paris for a second stay, before departing for Switzerland. While in Switzerland, William wrote to several close associates telling them that it was years since he felt as well as he was feeling. Clearly, the extended vacation was well overdue.

When returning to Paris, William began to suffer from intestinal trouble. He was admitted in the American Hospital in Neuilly-sur-Seine, just outside of Paris. William had three surgical procedures in a span of seven weeks in order to relieve his trouble. His first surgery was performed on June 27, 1930, several days after the onset and diagnosis of his ailment. Complications from that surgery necessitated a second surgery on July 11, 1930. As a result of William's condition, the Gallup's son and William's brother Harvey departed for Paris on July 16 on a ship named "Leviathan" in order to be with their father and brother, as they thought death was near.

The second operation was considered risky because of Mr. Gallup's age. His brother and son arrived in Paris just before the third surgery. On July 27, 1930 the third and final surgery took place. After the third surgery he slowly improved and it was thought the he would fully recover, albeit over a long haul. His condition was looking so favorable that his son William and brother Harvey arranged for trips back to America. On Wednesday August 6, 1930, both his brother and son left France on the steamship "Paris".

On Thursday, August 7, 1930, just one day after his son and brother left, William suffered a relapse which put him back in the hospital. His wife, Florence stayed by his side, accompanying him until his final breath. He grew weaker and his condition worsened until he passed away at nine at night (Paris time) on Saturday, August 9, 1930. He was seventy-nine years old. His official cause of death was listed was hypertrophy prostate and hypostatic pneumonia. His body was embalmed and placed in the Mortuary Chapel of the American Cathedral in Paris.

Arnold Print Works closed their mills on Monday, August 11, 1930 in honor of their former executive. The body of William Arthur Gallup began the long trek to his home on August 23, 1930. On October 28, 1930, memorial services were held in the Cathedral Church of St. Paul, where many of Gallup's friends and family from North Adams, Newton and Boston attended.

On February 17, 1931, the provisions of W.A. Gallup were made known. The estate was valued at $1,425,549.11[11]. This estate was split several ways. Trust funds of $30,000 were set up for both of his surviving sisters. Of the remaining estate, one-third was given to his widow and the remaining two-thirds were split evenly among his three living children.

William Arthur Gallup was buried in Hillside Cemetery next to his first wife Harriet Gallup. On the other side of his burial spot is William Arthur Gallup Jr., the second child born to Harriet and William.

The Children of Harriet and William Arthur Gallup

Technically speaking, the two surviving daughters did not have a direct impact on the Houghton Mansion. But I felt it was important to briefly discuss their lives since they were the stepdaughters of Florence Houghton Gallup and daughters of William Arthur Gallup, who did live at the mansion after Cordelia Houghton's death. The husbands of these two

---

[11] "W. A. Gallup's Estate Listed at $1,425,549." The Springfield Republican 18 Feb 1931: 2.

daughters also played a direct role in the Arnold Print Works after William A. Gallup retired.

Marian Gallup Flood

Marion Eugenia Gallup was born on July 14, 1883 in North Adams. Marion was only six years old when her mother Harriet lost her life. Marion was educated in the North Adams public schools.

On September 20, 1904, Marion married George Burnside Flood. After the marriage, the couple settled in North Adams and George started his career as a clerk in the Arnold Print Works, the firm where his father-in-law worked. Marion and George would then purchase a home in Blackinton and together had four children, Arthur, Harriet, George and Robert.

For the Flood family, as with most family members discussed in this book, religion was a key element of their lives. The Flood family would regularly attend and generously support St. John's Episcopal Church. George acted as a trustee and member of the finance committee of the church. Marion was a member of the Naomi Chapter, Order of the Eastern Star, and a member of the Fort Massachusetts Chapter of the Daughters of the American Revolution.

When William and Florence Gallup acquired the Houghton Mansion, their home located at 149 Church Street became available. On May 16, 1919, The Floods sold their Blackinton home and announced their plans to relocate into the Gallup home when it became available. At the time George Flood was moving up the ranks at Arnold Print Works to Assistant Treasurer working directly under his father-in-law.

When William Arthur Gallup retired and sold his interest to his other son-in-law Samuel Jones, Flood was promoted to the Treasurer. George retired from the Arnold Print Works at the end of 1930.

In 1931, George accepted a job with the Sprague Specialties Company shortly after the firm moved its operations from Quincy to North Adams. He would ascend within the firm to the position of Treasurer of Sprague Electric Company. He was also served on the Board of Directors for Sprague at a time when the impacts of the Great Depression were still widely felt.

Sprague Electric was founded by Robert C. Sprague as Sprague Specialties Company in Quincy, Massachusetts in 1926. He earned the capital necessary to open his business by inventing and patenting a paper capacitor and tone control for radios. By 1929, Sprague Specialties Company was outgrowing its facility in Quincy. When Sprague was looking for a new location for his growing company, he looked towards North Adams as that is where his father grew up. Sprague opened a plant on Beaver Street in North Adams. It was shortly thereafter that Sprague became the largest employer in North Adams, a spot once held by Arnold Print Works.

Not only was George the Treasurer of Sprague Electric, but he also served as a Treasurer and Director for a number of Sprague Electric's subsidiaries which included the Sprague Products Company based in North Adams, Ferroxcube Corporation of America, located at Saugerties, New York, and the Herlec Corporation of Grafton, Wisconsin. The Herlec Corporation would later become Sprague Electric of Wisconsin, Inc.

George also was named a Director of the North Adams Trust Company and a Vice President, Trustee and a member of the Board of Investment for the Hoosac Savings Bank. George served on the North Adams Planning Board for fifteen years and was also associated with the Y.M.C.A., serving as Director, Trustee and leader of committees. He served the Y.M.C.A. for fifty-one years. George was also a member of the North Adams Country Club, serving on the Greens Committee and taking a leading role in the design of the golf course. George was enthusiastic about playing tennis, partnering with his son George Jr. to win several local amateur tournaments.

In 1935 George Flood was named as a receiver for the Readsboro Chair Company, as the struggling company needed much needed help to survive. The firm was especially important to the community of Readsboro, Vermont as it was the only large industry in the small town.

As the Floods aged, they found it unnecessary to live in such a large home. Their children at this point had moved out. On March 27, 1954, there were rumors that the Floods sold 149 Church Street to a group of physicians who planned to convert the former Gallup residence into medical offices.

By the autumn of 1953, the health of George Flood began to deteriorate. Because of his health, he resigned from his Treasurer duties at Sprague

Electric in March of 1954, but remained a Director and worked as a consultant for the firm when his health allowed him to. George Flood passed away on November 21, 1954 at the age of seventy-four years old. Prior to his death, George was in critical condition for two weeks before he succumbed. Marion passed away on Christmas Eve of 1975 at the age of ninety-two years old. Burial of both George and Marion took place within Hillside Cemetery in North Adams.

Marian Gallup Flood's gravestone in Hillside Cemetery.

After the death of Marion Flood, 149 Church Street was purchased by a group called the Northern Berkshire Association for Retarded Citizens and begun renovations on the former Gallup-Flood home to accommodate twelve people. These residents were transferred from the Belchertown State School as the state looked to decentralize the facilities into smaller community-based homes.

The plaque on the home located at 149 Church Street lists the two prominent families that called the structure home.

One of the children of George and Marion played an interesting role in a fire at the Houghton Mansion that could have been catastrophic if not for a twelve year old boy walking to school in 1960. This incident is discussed later in this book.

Frances Dorothy Gallup Jones

Frances Dorothy Gallup was born on August 20, 1888. She was just over fourteen months old when her mother passed away. While her first name was Frances, she would go by her middle name of Dorothy throughout her life. On November 25, 1905 Dorothy married Samuel Mansfield Jones.

Dorothy was seventeen years old at the time of her wedding and Samuel was eighteen and a student.

Shortly after their marriage, Samuel was employed in the chemistry department of Arnold Print Works and the couple lived on Church Street in North Adams. On March 23, 1906, tragedy struck Dorothy and Samuel Jones less than five months after their marriage. Marian prematurely delivered a stillborn baby girl. The cause of death was attributed to Puerperal convulsions. The unnamed infant was buried the next day in Hillside Cemetery.

Samuel left the print works and would attend M.I.T. then travel abroad to Europe with his wife. Samuel received schooling in Europe and received a Ph.D. degree from the University of Basel in Switzerland. After he received his prestigious degree, he worked in various plants in Russia and Germany. The family then returned to North Adams and Samuel returned to Arnold Print Works.

In 1914, Dorothy and her two children were back in the United States visiting family. In fact, the Jones family was with Florence and William Arthur Gallup on August 1, 1914. It was that day when they were going to sail to Germany. This trip of course was called off as that day the declaration of war which began World War I occurred that day. It was of course, also this day when the car accident forever changed the Houghton family.

On August 20, 1915, the Jones family boarded a ship called the Dwinsk departing from Archangel. It would arrive in New York City on September 9, 1915. The family would then settle down in North Adams.

Dorothy and Samuel had four children: Florence (born approximately 1910), Edward (born approximately 1912), Anna (born approximately 1918), and Dorothy (born approximately 1926).

When William Arthur Gallup sold his interest and retired from Arnold Print Works, he sold his shares to Samuel Mansfield Jones who was named President and was the largest shareholder. He retained that role in the Arnold Print Works until the company's liquidation in 1942. After Samuel Jones purchased the print works, the family bought a large estate in Williamstown, Massachusetts where they moved in 1927.

Samuel Mansfield Jones passed away on May 29, 1954 at the age of sixty-six years old. He suffered from a cerebral hemorrhage that caused his death. For years he was suffering from arteriosclerosis, which is quite simply, the hardening and thickening of arteries that are often seen with old age. Samuel's remains were cremated. Dorothy Jones passed away on December 2, 1963 at the age of seventy-five at her winter home in Daytona Beach, Florida.

The Demise of Arnold Print Works

In 1935, the company once again faced financial difficulty. The company contended that price-cutting under the National Recovery Act had a substantial impact on the economic health of the company. On September 3, 1935 the company filed for bankruptcy protection. At the time the company still had 1,700 employees. Within the filing, the company listed both its assets and liabilities at just over eight million dollars. At the end of the fiscal year, the loss was reported at one-half of one million dollars.

It was increasingly difficult for Arnold Print Works to obtain cloth for conversion into draperies and other print goods that the company produced.

On March 30, 1942, the Directors of Arnold Print Works recommended the liquidation of Arnold Print Works. On May 1, 1942, the liquidation of the company was discussed during a stockholders meeting. The stockholders of Arnold Print Works then voted to dissolve and liquidate the corporation. At that time, the liquidation was scheduled to begin on October 1 of that same year. At the time it was estimated that the liquidation would net the shareholders $15 a common share. The Arnold Print Works established seventy-nine years prior, was no longer.

On Tuesday, November 16, 1943 the equipment and tools contained in Arnold Print Works went on sale through an auction. The auction was conducted by Samuel T. Freeman and Company for the Beacon Realty and Trading Corporation which owned the property. The boiler plant and machinery which once powered the complex was dismantled and sold to United Piece Dye Works of Lodi, New Jersey. It was the end of an era in North Adams, and the beginning of a new one.

The name Arnold Print Works lived on, however. The Jones Division plant of Arnold Print Works was located in Adams, Massachusetts. When the Arnold Print Works dissolved in 1942, the Jones Division was sold to the Aspinook Corporation. The Jones Division was renamed Arnold Print Works. In 1956, Aspinook was merged with U. S. Finishing Corporation and the new corporate offices were known as USF-Aspinook.

When the Arnold Print Works ceased operations, Sprague Specialties Company bought the Arnold Print Works facilities on Marshall Street and relocated all of their operations there. At that time, the Marshall Street complex consisted of twenty-six buildings, all of which were connected by a complex series of bridges and tunnels. When the company moved to the former Arnold Print Works, the name changed to Sprague Electric.

During World War II, the activities of Sprague Electric transitioned to wartime manufacturing. During the war, Sprague manufactured variable-timed proximity fuses. The fuse was either a small transistor or in some cases a receiver, that was built onto artillery in order for the artillery to detonate before impact to cause more damage. It was during this time that Sprague invented the Tantalum capacitor, which allowed for higher electron storage in a fraction of the size of the traditional design. The Tantalum capacitor is still used to this day. After the war, Sprague Electric reverted back towards commercial manufacturing and was considered an industry leader and the world's largest manufacturer of capacitors. Sprague Electric was sold to General Cable in 1978, taken over by Penn Central in 1981, eventually closing the North Adams operation in 1985.

87 Marshall Street was added in 1985 to the National Register of Historic Places.

6. Susan Houghton McKean: Her Life and Family

> **A day all about visiting family and friends turned into an event we are still discussing a century later.**

Susan Houghton was born on March 26, 1872 in North Adams. She was the third child born to Albert and Cordelia Houghton. When Susan was younger she would often prefer to be known as Susie, even using the nickname on official documents such as her passport application.

Susan attended the public schools in North Adams, and then she was enrolled in Miss Crighton's private boarding school in Englewood, New Jersey. This is the same boarding school that her sister Florence attended. After the boarding school in New Jersey, Susan spent two years abroad in Europe with her sister Florence and chaperone Mary Cady. The trip to abroad was to further her education and to see the historic sites throughout the continent.

According to her passport application, when Susan was nineteen years old she was five-foot five-and-a-half inches tall. She had light brown hair with brown eyes and a fair complexion. She described herself as having a high forehead, a Grecian nose, a small mouth and a dimpled chin with an oval face. This physical description is very similar to that of her sister Florence.

Throughout her youth, Susan was trained musically and she would often play piano for special functions. Keep in mind that her sister Alice was a trained singer, so I would assume the two sisters would accompany each other musically. Susan was involved in the Daughters of American Revolution, a charter member of the Fort Massachusetts Chapter, and would perform at several functions for that organization. Even in her later years, Susan would volunteer as a chairperson for music committees for several special functions.

Susan was closest in personality to her sister Alice in that she was heavily involved in the social circles of the time. Before she was married, she would travel around the Northeast and as far away as Chicago to visit close friends. As discussed in the history of Albert Houghton, Susan accompanied her father on board the ship Teutonic for a trip to England that was meant to rejuvenate a worn-out Albert Houghton.

Susan met Andrew McKean and they began dating. Andrew was born in Amsterdam, New York on December 29, 1870 to Reverend Samuel McKean and his second wife Katherine Porter McKean. Reverend McKean was a prominent Methodist minister and was pastor of churches in Greenbush, Saratoga Springs, Lansingburgh, Waterville, Fort Edward, as well as other communities in New York.

Reverend McKean was the pastor of the Methodist Church in North Adams from 1881 until 1883. In 1884, the McKean family finally settled down in Lansingburgh where the Reverend McKean became pastor of the First Methodist Church, later known as St. Mark's Methodist Church. Andrew was educated at North Adams Academy and Lansingburgh Academy. After those schools he enrolled in Williams College and graduated in 1892. While in college, Andrew was a member of the Zeta Psi fraternity. After he graduated from Williams College, he was a teacher for three years – first in Washington D.C, then in New York City. He moved to Troy, New York in 1895 and studied law under James S, Wheeler. In 1897 he was admitted to the New York State Bar and began his practice in Troy becoming a partner with Wheeler under the firm name Wheeler & McKean.

Susan and Andrew were engaged during the holidays in 1898, it was informally announced on December 31 at the Houghton residence. Andrew at the time of the engagement was already a well-known lawyer in Troy, New York.

The wedding announcement of Susan and Andrew took place at a function at the mansion. Houghton's daughters would throw several fancy social functions at the residence. This is the former parlor on the first floor.

The wedding ceremony took place on Wednesday, March 22, 1899 at the Buckingham Hotel in New York City. The Buckingham Hotel was the location where Albert C. Houghton and Cordelia spent their winters avoiding the treacherous travel from New York to North Adams. The wedding was a small function where only the closest of family and friends were invited. In total, twenty people attended the ceremony. The wedding ceremony itself took place in the hotel's parlors which were adorned by hundreds of roses, other cut flowers, ferns and palms. The father of the groom, Reverend Dr. Samuel McKean officiated the Episcopal ceremony.

Albert C. Houghton gave away the bride and her sisters Alice and Mary were the bridesmaids. Howard McKean who lived in New York City and was the brother of the groom served as the best man. After the ceremony the reception was held in the banquet room of the hotel. The head table was adorned by a centerpiece that consisted of approximately five hundred roses. If that were not enough an additional 300 roses were entwined throughout the table's decorations. Music was provided by the Lander Orchestra of New York City.

After the reception the newlyweds departed for a trip of six weeks through the Southern United States. When they returned from their honeymoon, the couple resided in Lansingburgh, New York. The couple would later move to Troy, New York.

Susan and Andrew had two daughters, Cordelia McKean Staniford and Florence Porter McKean Tompkins. The names were chosen to honor

Susan's mother and oldest sister. Cordelia was born on March 15, 1900 and Florence Porter McKean was born on January 6, 1903 in Troy, New York.

In 1905, Andrew's law partner James Wheeler died, and Andrew ran the law firm alone. He also served as a Vice-President and a member of the board for the Arnold Print Works from 1910 until 1926. He was also politically involved in Troy. He was a Republican and served as president of the Common Council in that town for two terms covering the years from 1906 through 1909. He was named as a delegate to the New York State Constitutional Convention in 1915 as well as serving on the Lansingburgh Board of Education. Andrew was on the board of directors for Russell State College. He was also a vice president and a member of the board of the People's Bank of Lansingburgh, a director of Union National Bank, and a trustee of the Troy Savings Bank. Andrew was also a member of several country clubs throughout the region taking up the sport of golf.

He did considerable work for the Troy Orphan Asylum and the Marshall Infirmary. He was also a trustee of the Leonard Hospital. Since his father and grandfather were pastors, religion was a very important part of Andrew's life. He served as an official of the First Methodist Episcopal Church in Troy, New York.

Susan donated much of her time to the Leonard Hospital and many other local charities. Susan became involved with the hospital because Andrew was also on the board of managers for that hospital. She was regarded as a socialite in both Lansingburgh and in Troy.

In January of 1925 Susan Houghton McKean set up a fund in order to memorialize her deceased sisters Alice and Mary. Susan donated ten thousand dollars to the Mohawk and Hudson Humane Society for the care of animals. As she presented the gift, she presented it as the Alice Houghton Wilkinson and Mary Cordelia Houghton Fund. Susan felt this donation was important due to both Mary and Alice having a love for the wellbeing of animals.

The North Adams Public Library was the recipient of a few donations from Susan McKean. What was interesting about the gifts is that they once graced the Houghton residence on Church Street. In 1933, Susan donated a bronze statue of "Nymphe de Diane", by the French sculptress, Signoret-Ledieu. The sculpture had for many years been part of the Houghton

Mansion. A year later, Susan donated a very pricy mantle clock with candlesticks that again had been proudly displayed in the Houghton residence years prior.

In 1937, Andrew and Susan moved out of Troy. They sold their home to the Leonard Hospital to be used as a home for staff – the house was later named "the Andrew P. McKean House". The McKeans moved to New York City residing at 111 East 48th Street in an apartment in Hotel Barclay. The McKeans also had a home in Florida where they would spend the winters.

As with many American families during World War II, the McKeans suffered from a personal loss. Private First Class John Hobart Thompson was killed in duty on January 26, 1945. The grandson of Susan Houghton McKean and the great-grandson of Albert C. Houghton lost his life in the bloodiest battle of World War II, the Battle of the Bulge.

Andrew passed away in July of 1954 at the age of 83 in their apartment in the Hotel Barclay. His funeral was held on Thursday, July 8, 1954. He is buried in Oakwood Cemetery in Troy, New York.

Susan died at the Manhattan apartment on Monday evening, September 12, 1955. She passed away in the same apartment her husband also died just fourteen months prior. Her funeral was held in New York on Friday, September 16, 1955. She is also buried in Oakwood Cemetery in Troy, New York.

Susan was the last survivor of A.C. and Cordelia Houghton's family. At the time of her death she had six grandchildren and six great-grandchildren.

Through Susan's Eyes: August 1, 1914

For Susan McKean and her family, August 1, 1914 was a day that was about visiting family. Living in Troy, New York, it was a bit more of an ordeal to visit with her sisters and parents. Her sister Florence practically lived across the street from her parents and sister Mary. It is unknown to me if Susan planned the trip specifically because Sybil and her husband and son were in town. I assume it was a major draw factor for her as Susan and Sybil were quite often in the same social functions previously. On a day that was about visiting family, it quickly turned to a day about a deep family tragedy. To the

McKeans, the beginning of August 1, 1914 was similar to the countless Saturdays before. Who would ever guess that this day will be one we are still discussing one hundred years later.

Since Mary and Albert were hosting the Huttons on a pleasure trip that morning, the McKeans were scheduled to visit later that day. The original plan was for them to drive from their home in Troy to the Houghton residence in North Adams. When Susan was told of the car accident, the plans changed. Either the news hit a raw nerve or Susan did not feel comfortable placing her family in an automobile. It is also possible that Cordelia asked her not to take a car so she would not have to needlessly worry about another loved one.

Either way, the McKeans delayed their departure so they can catch the train to North Adams versus driving in an automobile. Since Cordelia did not have the specifics of the car accident, Susan did not have any details herself. I cannot imagine how long those hours felt being separated by a distance and without knowing the status of her loved ones. All she knew is that it was serious. When the McKeans did step foot on the train, whatever communication between Susan and North Adams was cut off as there was no way to connect on the train. It is not known if she stepped foot on the train knowing that her baby sister was dead, or if she found out when she arrived in North Adams.

When the McKeans did arrive in North Adams, the aftermath was clear. Susan's youngest sister was dead. For Susan, this is the second sister she lost. Her father was injured and grief-stricken. Her mother again lost another child. Her friend Sybil was dead, and Sybil's two year old child was left without a mother. Widders, a man she had known her whole life, felt responsible and took his own life hours later. This is what the day turned into. August 1, 1914 was supposed to be a day about spending time with family and reconnecting with Sybil. This day turned out to be nothing but tragedy for Susan McKean and her family.

The Children of Susan and Andrew McKean

It is important to briefly discuss the children of Susan and Andrew McKean as they were the granddaughters of Albert and Cordelia Houghton. As children, they would often visit their grandparents, and as such, they walked through the hallways and played on the property. Their laughter as children became part of the fabric of Houghton Mansion.

Cordelia Houghton McKean

Cordelia Houghton McKean was married to Hobart Warren Thompson, Jr. who was born on February 20, 1897 in Troy, New York. Cordelia attended the Emma Williard School and then Madame Roeffel's School in New York. She continued her education at the Bennett School in Millbrook, New York.

During World War I, Hobart W. Thompson served as an Ensign in the United States Navy based out of Newport, Rhode Island. After the war, Hobart was enrolled in the Sheffield Scientific School which was part of Yale University. The Sheffield Scientific School specialized in scientific and engineering education. He would later move to Albany, New York and find a job in a securities firm before he met Cordelia. After their marriage Cordelia and Hobart had three children together. Mary C. Thompson was born around 1922, John Hobart Thompson was born around 1924, and McKean Thompson was born in 1926.

The union of Cordelia and Hobart unfortunately was not a lasting one, as they would get divorced. Both Cordelia and Hobart would remarry, however. Cordelia's second husband Foye Fawcett Staniford was born in Brooklyn, New York on April 8, 1890 to Charles and Julia Staniford. Like her first husband, Staniford served in World War I. He served overseas from April 30, 1918 to February 9, 1919. He was honorably discharged from active duty on February 14, 1919. His rank was First Lieutenant. This was also the second marriage for Foye Staniford as he was previously married to Gloria G. Staniford. Foye and Gloria had a daughter, also named Gloria, who was born around 1922.

Hobart W. Thompson Jr. would remarry as well. His second wife was named Marion. Marion was thirteen years younger than Hobart. With Marion, Hobart had three more children, all sons. Stephen was born around 1935, Michael was born around 1939, and Nathan was born in 1940. Hobart would become involved in real estate and would move his family to Stonington, Connecticut. Hobart would pass away between the years of 1940 and 1946, although I could not find the exact date.

Foye Staniford, Cordelia's second husband, was employed at the Mack International Motor Truck Corporation. He would rise through the ranks until he was named President. Foye and Cordelia had a son together, Foye F. Staniford Jr., who was born around 1932. Also living with the family were the three children of Cordelia and her first husband, Mary, John, and McKean. Keeping up with this large family was a household staff of four which included a chauffeur, a cook, a maid, and a waitress. Call me jealous!

On July 11, 1938, Cordelia spent the day at the beach at the Southampton Beach Club in Southampton, New York with her husband, and their friend Mrs. John Warner, who was the daughter of New York Governor Alfred E. Smith. Warner's husband was the head of the New York State Police. The two couples were in the ocean when someone made their way into a bathhouse that was used by the group and stole the jewelry that was taken off. Altogether the thief was able to get away with about fifteen thousand dollars' worth of jewelry. Remember that this is 1938; think about the jewelry's value in today's dollar.

Cordelia's son Hobart Thompson was sent overseas during World War II. After he graduated from Phillips Academy in Andover, Massachusetts, he entered into military service. He was largely stationed in America, until he was sent overseas around November of 1944. He was part of the Ardennes Counteroffensive, more widely known as the Battle of the Bulge.

The Battle of the Bulge was the result of a German offensive in the Ardennes region of Belgium, Luxembourg and France called Wallonia. The German military caught the Allied forces off-guard. This campaign resulted in a large loss of life for Allied troops, especially American forces. The German offensive began on December 16, 1944 and the battle lasted to the end of January, 1945. The Allied forces ended up repelling the German advances but the toll was extremely high for both sides.

It was estimated that of the American forces, over nineteen thousand were killed, fifty thousand were injured and twenty-two thousand were missing. These losses represent the bloodiest battle for the United States in the war. For the Germans, they lost a similar level of troops, but more importantly, the Luftwaffe, the well-known air fighters were left in disarray as well as many of the German units who had to hastily retreat. On what some consider the final day of the Battle of the Bulge, Private First Class John Hobart Thompson was killed in duty on January 26, 1945. The grandson of

Susan Houghton McKean and the great-grandson of Albert C. Houghton lost his life in the bloodiest battle of World War II.

Foye Fawcett Staniford passed away on May 22, 1964. Cordelia passed away in December 1970.

Florence Porter McKean

On July 7, 1923, Florence Porter McKean married Ralph Lewis Tompkins on the island of Nantucket. The groom was twenty-three years old and the bride was twenty. The groom was a salesman from the Bronx. Florence was living in New York City. This was the first and only wedding for both the bride and groom.

Ralph Tompkins was born on October 30, 1899 to Ralph S. and Lillian (Weller) Tompkins in Beacon, New York. The Tompkins family would later settle in nearby Newburgh, New York. Before World War I, Ralph was a helper at the Newburgh Shipyard. During World War I, Ralph was sent to battle as a Private. Later in life Ralph would again serve as a member of the New York Guard, rising through the ranks until he retired a 2nd Lieutenant. The New York Guard was formed as a result of World War I when the New York National Guard was sent to France. The New York Guard replaced the members of the National Guard and served to protect the reservoirs of New York City. Today the New York Guard supports the New York National Guard and its members today are typically retired members of National Guard and other military units.

After the war, Ralph attended Princeton University. After Ralph and Florence were married, the couple settled down in New York City. Their family consisted of two children, both of them girls. Suzanne was born in approximately 1925 and Janice was born in approximately 1927. It is interesting to note that the family of four at one point had a household staff of four. So when you put this book down and have to do the kid's laundry, think of having one staff member per family member. Ralph was a proprietor of a woolens mill.

Florence McKean Tomkins became a widow in 1971 when her husband Ralph passed away in August of that year. Florence passed away on July 11, 1991. She is buried at the Old North Cemetery on Nantucket next to her husband.

7. Alice Houghton Wilkinson: Her Life and Family

> Sometimes God calls us home early.

Alice Houghton Wilkinson is a central figure in the trials and tribulations of the Houghton family. Sadly, her story is never told. While she did not live inside the halls of Houghton Mansion, she did grace the hallways of the mansion many times, as did her husband and young son. The story of Alice Houghton Wilkinson is one that is far too short. If her narrative was allowed to continue, who knows what she would have accomplished.

Alice Josephine Houghton was the fourth daughter born to Cordelia and Albert Houghton. Alice was born on April 17, 1875 in North Adams. Except for her boarding school in New York City and time spent abroad in study, Alice resided in North Adams for her entire life. Alice attended the public schools in North Adams, and then attended a private boarding school, Miss Peeble's Boarding and Day School for Girls, which was located on East 57th Street in Manhattan.

Alice spent a year traveling and studying abroad in Europe. During this time abroad, she was accompanied by her younger sister Mary and their chaperone Mary Cady. Like her sisters Florence and Susan, the group took in many European landmarks and spent the most time in Germany. It is not known why Alice and Mary spent only one year in Europe while Florence and Susan spent two years abroad.

Alice returned to Europe a short time later when she accompanied her father Albert C. Houghton and sister Susan on board the ship Teutonic for a trip to England. The ship departed from New York City on April 6, 1898. The trip was in reality a trip to restore her father's health. This may have been the first extended vacation that he ever took. He was no longer the Mayor of North Adams, a responsibility that was even more impressive considering how hard he worked within all of his business endeavors and with all the other appointments to various boards. The Houghton family returned to New York City on April 27, 1898.

While Alice was growing up, she was friends with children of several prominent families in North Adams. She was very active in the social scene with well-known offspring in town. She hosted parties at popular locations such as Idlewild with the likes of Stella Cady (the sister of Sybil Cady Hutton) and her future husband Edward S. Wilkinson Jr.

When the Houghton family moved to their new home, the structure we know call Houghton Mansion, Alice remained in the home at 36 Church Street. This is significant as a Wilkinson family, including Edward S. Wilkinson Jr., lived at 34 Church Street. Edward at the time was a bank clerk at Adams National Bank; his father was the President of the bank at this time. To show how close the families we are studying were, Sybil Cady was living at 37 Church Street at this time.

On Wednesday, July 27, 1898, during a whist party – a card game that was very popular at the time – Alice and Edward announced their engagement. This whist party occurred at the Houghton Mansion. Since Alice and Edward were both very popular and prominent youths, the news of their engagement was both exciting but it also disappointed others who may have had their eyes on either of them for themselves.

The wedding of Alice and Edward took place on Wednesday, April 19, 1899. Both the bride and groom were twenty-three years old. This was also the first marriage for both the bride and groom. The wedding ceremony took place at five in the afternoon in the Buckingham Hotel in New York City.

The hotel was decorated with hundreds of roses and other cut flowers. Alice's wedding took place mere weeks after her older sister Susan's wedding. In fact, the Reverend Samuel McKean, Susan's father-in-law officiated Alice's wedding. The Episcopalian wedding service was used and was witnessed by thirty of the bride and groom's closest friends and family. Mary C. Houghton was the maid of honor.

After the ceremony there was an elaborate reception that also took place at the Buckingham Hotel. The parlors and banquet room of the hotel were adorned by large quantities of roses and other flowers. During the reception, there was an orchestra providing the music for the bride and groom and their guests. After their wedding, the bride and groom took a lengthy honeymoon. When they returned to North Adams in June, they moved into the home of Edward's parents which was just yards from Houghton Mansion. Shortly after their marriage, however, the couple moved into a home on Elmwood Avenue in North Adams.

Alice Houghton and Edward Wilkinson would move into his parent's house temporarily after marriage. After Alice's death, her widower and young son would move into this residence, just yards away from Houghton Mansion.

Alice and Edward's marriage was described as being a very happy union. Alice was very social and she was described as being cheerful and very friendly. She made many friends throughout her short life. Whoever met her would soon be considered a friend. She took special interest in planning or being part of social engagements for the youth of North Adams. In fact, she was described as having extraordinary musical talent, to which she was happy to showcase that talent at many of these social gatherings. Alice was very active in many charitable functions serving on many committees for such social affairs.

Together Alice and Edward had one child, a son named Edward Shepard Wilkinson III who was born on May 20, 1901. Unfortunately his life is yet another tragic story in the history of this family. We will explore the short life of Edward a little later on.

One Final Visit to New York City for Thanksgiving

As mentioned earlier, Albert C. Houghton, Cordelia and Mary would relocate to New York City in the winter so that Mr. Houghton can work in the New York City office without having to travel from North Adams to the city in harsh conditions.

For the Thanksgiving holiday in 1906, Alice intended to travel to visit her family in New York City. Alice was feeling ill for several weeks before, but her health improved so that she was able to make the trip. Alice left North Adams on Wednesday, November 21, 1906, Thanksgiving was the following day. Her husband Edward remained in North Adams to attend to business. Alice took the railroad down to New York City.

The Houghton family enjoyed Thanksgiving and everything seemed to be great. Then suddenly on Tuesday, November 27, the normally healthy Alice felt ill again. Her condition deteriorated rapidly. News of Alice's condition reached her husband in North Adams. Her concerned husband rushed to New York City to be with his ailing wife.

Alice was diagnosed with appendicitis and had an emergency operation at the Murray Hill Hotel that evening. Since Alice was a member of a prominent family, she received care from those medical professionals that were deemed as eminent surgeons. This was supposed to a standard procedure and she was expected to have a quick and complete recovery.

Alice, however, suffered complications from the surgery and remained in the hotel room. She received round-the-clock care, but she deteriorated nonetheless. On Friday, November 30, 1906, Alice succumbed at the age of thirty-one. She left behind her husband of nine years, and more tragically, a son that was six years old. The news of Alice's passing made it to North Adams rather quickly. The somber news of the death of a young, vibrant, cheerful and prominent member of the community shocked many.

The body of Alice made the final trip back to North Adams in the evening of Saturday, December 1, 1906, where she was brought to William Arthur Gallup's house on Church Street in North Adams. The funeral was originally to take place in the Baptist Church. However, the location of the funeral was changed to take place at her home located on Elmwood Avenue. The home was packed with people paying their respects to a young woman who was widely known for her sunny disposition.

Suddenly a holiday weekend in which we are supposed to celebrate all of our blessings turned into one in which the Houghton and Wilkinson families lost one of their own blessings – a loved one.

Alice was buried in Hillside Cemetery in North Adams. Unfortunately for the Houghton family the pain and suffering did not end with the untimely loss of Alice, but her young son also experienced a similar fate just two years later. Shortly after Alice's death, the Houghton family experienced great difficulty due to the financial crisis that would threaten Arnold Print Works and the reputation and wealth of many of the family members. These days were indeed gloomy and dreadful ones to all those impacted. The once cheerful home lost a major part of its charm. The laughter and the singing from within its walls would fade.

After the death of his beloved wife, Edward Wilkinson could not bear the thought of living in the home he shared with his wife. His son was young and needed care while he worked. Edward's mother lived in a home immediately adjacent the Houghton residence. Edward would move into his mother's house which allowed for his son to be very close to all of his living grandparents.

The gravestone of Alice Houghton Wilkinson. Sometimes God calls us home early. Her death marked the beginning of a tragic and trying time for both the Houghton and Wilkinson families.

Edward Wilkinson III

Edward Shepard Wilkinson III was born on May 20, 1901 in North Adams. In the very short time on this planet, the little boy lived a tragic life. At the age of five years old, he lost his mother. Alice was a very good mother to her son and her overall happiness and joyful personality provided little Edward with a healthy home life. He was described as being very bright and like Alice, he was very cheerful and loved to spread smiles to whoever he would meet. To his father, he certainly reminded him of his cherished wife.

> ## The Wilkinson family again lost its sunshine, gone now was a mother's song and a son's laughter.

After the death of his mother, young Edward's life took a turn for the worse as his own health deteriorated. In the spring of 1908, Edward's father and grandmother took him out west in the hopes that the change of climate would help his condition. In the previous winter, he suffered from a very serious case of pneumonia which threatened his life. While in Phoenix, Arizona, he contracted Scarlet Fever. That illness ran its course through the little boy. When he recovered slightly, he was taken to Pasadena, California, although he was still very weak and fragile due to battling both pneumonia and Scarlet Fever.

As he was in Pasadena, he received the best medical treatment for that time. But unfortunately his health grew worse again. While weakened he contracted rheumatic fever. As a result of this illness, his heart valves were badly damaged, a condition called rheumatic endocarditis. Just several days after his seventh birthday, Edward passed away in Pasadena on Tuesday, May 26, 1908.

The death of his son greatly impacted Edward Wilkinson Jr. In a very short period of time, he lost his wife and his son. The once happy family was torn apart and Edward was now alone. Edward returned to North Adams with the body of his son on Sunday, May 31, 1908. Little Edward S. Wilkinson III was buried in Hillside Cemetery next to his

The gravestone of Edward Wilkinson III. The reunion with his mother did not wait long. Gone was the sound of a child's laughter from within the home adjacent Houghton Mansion. A grieving father lost two beautiful souls in just two years.

mother, Alice Houghton. The Wilkinson family again lost its sunshine, gone now was a mother's song and a son's laughter.

Edward Wilkinson Jr.

Edward Wilkinson lost both his wife and his son in a short amount of time. He was understandably devastated by both tragic events. Edward never remarried, but he dedicated himself to his business and to the many civic duties he chose. When he lost his family, he realized how lucky he was to have them in his life, so his sense of giving back to his community was awakened.

Like others we were introduced throughout this book, Edward S. Wilkinson Jr. was an important figure to both the community of North Adams, as well as to the Houghton family. The Wilkinson family had roots in North Adams even before it became North Adams. Edward Shepard Wilkinson Jr. was born on October 14, 1875 to Edward and Eliza Cornelia (Quackinbush) Wilkinson.

In addition to Edward, his mother and father had three more children. Sadly, Edward is the only one who made it past childhood. Their first child, Mary Eliza, was born on August 9, 1865. Mary would be called "Birdie" throughout her young life. Birdie passed away on March 22, 1872 after suffering from a gastric ailment, she was

The gravestones of Edward's siblings. L – R: Florence, Anna, and Mary Elizabeth "Birdie". Edward's sisters all died during childhood.

only six years and seven months old. Anna Belle Wilkinson was born on January 28, 1868. Florence C. Wilkinson was born on October 30, 1877.

I could not obtain the dates on when Anna and Florence died, but the Wilkinson family plot contains the graves of three children and Edward was described as an only child, so it is evident that his two other sisters passed away when they were children.

His father Edward Wilkinson Sr. would become the third Mayor of North Adams as he was elected in 1901. Edward Wilkinson Sr., however, died during his term as Mayor. Mayor Wilkinson died on October 14, 1902 at a hospital in Albany, New York as a result of blood poisoning after a surgery for kidney failure. Edward Sr. passed away on Edward Jr.'s birthday.

Edward Wilkinson Jr. was educated in the North Adams public schools. He was later enrolled and attended Worcester Academy and later Brown University. While at Brown, he was a member of the Delta Kappa Epsilon fraternity. After he graduated from Brown University he returned to North Adams and was hired as a clerk in the North Adams National Bank, the institution in which his father served as President. He later was hired as an Assistant Treasurer at Arnold Print Works, where he was placed in charge of purchasing. Edward was also a Mason, a member of the Greylock Lodge.

When Edward was young, he was part of the social scene in North Adams. He would hold various charity functions, one such party was a charity ball with sleigh rides through North Adams. One of his guests was Alice Houghton, the woman he would later marry. As it has been told, many young men and women were disappointed when Edward and Alice were taken off of the market.

Edward was known for his remarkable sense of humor. When his wife was alive, the combination of Edward's humor and Alice's cheerfulness made their home a very cheerful place and a warm and loving environment for their son.

In 1902, after his father's passing, Edward was named as a Director of the North Adams National Bank, a role he held for twenty-eight years before retiring. He later returned in that same capacity three years after he initially retired from that position.

Edward was despondent when his wife Alice passed away as a result of her appendix operation. Having to care for his young son kept Edward's spirits up as it has been said that their son carried many of the same personality traits that his mother had. But the death of Alice greatly troubled her husband. As the result of her death, Edward's health began to fail. He tried to fight through his pain to continue his work as the Assistant Treasurer at Arnold Print Works. When his son's health started to fail, Edward did whatever he could to try to save his son. The stress of losing his wife and now his own son's failing health was giving too much stress for Edward to carry on his duties. In January of 1908, Edward resigned his position with the Arnold Print Works. This was in the midst of a major financial crisis at Arnold Print Works as well.

Since his son was suffering from multiple respiratory ailments, Edward moved to warmer climates in an attempt to nurse his child back to health. Unfortunately it was too late, and Edward had to bury his son next to his wife.

After the death of his wife, Edward Wilkinson moved into the home that his parents built. Edward moved in so that his son would be close to his mother and the Houghtons.

Religion was important to Edward and as such he was a deacon of the First Baptist Church in North Adams. His father served as the Superintendent of the church's Sunday school program and was a trustee of the church. Because of his father's prominent role, the church was very important to Edward as he himself, served as a trustee and members of various committees within the church.

Eliza Wilkinson, the mother of Edward developed dysentery in late August, 1912. At this time she was nearly sixty-eight years old and the illness took its toll on her body. Eliza passed away in the home she shared with her son on August 27, 1912. She was buried in the Wilkinson family plot within Hillside Cemetery.

Edward had a role in the car accident of August 1, 1914. As he was golfing at a local country club, Cordelia was able to contact him regarding the car accident. When Edward found out that Cordelia did not have the details necessary to know the status of her loved ones, he rushed away to try to find out some information to bring back. When the tragedy's aftermath became clear, Edward was with the family to help them grieve and cope with all of their losses. Edward was still very close to the Houghton family and the tragedy of that fateful day impacted him deeply as well.

After the United States entered World War I, Edward was named a member of the personnel board of the War Work Council. He initially served the

Northern Berkshire region before he traveled the country enlisting on average one thousand men per month for duty as Y.M.C.A. secretaries. He was then sent to London as a member of this board.

Edward also enlisted to serve in the Y.M.C.A. Edward chose this work because he was above the age limit to serve as an active soldier for the United States. He travelled the country visiting several camps and working on enlisting volunteers for the Red Triangle. He was appointed as the Secretary of the Pennsylvania War Work Council. That particular chapter was formally recognized as a model chapter for which others should be patterned after. The duties of the position involved selecting men for overseas service in the Red Triangle. After the war and the board was demobilized, Edward Wilkinson was requested to remain in Philadelphia to help launch educational programs for soldiers in France.

In April of 1919, he was sent to France to continue his work there. Shortly after arriving in France, he was named as the head of the Y.M.C.A. operations in Italy. Due to the quick demobilization in Italy, he was never sent there. He boarded the ship Rotterdam and arrived in New York City on July 22, 1919. On Wednesday, August 6, 1919 Edward returned to North Adams after a year-and-a-half deployment.

Edward kept the legacy of Alice alive by dedicating himself to many of the causes that she held near and dear to her heart. Alice was very interested in the issues of the youth, so Edward was very generous in his support of local youth who were seeking college education.

Edward unsuccessfully ran for mayor of North Adams in 1924. Wilkinson and an attorney by the name of J. Bernard Boland were both seeking the Republican nomination to run for mayor. In the interest of showing party unity, Boland dropped his candidacy so that Wilkinson would be the Republican nominee. His opponents ran a somewhat negative campaign against him, questioning his motives. Wilkinson ran a clean campaign as he decided not to attack his political opponent.

Edward was defeated by William Johnson, an Independent running as a "People's Candidate" but had the endorsement of the Democratic Party. As late as the day before the election, the local press and many others predicted victory for Wilkinson. The margin of victory for Johnson was seven hundred and eighty seven votes[12]. Although he was gracious in defeat, it was particularly painful for Wilkinson, so much so that he decided to forego any thought of running again for any political office. He did not disappear from the public view, however. In fact, his involvement in the community actually grew. Many voters would later regret turning their back on Edward. Edward was asked to run several times, and each time he politely declined their requests.

In April of 1926, Wilkinson lost both his uncle and aunt in what we typically see as broken-heart deaths. On April 18, 1926, Sarah Louise (Bliss) Wilkinson passed away. Her funeral was scheduled for the afternoon of Wednesday, April 21. While her husband, Warren J. Wilkinson's health was deteriorating over the previous two years, he passed away mere hours before his wife's funeral. Sarah's funeral was postponed so that a joint funeral could be held the next day in their home on Quincy Street that they shared for many years. The couple was married for just under fifty-three years and together they embarked on the journey to Heaven.

Edward would leave North Adams in the winters and spend his time in warmer climates. He had established business interests in both Pasadena and Los Angeles. He would also spend considerable time in both St. Petersburg and Palm Beach, Florida.

His travels allowed him to become a member of clubs throughout the country. He was named a commodore of the New York Yacht Club and a member of the University Club, also in New York. He was a member of an exclusive and small club called the Bohemian Club. This club is unique as its meetings were held in a California grove, and another member happened to be President Herbert Hoover. In fact, Wilkinson and President Hoover were rather close.

Locally, Edward served as a member of the local Rotary Club, held the Vice-President role of the Richmond-Wellington Hotel, and Vice-President of the North Adams Hospital. Edward was also named a Director and President of the North Adams Community Chest. More importantly to the history of the Houghton Mansion, Edward was also a member of the Greylock Lodge. Could this connection be the driving force of the Masons later acquiring the property? In the final years of his life, Edward Wilkinson

[12] "Vote for Mayor in Former Years." *The North Adams Transcript* 16 Dec 1926: 2.

became an avid traveler, with several trips to Europe and other trips around the world.

It would become quite the task to sort out and describe all the philanthropic causes that Wilkinson was attached to - not to mention it would have been a daunting read. As mentioned earlier, when his wife passed away, he seemed to become dedicated solely on honoring her memory by being that ray of sunshine that she was described as being.

I believe I can relay his overall generosity with one example rather than lull you into a coma with dozens of tales. During the winter of 1934, Edward noticed that a visiting nurse by the name of Mabel Rice was traversing the snow-covered roads in a somewhat dilapidated vehicle. Understanding the need for Miss Rice to attend to many people in the community, he decided that her vehicle was not only a risk for her, but also her patients that counted on her. Edward Wilkinson decided to take his own vehicle to a garage and had it restored to a new condition. He then took the restored auto to the Visiting Nurses Association with the instruction that it should be given to Miss Rice so she could make her rounds in a safer and more amenable vehicle. While we take little things for granted nowadays, heat was considered a luxury in automobiles, Edward made sure that her new vehicle was equipped with heat, for her comfort.

In 1935, Edward would purchase the controlling interest of the Sands Springs Corporation in Williamstown, Massachusetts. When he purchased the controlling interest, he was named as President of the corporation. The Sand Springs Corporation produced beverages utilizing natural springs. The company was well-known locally for its ginger ale, a claim by locals at the time to be the finest ginger ale in the world. But prior to the carbonated beverages, Sand Springs has a rich history all its own.

Even before the colonists arrived in the region, the location was a favorite of native tribes as it was considered to have curative properties. The springs flowed at a constant temperature of approximately seventy-five degrees and a modern analysis found mild radioactivity in the water. In 1896, Dr. S. Louis Lloyd began to develop the area around the spring utilizing the "curative" nature of the springs. Lloyd had built a grand resort and sanitarium with indoor pools and baths so people can soak in the waters. To further tap the water's earning power, a bottling plant was built and the water was bottled and sold. As with many similar developments across the country, people fell out of favor of handing over hard-earned dollars to take a bath, so the resort shut down, but the bottling operation continued. Profits were maximized when the spring waters were flavored. The company has been described as one of the pioneers of the soft drink industry.

After the death of Dr. Lloyd, his widow, Grace operated the bottling business for another fifteen years. After Grace Lloyd passed away, the heirs of her estate operated the business for two more years before they partnered with three gentlemen to form the Sand Springs Corporation. The new corporation was in business for only one year when Edward Wilkinson purchased the controlling interest. His tenure of President of the Sand Springs Corporation was short lived however.

The gravestone of Edward S. Wilkinson Jr. At long last, he was able to reunite with his wife and young son. Edward would never remarry and worked to keep his wife's legacy alive through his many philanthropic endeavors.

Edward Wilkinson Jr. passed away in his bed at his North Adams home on 164 Church Street on June 12, 1939 at the age of sixty-three. At eight in the morning his housekeeper prepared breakfast as usual and checked in on him when he did not appear. His death was unexpected as he was in relatively good health. The day prior to his passing, he attended the Sunday morning service at First Baptist Church, and then went to his newly purchased farm and summer home in Pownal, Vermont to check in on the property. Edward's farm was not to be taken lightly as it was an estate that was one hundred and fifty acres and contained a farmhouse and several large barns. Edward then returned home and retired for the evening at around nine. A cerebral hemorrhage was determined to be the cause of his death. His death was considered immediate and likely happened in his sleep.

Before his death was known in the community, on Monday June 12, it was announced by the North Adams Chamber of Commerce that Edward was elected to serve a two-year term as one of twelve directors of the organization. One of the other members elected and announced that day was George Flood, the son-in-law of William Gallup and the Treasurer of the Arnold Print Works.

On Wednesday, June 14, 1939, the funeral for Edward was held. On that day, the shades of North Adams City Hall were ordered shut and the flag was lowered to half-mast. There was a brief service at his home before his closest family and friends. His remains were later brought to the First Baptist Church in North Adams where a more formal service was held. The church was filled to capacity as he was very involved in the community and was a generous benefactor for many in the community. The church itself was filled with flowers from many in the community and even outside of the region. After the funeral, he was buried with his wife and son in Hillside Cemetery. At last, Edward Wilkinson was reunited with his loved ones.

The Wilkinson family plot in Hillside Cemetery in North Adams. The three gravestones in front of and to the left of the very large obelisk belong to Edward Wilkinson Jr., Alice, and Edward Wilkinson III. Next to them are the gravestones of Edward Wilkinson and Eliza Wilkinson. The gravestones of Edward Jr.'s sisters, who all died in childhood are also visible.

8. Mary Cordelia Houghton

> A parent should never bury their child; unfortunately, this is not a perfect world.

Mary Cordelia Houghton was born on July 25, 1877 in North Adams. Mary was the last child born to Albert C. and Cordelia Houghton. Mary has often been described as "Daddy's little girl". She was known for her innate sense of gentleness and in the fact that she put other people's welfare before her own. This level of sacrifice became apparent during the final years of her short life.

Mary initially attended public schools in North Adams, before she received further education from both private tutors and private boarding schools. Part of her schooling sent her to New York City. It is unclear if Mary attended the same boarding school as her older sister Alice.

Mary also spent a year studying abroad in Europe with her sister Alice and their chaperone Mary Cady. Mary Cady was the aunt of Mary's friend Sybil Cady Hutton. Mary Cady was actually born and raised on the property that would later become the Houghton Mansion. Each of the surviving Houghton children had the chance to spend a considerable time in Europe to further their education.

Mary spent her entire life in North Adams except for the time in boarding school, her time abroad and her winters spent in New York City. One question that lingers is why Mary did not get married. All of Mary's sisters married prominent men, but yet, Mary remained single. It is often said that Mary gave up finding a suitor because she made the ultimate sacrifice to take care of her ailing father. It is true that her father's health began to fail

as a result of the stress of the 1907 panic and Mary did take care of her father. But at that point, Mary was thirty years old. I realize that I cannot compare the Houghton children, but all of her sisters were married well before this age. In fact, the average age of a bride getting married for the first time in 1907 was around 23 years old.

Mary Houghton lived within a suite on the second floor of the mansion. The wall between two of her rooms was removed during the construction of the lodge.

The answer as to why Mary remained single may be lost in history. All we are left with are assumptions. Was Mary painfully shy? Being a "daddy's girl", did possible suitors have an impossible task of not being good enough for young Mary? Did she not find someone to settle with? Was Mary ahead of her time and believed that she did not need a man to take care of her? Was there another reason? The answer at this point is still a mystery. If Mary is indeed in the Mansion as a spirit, she is not spilling that particular secret.

My theory on why Mary was single, and remember this is my theory, is that Mary found it difficult to find someone who was not interested in advancing their own career. According to descriptions, Mary was pretty and was a sweet young woman. The Houghton family was a prominent family in the region and as such their daughters were prominent members of society as well. Her sisters Florence, Susan and Alice married well-to-do men who were up and comers.

Mary may have had different aspirations, maybe Mary wanted to focus on family rather than have her significant other worry so much about business. She may have seen first-hand the stress and struggles of being prominent in the community and would not want that to be the focus of her life. There must have been a line of suitors for the hand of Mary. However, Mary may have seen through so many who were only interested because she was the daughter of someone with great wealth and influence. For some children of the rich and powerful, it is extremely difficult to find a love not interested in their own aspirations of wealth and prestige.

I believe that Mary would have settled down in an instant had she found her ideal match. When she started to lose faith that she could, coupled with her father's health, she thought it was best to put aside her dreams. I believe that this decision would come back to Mary as a significant level of regret.

One rumor that has been floated around was that Mary and John Widders had a secret relationship. I do not necessarily prescribe to this accusation as there is no empirical evidence to suggest this to be true or false. I feel strongly that this is a story that has been passed down to make the personal history more like a soap opera than reality. There are only two people who would know for sure, and they are no longer with us – in body form.

I am less likely to buy into the Mary and Widders relationship because of several factors. Mary and John were very different in regards to both economic and social status. Fast forward to the present day, people tend to seek those similar to themselves. Back then, the mixture of social and economic classes was even rarer than it is today. There was also quite a bit of age difference between the two of them as well. Another thought I have is that Mary is commonly referred to as "Daddy's little girl", would Mary risk alienating her father by having a secret relationship with someone of a different economic and social status; with such an age gap; and the employer-employee connection? I am not saying that it definitely did not happen, but I am looking at it with a healthy dose of skepticism and the belief that life is quite often more mundane than tales meant to romanticize a story.

Mary was described as living a quiet life. She was devoted to her father and devoted the final seven years of her life to care for her ailing father. She did not appear to be the social butterfly that her sisters Susan and Alice were.

She appears to be more similar to her mother Cordelia and sister Florence in that the spotlight thrust upon her made her uneasy.

One interesting bit of history that shows the pull of the Houghton family is when Albert was on business in New York City in September 1905, word got to him that Mary was suffering with appendicitis. In order to get home, a special train was arranged that brought A.C. Houghton to North Adams at two in the morning. The train also carried two prominent surgeons from New York City who assisted in Mary's surgery. Mary recovered fully from the surgery. This incident was approximately fourteen months prior to Alice Houghton Wilkinson passing away as a result of an appendectomy.

Mary was heavily involved in the Fort Massachusetts Historical Society, at one point being elected as the assistant treasurer of the organization. Mary's brother-in-law William Gallup was the Vice-President. Like most in her family, she was also proud of her ancestry and the ties to the founding of the country.

As much as we focus on Mary's lack of a husband and children, she was hardly alone. Living close by was her sister Alice and her family. Living almost across the street was her sister Florence and her family. Her sister Susan would often visit with her family. Mary also had many cousins who lived in the area. So while Mary did not have a husband or children of her own, she did find plenty of companionship and held her share of babies.

This is the view from a window in Mary's bedroom. The constant reminder of the loss of her sister Alice and her nephew Edward was difficult for Mary to endure. The Wilkinson residence is in the background.

Mary was in New York City during Thanksgiving of 1906, as was quite often the case; the Houghton family would live in a hotel in New York City so Albert Houghton did not have to travel in the winter. Since it was a holiday, Alice joined the Houghtons. Mary was present when her sister Alice passed away. Her death impacted Mary, as you can imagine.

One of Mary's bedroom windows faced the Wilkinson home where Alice's widower and son lived after her death. When Alice died, the family lost a large part of its soul, and this provided Mary a grim reminder whenever she would look out the window. Alice had an infectious spirit, one that brought happiness to many people. It was impossible for Mary to look out that window and not see the void created by the loss of her sister. Mary also could not avoid seeing the pained look in her brother-in-law's eyes. Even more tragic, Mary saw the loss in the face of her nephew.

Mary would continue to see her nephew and I would assume that Mary tried to console the young boy. It must have been difficult for Mary as Edward Wilkinson III was described as having the same infectious good spirits that his mother possessed. Whether or not he retained this spirit after his mother's death is unknown to me. Obviously Mary was close to her nephew, especially because of the proximity. Mary enjoyed the time with all of her nieces and nephews; they were a source of pride for her.

Sadly, when Edward Wilkinson III's health began to fail, it was troubling for Mary. In an attempt to improve his health, his father brought him west to a better climate. When the Wilkinsons departed, that was the final time Mary would see her nephew alive. When the body of little Edward was brought back to North Adams to await his funeral and burial, that home next door became even more vacant. Mary could not avoid seeing that once happy home from her own bedroom. With each and every day, a glimpse of that home would remind Mary of two significant losses in her life.

August 1, 1914 was supposed to be a pleasant day for Mary. She was spending time with her friend Sybil and her husband who just arrived to start the family vacation. A pleasant summer morning, a day that started with so much promise of a relaxing and fun-filled day turned tragic for Mary. She was in and out of consciousness, and she felt extreme pain from her serious injuries. By 3:00, her physical vessel passed on. Her spirit may not have.

The loss of Mary greatly distressed Albert C. Houghton. For a man who witnessed so much personal loss in his life, this may have been the toughest. The final days of Albert Houghton's life were one of severe anguish. This pain, compounded with the loss of Sybil and John was too much to bear.

Photograph of the gravestone of Mary C. Houghton in Southview Cemetery, the third daughter that Albert and Cordelia had to witness the burial of. A parent should never bury their child, but unfortunately this is not a perfect world.

Part of me wonders if Albert felt a bit guilty about Mary. Was she so dedicated to him that she gave up her chance to be a wife, a mother? If she was married, would she have been on that trip? Would she be alive? These are questions I am projecting in Mr. Houghton's mind. Typically survivors of accidents in which there are other fatalities experience survivor's guilt. I would expect Mr. Houghton experienced this guilt, but he may have had other questions running through his mind. If his spirit is restless, could this be part of his distress? Whatever the questions running through his mind, burying his third daughter was too much to bear.

The funeral of Mary was held at the Houghton Mansion at three in the afternoon on Tuesday, August 4, 1914. The funeral was private and the family requested that no flowers be sent. However, this request was ignored and the family received an outpouring of flowers. Reverend James F. Bisgrove of the Methodist church officiated. Mary was buried in the family plot at Southview Cemetery in North Adams.

Mary passed away without writing a will and left a sizable estate. Approximately two weeks after her death, the probate court granted the petition allowing for William A. Gallup and Andrew McKean, her brothers-in-law to be the administrators of her estate. The value of Mary's estate was estimated over $300,000.[13] Her estate included a $100,000 bond on the A.J. Houghton Company, a $140,000 life insurance policy on her father, and

---

[13] "Inventory of Houghton Estate." *The Springfield Daily Republican* 9 Dec 1914: 14.

cash in several bank accounts in New York City and North Adams. She also owned stock in Fisk Rubber Company, International Trust Company of Boston, New England Power, and Worcester Suburban Electric Company. Her estate also consisted of sizable value in jewelry, clothing and other personal effects.

Her estate also consisted of the Houghton property, which included the Houghton Mansion, the barn and the greenhouse. Tragically enough, as part of Mary's estate, the value of the automobile which led to her death was included as part of her inheritance. Since Mary's sisters Florence and Susan were married and had sizable personal wealth, Albert Houghton had Mary as a beneficiary for the home and his life insurance so that she would have place to live and a source of income for her to live off of. Accounting for inflation, in today's dollars, Mary's estate would be worth around seven million dollars. According to the executors, Mary intended to leave her estate to her parents, of course Albert passed away by then.

In 1930, the North Adams Hospital opened a new maternity wing that was considered state of the art for that era. Many of the wealthy and powerful families in North Adams contributed handsome sums to make the new maternity wing a reality. Mary's sister and brother-in-law Florence and William Gallup donated to have a room in the maternity wing named the "Mary Cordelia Houghton Room". What is telling for me is that the Gallups could have had the memorial for Alice Houghton Wilkinson. The fact that they donated a room in the memory of Mary tells me that she wanted to be a mother, that she enjoyed children; but sadly as we know, she was never given that chance.

Through Mary's Eyes: August 1, 1914

For Mary, the events of August 1, 1914 started a couple of weeks before that fateful day. Mary's friend Sybil was back in North Adams visiting her family for the summer. Along with Sybil was Robert Jr., her two year old son. Mary was quiet and was not a social butterfly like her sisters Alice and Susan. She may have been more like her older sister Florence, who was not comfortable in the spotlight. Mary also resigned herself that she was not going to get married or have a child. Mary had a motherly instinct though, she was tender and loving. As her father's health was deteriorating, she gave up any chance she had of a family of her own to take care of her father.

Seeing that Mary's life consisted of these caretaking duties, a visit by a friend was welcomed. She had a chance to relate to someone close to her age. She also had a chance to spend time with a mother to a young child and she saw the interaction between the two of them. Sybil's husband Robert was going to take a vacation and joined Sybil in North Adams on July 31, 1914 for the start of what should have been a relaxing time. I cannot guess whose idea it was to all drive to Bennington, Vermont in the family's new car, but Mary would have been excited to be with a married couple her age for a day away from caretaking.

On August 1st as she took her seat with Robert and Sybil, what must have been going through her mind? Did she see the smiling Sybil and Robert and have some envy, wishing she too could be sitting next to someone? When the car approached that work team, did she see the danger that was ahead or was she focused on a topic of the moment?

The moment the car started to roll, what flashed before her eyes? Did she see the smiling faces of her friend and her husband? Did she think about what she had given up? These moments are important because these moments are the strong anchors that can bind a spirit to this realm. Odds are if she were content in life, these anchors would not be formed.

In what I consider a cruel twist of irony, the automobile that claimed the life of Mary Houghton was part of her estate after her death. Here is an illustration of a similar model Pierce Arrow touring car from that era.

I do not want to imagine the pain Mary was in when she remained in the car as it rolled over three times with her in the seat. All the thrashing and slamming that Mary was subjected to while the car flipped over took an immense toll. As the car stopped, she remained in the seat, her spine broken, her facial bones badly fractured. There was also the pain of severe internal injuries. Mary was at the time conscious. She must have heard that Sybil was dead, either overhearing the conversations or just by deducing based on the reaction Robert must have had. She must have witnessed the reaction when Widders or her father saw the condition she was in. Most unfortunate of all is that she felt the intense pain as she was telling others about her pain and where it hurt.

As she was in the vehicle, it started to get foggy as she was drifting in and out of consciousness. She must have heard the sound of the commotion, the people running to help. It must have seemed like an eternity for her before she could be seen by a doctor. When they finally did arrive and carefully removed her out of the wreckage they carried her gingerly up the very same embankment that the car rolled down. There were no ambulances to carry her, so she was placed in a vehicle that provided little comfort for someone with a broken spine. All those bumps and those sharp turns must have been Hell on poor Mary.

As she regained consciousness, she found herself in the very hospital that her family spent so much time and money as benefactors. Did she hear the discussion that any operation had to be delayed until she stabilized? Slowly she deteriorated, in tremendous pain. Those thoughts of her friend and her husband must have resonated in her head. She must have relived her life, her decisions, having seen her sisters marry and have children. Are these the final thoughts before her spirit left her body?

The doorway to Mary Houghotn's bedroom. After Mary's death, how many times did Cordelia pause outside of her suite? This room became a daily reminder of another daughter that had died. Gone from within the walls was a compassionate young woman.

9. The Man Known as John Widders

> **It was a large piece of cold metal that drove off the road; it was a small piece of cold metal that would take another life.**

One of the most interesting revelations of the people involved in the tragedy that forever changed Houghton Mansion is that the man that we call John Widders was in fact not who he said he was. When John was alive, he was very secretive about his life and would have been happy to be merely an unknown blip on the radar. Because of his role in the tragedy that unfolded on August 1, 1914, he became much more than a blip, but a central figure in the chain of events that still captivates people to this very day. After his death, his real past that he worked so hard to conceal for many years came bubbling to the surface in a very public way.

The man known as John Widders was actually John Winters. I admit, it is a bit anticlimactic to have such a similar alias. I guess you can say that creativity was not a strong suit for John. You will notice that I use his alias throughout the book as it is what most people are accustomed to. There are two stories of John – the real one and the one that he told. We will start with the doctored history before we discuss what is actual history.

John Widders

The man known as John Widders was supposedly quite the character, although one that many found to be very secretive. Many people in town considered John an acquaintance or friend, but even to his closest confidants, he would fail to discuss his childhood. Some had an inkling that he was not who he said he was, but he offered no clue and quite frankly, since he was harmless, people did not press the issue too much.

John told those he was closest to that he was born in New Jersey and moved to New Hampshire. It was there in New Hampshire where he claimed that he ran away from home. He told some people that he had run away from home to join a travelling circus. He had implied many times that he had no living relatives, although he let it slip on several occasions that he thought his sister was still alive. For most people that knew him, John Widders' history started the day he stepped foot in North Adams. Some people have claimed that he admitted to them that Widders was a fake name and that he specifically told them that he did not want his real name known since he was ashamed of his family.

What was known was that John Widders was a very reliable man; this is the trait that lured Albert Houghton into hiring him and keeping him as a trusted employee for many years. He was described as very honest when you get past the fact that he would not divulge his history. As you will learn, his past hurt him deeply and it was this pain he was trying so valiantly to suppress. Since John was an employee of the Houghton family for several decades, the family became attached to him as he was attached to them.

John Widders arrived in North Adams in 1870 at the stated age of twenty-nine. He originally came to the area because he was hired as a tip-cart operator during the construction of the Lebanon Springs Railroad. He was hired by Frank Chase to work on the rail line. He was quickly hired by James H. Flagg, who operated a livery stable in North Adams. This was the same Mr. Flagg who had connections to Andrew Jackson Houghton, older brother of Albert C. Houghton. Over the course of two years, Widders routinely drove Albert Houghton over the Hoosac Mountain so he could catch a train to Boston for business. These trips to Boston would occur approximately two to three times per week. The Hoosac Tunnel would later simplify the connectivity of the rail to Boston.

Houghton valued John so much that he offered him a job to tend to Houghton's horses in his stable. John worked continuously for the Houghton family for forty-two years until his death. At one point in time, Widders was responsible for all of the horses in the stables of Arnold Print Works and Houghton's private stable. He became quite the expert in horses and was even granted the responsibility of purchasing horses for Houghton's personal and business stables.

As Houghton spent less and less time with the Arnold Print Works, John's duties were then changed to take care of the Houghton family's personal horses and stables as well as being the Houghton family's coachman and then chauffeur.

John was a boarder for many years in some of the hotels within North Adams. Between 1890 through 1900, John boarded at the Wilson Hotel. Between 1901 through 1905, John had a room at the Wellington. From 1906 through 1908, John rented a room at the Richmond. John returned to the Wilson in 1909, before moving onto the property of Albert Houghton in 1910.

It was said that John had very comfortable living arrangements in the upper floor of Houghton's stable which included a bedroom, private bathroom and a parlor. Since John was a perpetual bachelor, he often dined at the local hotels and restaurants. There is a room on the third floor of the mansion which is often called Widders' room; I am not aware why this room is closely associated with him if his living arrangements were more than likely above the stable on the Houghton property.

John was thrifty and squirreled away his salary. He actually invested his money very wisely and accumulated a sizable estate. Even though he had enough money to retire comfortably, the thought of not working for the Houghton family was a thought that may not have crossed his mind. He was never married.

On Thursday, June 4, 1903, John Widders had an incident in North Adams that bears some semblance to the tragic events which would unfold more than a decade later. Widders was driving a team of six horses on Furnace Street in North Adams. That day the horses were pulling a boiler from

Arnold Print Works to the rail yard. At the time the North Adams Gas Company was digging a ditch on the right side of the roadway and the passage was extremely narrow. The rear set of wheels under the boiler came too close to the edge of the embankment and the soft earth was no match for the heavy load. The back end of the load began to slide towards the Hoosac River below. As the load was sliding Widders pulled the horses to the right and was able to have the front wheels of the load get caught on a large boulder preventing the load from completely overturning. Widders was thrown from the load but was uninjured.

In the spring of 1914, Albert C. Houghton purchased the family's first automobile and convinced John to learn to drive. As one can imagine, the change from a horse to an automobile was not a simple changeover. It is important to note, that generally, it is much easier nowadays to drive an automobile, with decades of engineering improvements. The first automobiles were not that easy to maneuver and were a bit temperamental.

John Widders was uncomfortable with the switch and would need months of practice to be comfortable behind the wheel. Even with months of practice, he drove at slow speeds because his comfort level was never high. John managed to drive only two thousand miles behind the wheel of an automobile. Widders initially refused to drive, but Albert Houghton convinced him that he could safely operate an automobile.

The Houghton family plot located in Southview Cemetery in North Adams. The four gravestones in the foreground are the burial spots for Laura, Mary, Albert and Cordelia Houghton. The lone gravestone located in the background was the final resting spot for the man who preferred to be called John Widders. John is now forever linked with the Houghton family.

It has been said that John Widders' health was beginning to fail in the spring and summer of 1914. This may have been a contributing factor in the accident. After John Widders' suicide, his funeral was held at five in the afternoon on Tuesday, August 4, 1914 which was the same day as Mary Houghton's funeral. Widders' funeral was held at the Methodist Church in North Adams with Reverend James F. Bisgrove offering the rites. As John was a long-time employee and revered by the family, he was given a spot within the Houghton family plot.

It was after his death that the real John Widders came into the conscious of North Adams.

The Real John Winters

After the man known as John Widders died, the truth began to unfold. On Friday, August 14, 1914, it was discovered that he had not made out a will and the somewhat sizable estate he had amassed had no heirs. It was said that before the accident and his suicide, he was thinking about writing a will to distribute his wealth, but the accident occurred before he had the chance to. If he had only written a will, his true identity may never have come to light.

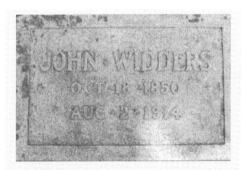

The gravestone of John Widders contains a rather significant error – his birthdate. Since he was less than truthful about his past, we are reminded of the lengths he tried to cover his history. The gravestone lists a birthdate of October 18, 1850.

Since Widders had no known living family, it was thought that his estate, which was estimated at fifteen thousand dollars, would go to the coffers of the Commonwealth of Massachusetts. In his lifetime, he had slipped on a few occasions that he had a sister, but he did not know whether she was dead or alive. Since no will was filed or found and no relatives were found, a public administrator by the name of Mr. W.H. Woodhead was named the administrator of the estate. It was shortly thereafter that an alternate story of John began to emerge. At this point, however, some of the money was already distributed leaving a slightly smaller estate.

In the month of September, 1914, attorneys with the Adams law firm of Shaw & Harrington filed a petition with the probate court on behalf of Mrs.

Henrietta Ostrander. Mrs. Ostrander was eighty years old and was at that time living in Salisbury, Connecticut. In the legal claim, Mrs. Ostrander claimed that she was in fact the mother of John Widders.

A former resident of North Adams who moved to Salisbury relayed a story to Henrietta regarding a man and his death and that he had no known relatives. Henrietta was not living in the best of financial circumstances and immediately claimed that she was the mother of John. Ms. Ostrander was unable to read the news stories of the accident since she was unable to read or write. Henrietta retained a local law firm Warner & London to represent her in claiming the estate. The law firm prepared the affidavits and forwarded them to the Adams law firm of Shaw & Harrington. At the time of the filing of the affidavit, Henrietta was receiving aid from the town of Salisbury. She was also very ill and was unable to care for herself.

Many would assume that Henrietta might have been after a payday and concocted a story to improve her financial situation, so of course this situation resulted in a long and drawn out court process in order to determine if this woman's claims were fact or fiction. The drama unfolded inside the District Court where the hearings were presided over by Judge E. T. Slocum of the Probate Court. If the estate was not to be granted to Mrs. Ostrander, Widders' estate would have gone to the Commonwealth of Massachusetts.

In the affidavit, Mrs. Ostrander was said to be born in Mount Washington, near Pittsfield, as Henrietta McLean. When she was sixteen years of age, she married John Winters. After their marriage they lived in North Adams, Hillsdale, New York, and Salisbury, Connecticut. They moved to North Adams in 1852 where her husband found a job working for his uncle. While in North Adams, Henry, Lydia and Mary were born. About two years later, they moved to Hillsdale, New York, then finally to Salisbury.

While living in Salisbury, John was born. The family would then welcome another child by the name of Martha. Shortly after Martha's birth, his father abandoned his mother and his sisters. Unable to provide for her young family, Henrietta's brother Hiram McLean took the children into his home in Mount Washington. When John was five years old, custody of John was given to Shakers in Mount Lebanon, New York. When John went to the Shakers, his mother and John failed to see each other from that point forward.

John lived with the Shakers for ten years, when at age fifteen he was hired by a contractor named Frank Chase. Frank Chase was working on building a railroad line through Lebanon Springs, New York. John was employed to be the driver of a tip cart. After a year, Chase took John with him to North Adams where Chase had a subcontract on the construction of the Hoosac tunnel. It was at this point that John settled in North Adams until his death. He was then hired by J.H. Flagg and then by A.C. Houghton.

Sometime after John was abandoned, Henrietta remarried to a man named Myron Ostrander and had two more children, George and Lester Ostrander. George and Lester later settled in Salisbury and Norfolk, Connecticut, respectively. When Henrietta remarried, she took back both Mary and Lydia into her new home, but not John. Both Mary and Lydia were married and settled in Salisbury. Mary became Mary Rossiter and Lydia became Lydia Hiserodt. I could not discover what happened to Henry or Martha. While I could not find records, they most likely died young.

On December 28, 1914 Judge Slocum visited Cordelia Houghton in order to secure a disposition to be used in his ruling. He visited Cordelia because her health was deteriorating after the loss of both her husband and daughter Mary. After Cordelia's statements were recorded, a hearing continued in the probate court. William Arthur Gallup and Albert Willmarth testified that they did not know of John having a different name. There were a total of five witnesses that afternoon and none could state his age. Albert Willmarth testified that John Widders once remarked to him about the town in New Jersey where John repeatedly said he was from.

At the court hearing, evidence was brought forth showing that when John paid his taxes he used six different spellings of a last name, including Widders, Withers and Widows. During this hearing a testimony was provided by a witness by the name of Samuel Starkweather, who was an acquaintance of Ira McLean, the brother of Henrietta Ostrander. Starkweather testified that before the accident John stated that he was Henrietta's son. Starkweather also testified that a janitor at Williams College was also at the Shaker community when John was there and at that time he was known as John Winters.

On Thursday, March 11, 1915, there was a final hearing in the matter of Widders' will. Some people had serious reservations regarding the validity of Mrs. Ostrander's claims. More specifically, regarding the difference in the age and the last name itself. Widders for some reason claimed to be older than he really was. One of the final witnesses called by Attorney Shaw was a Mrs. Augusta Marshall, who at the time was living in North Adams.

Mrs. Marshall testified that John lived at her home in Petersburg, New York. She testified that John had told the Marshall family that he had run away from the Shaker home in Lebanon. According to John, he ran away because they were abusing him. She also claimed that at one point he told her that his mother's name was Henrietta and that she lived in Salisbury, Connecticut. Mrs. Marshall testified that on one occasion John sent five dollars to his mother, addressing it to "Mrs. Ostrander".

Also lined up to testify that day were two men, Charles Jones and George H. Lewis. Both Mr. Jones and Mr. Lewis testified that John had acknowledged his relatives to them. Supposedly before the accident and suicide, one of the Winter's sisters was overheard by Mr. Frank Goodell of Williamstown say that Widders was in fact her brother.

In the final week of March of 1915, the court ruled that there was enough evidence to legally declare Henrietta Ostrander the mother of John Winters, the man we know as Widders. Judge Slocum declared that Widders' identity was in fact John Winters. Attorney Fred R. Shaw was named the administrator of John Winters' estate on behalf of Mrs. Ostrander. The court ruled that Henrietta was the lone heir of John and as such was entitled to the estate, which at that time was listed as ten thousand dollars. There was some devaluation and then an increase in the size of the estate since much of it was in stocks and bonds which varied wildly during the time of the hearing.

It only makes sense that John Widders or Winters would fail to discuss his past. How can one relive the pain of having your own mother abandon you? Is this why John did not divulge his past? Was abuse at the hand of the Shakers another reason he was tight-lipped or was this yet another story to hide his past? One person can talk about this – and that is John himself, but his spirit appears to be as secretive as he was a century earlier.

Interestingly enough, the New York Census in 1860, seemed to confirm Henrietta's story. In Stephentown, New York in the county of Rensselaer there was a Winters family. Within a household, the census lists John

Winters (age 28) as head of household; Henrietta his wife (age 23), Lydia (age 7), Mary (age 5), John (age 4 years), and Martha (9 months old). The first born child, Henry, did not appear in this census, which leads me to believe that he was deceased at this time.

Another bit of intrigue is one of the recordings we captured in the basement of the Houghton Mansion appeared to have said "McLean". At the time, we had no idea of the significance of this name. But it is now known that Henrietta's maiden name was McLean and the uncle who took John and then handed him over to the shakers was also a McLean. Is this a coincidence or was John finally starting to come clean on his past?

Through John's Eyes: August 1, 1914

Throughout this book, I reintroduced the tragic events that unfolded on August 1, 1914 through the perspective of each person who had a significant role in the day's events. There is no darker place to be during and after the events than revisiting the tragic day through John Widders' perspective.

For John Widders, the morning of Saturday August 1, 1914 started out like thousands of others before. John rose out of his bed at an early hour. He walked downstairs into the stable to take care of the horses. This day is different, however, as he is to drive the family's first automobile later that morning. The changeover from a horse to a machine was hard on Widders. Even though he has been practicing for months, he was not comfortable behind the wheel of a car. For decades, he has been a horse man, now he was asked to pilot something with cold steel versus a pulse. A horse has intelligence; a car relies on the quick thinking of the person behind it. Plus John Widders was no spring chicken anymore, for that era.

Widders pulls the car under the covered porch on the side of the mansion. He watches as Sybil, Robert and Mary get into the rear of the Pierce Arrow. He knew Sybil since she was a little girl, now she is all grown up with a child of her own. He has also watched Mary Houghton grow up from a little girl to a woman. Widders watched as his longtime employer Albert Houghton entered the front seat next to him.

As they pull out of the Houghton driveway, for what would be Mary Houghton and Sybil's final day, I often wonder if the Hutton's child Robert was either looking out the window of the Cady residence or outside waving his parents off. If so, that would be the last time he saw his mother alive. A half-hour into their trip, Widders and the automobile encounter a work crew on the right side of the road. Since Widders did not drive over twelve miles per hour, what should have been a simple maneuver was the beginning of the end.

Widders turned to the left; he claimed the engine was racing as he made the turn. Turns out, he may have accidentally stepped on the gas pedal. As he maneuvered around the work team, the car's left tires slipped off the roadway. The automobile started to overturn; it was at this point where everybody in the car must have known something was amiss. John Widders was thrown from the automobile during one of the auto's three revolutions. When he came to realize what happened, he would have seen and heard things that still haunt his soul to this very day. As he looked around the debris-filled chaotic scene, he would have either seen or heard the commotion of Sybil Hutton lying motionless, her body horribly crushed, her husband holding her. He would have come across Mary still remaining in the car, in excruciating pain. He would have seen Albert Houghton clutching his arm and shoulder panicking over the condition of his youngest daughter. John Widders would have heard the commotion of the roadway workers as they were running to aid the accident victims.

While all of this was going on, that moment in time where Widders turned that wheel, must have been replayed itself over and over again in his mind. I wonder what the thoughts were as he saw the car, that damn mechanical device that he was so wary of. Did he recall years prior when he almost lost the boiler and it was through his quick thinking that he was able to prevent a similar fate, that event was almost eerily similar. All of those years that Widders worked with horses, he had the chance to appreciate that the horses have intelligence. A horse can make up for human error because they have thought. A cold, mechanical device had no means of correcting human error. Did this cause resentment in Widders? Did Widders think that time was passing him by and he cannot keep up with the latest and greatest inventions?

Widders remained while the injured were removed from the scene and while Sybil's dead body was finally removed from the scene accompanied by her injured husband. Widders was questioned by investigators to see what happened. In his mind he would have to relive that moment in time in which chaos was born - one split second that changed the course of history.

After Widders was checked out medically and questioned by the police, he was brought back to the Houghton residence. The same residence he left just hours before. He must have thought back to being in the car, pulling out of that driveway with smiling, happy people – how times changed! As he entered his living space, I cannot tell whether any member of the Houghton family talked to him, but he certainly would have heard all the crying over the loss of Mary and Sybil. This was a family in mourning, and not only was he probably also in mourning for them since he was so close to the family, but he also had to bear the reality that it was on his own hands.

John was not alone; two of his closest friends were there for him. But it was not enough. John was inconsolable as he shouldered the blame. Inevitably he had enough between the replaying of the incident in his head, the visuals and the sounds that were trapped in his memory, and the sounds of wailing and crying of a family that meant so much to him. The Houghton family was the only family unit that was known to him as growing up, John was deprived of one by a runaway father and a mother who could not support him.

During the night, John made that decision that there was no way he could live with this guilt and regret. He bargained in his head that dying was the easiest solution to solve his pain. I cannot fathom the thoughts that must have been in his head as he was rationalizing his decision. How could he look at the Houghtons again for what he has done to them? How can he live in a home that was devoid of a child's love for her parents? What did the Houghtons think of him? These questions must have been asked in his head. "What did I do?"

Even though he was cleared in the accident, it did not matter. For John, he could not handle it anymore. His mind was made up; there was no talking him out of it.

Could John Winters be hiding in the solitude of this third story room? While it is apparent he lived above the stable, many clues are present that suggest he likes to be alone in this space.

He hatched a plan; he knew the stable as well as anyone. He knew there was a gun at the stable to take care of injured horses. He had to get out of that room and get that gun. John then mentioned he ought to take care of the horses. His close friend thought that would be the best thing for him to get his mind off of the tragedy. He took care of his horses and went outside for a smoke. He excused himself briefly and went into the stable. He found the gun, picked it up in his hand and pressed that cold metal against his head. It was a large piece of cold metal that drove off the road; it was a small piece of cold metal that would take another life. As his finger was on the trigger, whatever thought was on his mind carried over when that bullet ended his life. This is why I find it dismaying that some treat him as a carnival attraction.

10. Sybil F. Cady Hutton

As the automobile left the Houghton property, a two-year old waved farewell to his mother. Tragically that would be the last memory of his mother alive.

Sybil is often an afterthought or a brief mention when most individuals recount the details of the car accident that took place on Saturday, August 1, 1914. To many, she was the "other woman" killed in the accident, or simply the first casualty of the events of that day. This lack of emphasis on Sybil's life may be due to the fact that her spirit is generally believed not to be located within the mansion. In my opinion, Sybil's death was perhaps the most tragic of any involved in the accident.

Many think that the death of Mary Houghton was notable because she was the daughter of a very wealthy and prominent family. Sybil too was a daughter of a wealthy and prominent family. The lack of emphasis on Sybil is simply the fact that her "ghost" is not haunting the hallways of Houghton Mansion. It is my goal to give her the honor she deserves, the chance for her life story to be told, so that if her spirit is restless somewhere, whether it is the embankment where she lost her life, or where she lived before her untimely end, she will be comforted knowing that her life story has been told and she could move on.

Sybil Frances Cady was born on July 10, 1880 in North Adams, Massachusetts to William and Harriet (Ballou) Cady. William G. Cady was a prominent shoe manufacturer in town and Sybil's uncle H.T. Cady succeeded Albert C. Houghton as the second Mayor of North Adams. The Cady family was very close to the Houghton family and was one of the prominent families that helped not only govern the community but the local economy with their enterprises. In fact, for many years the Cadys and Houghtons were neighbors in several locations. Members of the Cady family were descendants of one of the pioneering families of the region. In fact, Sybil was a descendent of passengers from the Mayflower. Sybil's mother also had a direct lineage to Hosea Ballou, who founded the Universalist religious denomination.

Sybil's father was born on September 17, 1838 in Southbridge, Massachusetts to Alanson and Jane A. (Bradford) Cady. The Cadys later moved their large family to North Adams where Alanson became a farmer. The Cady family consisted of eleven children. Interestingly enough, the family was raised on the corner of Church and Pleasant Street, where the Houghton Mansion now stands.

Sybil's parents were married on May 14, 1867. At the time of their marriage, William G. Cady was twenty-six and Harriet E Ballou was eighteen. At the time of their marriage, William was listed as a manufacturer.

Brothers William G. and H. T. Cady constructed a large shoe factory on the north end of Holden Street. In 1880, the same year Sybil was born, William "retired" and brother H.T. Cady ran the business before he sold it. Retirement did not last long as just three years later, William partnered with S.H. Fairfield to begin a new shoe manufacturer called W.G. Cady & Co. on Ashland Street. William retired again because of health issues only to begin a new shoe manufacturing company in Greenfield, Massachusetts. He later became manager of the North Adams Brick Company. Clearly, retirement was not in this man's vocabulary.

William became a selectman of North Adams, and H.T. later became mayor. William also was a private in the 8th Massachusetts Regiment actively serving between the years of 1864-65, the tail end of the Civil War.

Sybil had one other living sibling, a sister, Stella Ballou Cady who was born on April 3, 1877. The Cady family had one other daughter, Bertha Harriet Cady who was born on March 6, 1873, but she experienced severe spasms and passed away on April 3, 1874, a little more than one year old.

As Sybil was from a prominent family, her education was extensive. After she attended public schools in North Adams, she was sent to a private school in Northampton, Massachusetts. Sybil also attended Dean Academy in Franklin, Massachusetts. Sybil was very involved in committees for many charitable functions within North Adams. She would often be on planning committees with her sister Stella and several of the Houghton sisters. Sybil was also involved in the Universalist church in North Adams. On several occasions she appeared in concerts put on by the Ladies' Aid Society of that church, oftentimes performing solos. Sybil even had a bit of an acting bug in her, appearing as an extra at the Columbia Opera House in a play called "Evangeline" in 1895.

On April 16, 1901, Sybil's sister Stella Ballou Cady married Robert Torrington Furman from New York in the Universalist Church in North Adams. Robert was born in Sunbury, Pennsylvania to William S. Furman and Annie (Torrington) Furman. At the time of their wedding the bride was twenty-four and the groom was twenty-six years old. Stella and Robert moved to Manhattan and lived in a building located on 83rd Street. Robert earned a living by selling insurance.

As I mentioned the Cady family lived near the Houghtons on several occasions. When the Houghtons moved, the Cadys were never far behind. Sybil would move into the home across from the Houghton Mansion around the turn of the century.

After Sybil graduated she decided that she wanted to work as a nurse. She moved to New York City so that she can learn and work at The Presbyterian Hospital in New York City. The 1905 New York Census listed her as living at the Florence Nightingale Hall in the School of Nursing Department. While working at the hospital, Sybil met an intern named Robert LeRoy Hutton who graduated from Cornell University in June of that same year. Robert was a specialist in internal medicine and later became a well-known diagnostician.

Sybil graduated from the Presbyterian Hospital Training School is June of 1907. After graduating, she started to work in the hospital as a nurse. Sybil rose through the ranks and became the head nurse at the Presbyterian Hospital. While most daughters of wealthy industrialists did not work but instead focused on being active in the social scene, Sybil did not. She preferred to take care of others and that involved her training for a job and holding a job – something that was uncommon for the young women in this book.

In 1906, Sybil became an aunt when her sister Stella and husband Robert welcomed Robert Torrington Furman Jr. into the world. Less than four years later, another son William C. Torrington was born. Shortly after William's birth, the couple moved to Pittsburgh when Robert became the General Manager of a life insurance company located in that city.

Robert and Sybil started to date and then became engaged. On June 22, 1909 Sybil married Robert in North Adams. At the time of their wedding Sybil was twenty-seven years old and her husband was twenty-eight. Reverend George Mayo Gerrish presided over the rite of matrimony at the Universalist Church. The event was billed as the social event of the month in the local press since Sybil was the daughter of the prominent Cady family. Sybil's sister Stella was the matron of honor. After the ceremony, there was a reception for twenty-one guests at the Richmond, a hotel in North Adams. At three in the afternoon, the bride and groom departed North Adams for their honeymoon.

After the honeymoon Sybil and Robert returned to New York City in which they would call the city their home. The couple resided on East 71st Street. Sybil resigned her job as head nurse when she became pregnant. Sybil and Robert welcomed their son Robert LeRoy Jr. into the world on June 3, 1912. Her husband Robert became a consulting physician at Lincoln Hospital in 1913, where he would remain until his retirement in 1947.

One odd bit of trivia about the Hutton household is that one of their maids was a passenger on the Titanic. She was coming to the United States to start a new life when the tragedy hit. The sinking of the Titanic occurred in 1912, so the wounds of that tragedy were still very fresh in the minds of many.

On July 2, 1912, Sybil's father suffered a cerebral hemorrhage at his home at 181 Church Street and died instantly. William G. Cady was seventy-three years old at the time of his death. He was still working as the manager of the North Adams Brick Company at the time of his death. William G. Cady was buried at Southview Cemetery in North Adams on July 5, 1912.

Sybil returned to North Adams on vacation in July of 1914 in order to spend time with her family. Robert joined her later in the afternoon on July 31, 1914. His trip was delayed when the train he was riding in derailed. The automobile ride on August 1, 1914 was the first event for the married couple on their long awaited vacation together. Her husband found it difficult to leave his medical practice, so this was a welcomed breather. She said goodbye to her toddler son and joined the Houghtons on that fateful trip. Sybil was only thirty-four years old when she died tragically as a result of the car accident.

The private funeral for Sybil was held at the family's house on Church Street on Monday, August 3, 1914. Reverend Gerrish, who presided over her marriage just five years earlier, presided over her funeral. The next day her body was transported to Ridgewood, New Jersey to her final resting spot in Valleau Cemetery.

With the prospects of raising his young son alone along with a demanding job, Robert hired two Irish immigrants to help with the household and tending to Robert Jr. The young widower became a medical examiner for the Selective Service during World War I – he would later reprise that role for World War II. Robert had varied talents through his life. He was a church organist as a young man for the Madison Avenue Presbyterian Church. While at Cornell he was on the crew team, and then was a hammer thrower on the track team. In his later years he was a Civil War buff, collecting many books, relics and photographs related to the war. He was also an amateur photographer and received many prizes for his work when he entered them into exhibitions.

Sybil's widower Robert married Ellen A. Frost, who was born in July, 1886 in Michigan, but raised in Livingston, New York. Prior to her marriage, Ellen was still living at home and worked as a parish assistant. Together they had a daughter Barbara, who was born on July 4, 1918.

By 1920, Sybil's sister Stella and her family moved from Pittsburgh to the Bronx, where her husband was employed in the manufacture of dyes. In April 1923, Harriet Cady, Sybil's mother, was visiting her lone surviving daughter in New York City. After she spent time with Stella and her family, she headed up to Albany, New York to visit her brother before she was to return to North Adams. Sybil's mother Harriet Ballou Cady suddenly passed away on April 12, 1923 at the home of her brother William Ballou in Albany, New York at the age of seventy-four. She had been ill for only a few hours. Her body was transported to the home of her nephew W. A. Ballou Jr. who lived on Arnold Place in North Adams. Her funeral was held on Saturday, April 14 at the North Adams Universalist Church.

Ellen Frost Hutton, Dr. Hutton's second wife, passed away in 1957 and is buried in the family plot alongside her husband and his first wife Sybil. Robert, Sybil's husband, passed away in 1964 at the age of 83.

Through Sybil's Eyes: August 1, 1914

When Sybil opened her eyes on the morning of August 1, 1914, she woke up to familiar sights and sounds. Gone were the sounds of the hustle and bustle of New York City, instead of street cars, she may have heard song birds serenading the locals. Instead of seeing tightly packed multistory structures, she would have seen the hills and mountains. While Sybil had been in her native North Adams for several weeks, the morning was special because besides her was her husband Robert, the love of her life.

If Sybil's son Robert Jr. was like a typical two-year old, he would have been up and climbing into the bed with his mother and father to greet them or to wake them from their slumber. Robert Hutton was not too keen to the idea of taking a ride that morning because of his experience in a train derailment the previous day. For Robert, this trip was a way to get away from his medical practice and to recharge. August 1, 1914 was the first full day of vacation where Robert and Sybil were together.

After breakfast, I would assume that Sybil gave her two-year old son a hug and kiss and told him that they would return soon. Sybil was comfortable leaving her precious son in the hands of her aunt, Mary Cady. When Sybil let go of young Robert, no one knew at the time that it would be the last time Sybil would hold her son in the flesh. Together Sybil and Robert took the very short walk to the residence of Albert C. Houghton.

Robert and Sybil would greet Albert, Cordelia and Mary Houghton. They soon would enter the 1914 Pierce Arrow car chauffeured by a man who called himself John Widders. One of the final sights Sybil saw was the covered car port to which she began her final journey. A journey that was supposed to have a return to North Adams, not a trip to the afterlife. I am assuming that Mary Cady and Robert Hutton Jr. may have waved off the automobile. If so, this was the last he saw his mother in her flesh.

Seated with her and her husband was her good friend Mary Houghton. Sybil was happy to visit a dear friend and had the pleasure to watch Mary play with her son Robert in the previous days. Mary's innate compassion and nurturing spirit showcased itself when she lit up during the time she spent with Robert. During the final few days together, it is expected that there were a surplus of laughter and good times. Sybil felt blessed; she had a loving son and a devoted husband.

I wonder if Sybil looked at Mary and felt a bit of sadness that her friend did not have her love to share with a husband or children. Sybil saw how Mary lit up when seeing her own son and wondered why Mary did not have the same blessing. Sybil felt lucky as she sat next to the doctor who swept her off of her feet when she was a nurse. All she needed to do was to look at Mary to see how lucky she was. I am sure the mood in the car was light, and it was filled with great joy.

All of that changed rather dramatically in a blink of an eye as John Widders turned left to avoid the work team. Sybil would close her eyes for the final time, her life taken by those very same hills she woke up to earlier in the day. Her body would return home, although her young son lost his mother and her devoted husband lost his wife. Life can be so cruel in that it can be taken away in a split second.

Robert LeRoy Hutton Jr.

Perhaps the most tragic participant of the August 1, 1914 was the story of Robert Leroy Hutton Jr. While he was just over two years old, and was not in the automobile at the time, young Robert lost his mother.

What ever happened to Robert Leroy Hutton Jr.? Robert Jr. went on to Choate and then Princeton University where he graduated in 1934 with honors. While at Princeton, he served as associate editor of the school's newspaper, was advertising manager of the Princeton's Athletic Association and led a student club. He served in the United States military in the office of the OSS, a precursor to the CIA.

After the military, he went into advertising and public relations and was called a pioneer in promotions for television stations. He worked for a large advertising agency as well as a publication before he was hired as Vice President of Edward Petry & Company.

Robert married Mary E. Best on October 13, 1939 in Watertown, South Dakota. Robert and Mary were both 27 years old at the time of their marriage. For Robert, it was his first marriage, for Mary – her second as she was divorced. Robert and Mary stayed married until Robert's death. At one point in time they also lived in Minneapolis.

Robert and Mary welcomed a daughter, also named Mary on July 30, 1948. After his retirement in 1977, Robert and his wife moved to Maryland to be closer to their daughter and granddaughter. After years of battling Parkinson's disease, Robert Jr. passed away in a Maryland hospital on September 17, 1991. Robert Jr. was laid to rest at the Hutton family plot with his father and his mother, Sybil.

The Tragic End of Henry A. Cady

On Tuesday, November 30, 1897, tragedy struck the Cady family. While the tragedy did not occur within the walls of the Houghton Mansion, it was within very close proximity and it is quite possible that the energy associated with this event could easily migrate to the mansion. It is a known phenomenon that restless spirits can be drawn to locations where there are continuous paranormal investigations. This is because those spirits that are restless can feel an open channel of communication and with repeated investigations, the energy of Henry A. Cady may make his presence known, if he is indeed restless.

Not only did this tragedy impact the Cady family, but at one point Henry Cady actually lived on the land in which the Houghton Mansion sits on, so his spirit does have an attachment to the land. His family had a close connection with the Houghton family as well. With all of these ties, it is not out of the realm of possibility that his spirit or energy associated with him can be at the mansion.

Henry A. Cady was Sybil's uncle and one of the many children of Alanson and Jane Bradford Cady. Henry lived with his sister Mary A. Cady, who incidentally was the chaperone for all of Albert C. Houghton's daughters when they travelled abroad in Europe. Mary and Henry lived in W.G. Cady's Church Street home which was across the street from the Houghton residence. While Mary was visiting a friend, Henry met his gruesome death.

Henry Alanson Cady was born in North Adams on August 28, 1841. He spent his entire life in North Adams. He was a bachelor for his entire life as well. He worked as a foreman in the various shoe factories that were owned by his brothers William G. and H. T. Cady. In 1893, at the age of fifty-one, he had to retire because his health was deteriorating and he could no longer perform the duties of foreman.

Although his health prevented him from working as a foreman, he had absolutely no interest in sitting still. In 1896, Henry Cady announced that he was a candidate for the legislature of Massachusetts. He reportedly was urged by many of his friends and family to run on the Democratic ticket. Although he was a lifelong Democrat, Cady too was against Bryan and was supporting McKinley, the Republican for President. Cady would ultimately lose the election, but it was a close margin. Those supporters of Cady circulated a petition for a recount to take place.

Henry did not like being idle and slowly his mind started to fail and he became despondent. Prior to his illness, Henry was described as being very intelligent, very frank, and very sincere. In November of 1897, Henry began to act erratically. His family thought he was becoming delusional and they attributed his condition to the fact that his poor health caused him to retire. Nowadays, mental health is better researched, so a logical explanation may have been missed. He may have been battling Alzheimer's or dementia. Henry started to discuss to many people that he felt there was a large conspiracy to ruin the Cady family. But as quickly as these episodes started, they ended just as quickly. No one expected anything out of the ordinary to happen.

On Tuesday, November 30, 1897, the Cady's servant did not notice anything in Henry's behavior that was deemed out of the ordinary. Around eleven in the morning he walked into the basement of the home supposedly to take care of the furnace. Although he was gone longer than expected, his demeanor seemed normal, so the servant thought nothing of his prolonged absence. At some point after the usual lunch time the servant became concerned when Henry did not return upstairs. Panic began to set in and the servant ran to the nearby home of W.G. Cady's driver Eugene Coon. Coon and the servant returned at once to the home and into the basement to investigate.

Around 3:30 in the afternoon, Mr. Coon discovered the body of Henry lying on the basement floor in a pool of blood. Upon closer inspection he found that Henry was lying motionless and his throat had been slashed. Mr. Coon then ran to the home of H. Torrey Cady and told him of his brother's condition. H.T. Cady then called three different doctors by telephone. The three doctors arrived at once and examined Henry's body. The doctors concluded that Henry was dead for at least two hours. They also found the blade of a safety razor near his body. When going through the home, they also discovered a farewell note to his family. Henry Cady was fifty-six years old when he took his own life. His funeral took place on the Friday afternoon in the home in which he slashed his own throat.

Even though Henry took his own life in a very tragic way, there is no evidence whether his residual energy or his spirit is present at the Houghton Mansion. I included this bit of history because it is not out of the realm of possibility that he can be responsible for some of the activity. Several factors contribute to my belief that the odds are higher than usual that he may be responsible for some of the activity. The factors I see that raise the risks include the fact that he committed suicide, that his mind was in a frantic state the moment of his death, and that he was battling a possible disease which deteriorated his cognizance. Only further investigation may answer the question of whether or not Henry is present. As mentioned earlier, he has a connection to the land that Houghton Mansion stands on, and we do know that spirits can travel to locations where there are people who are sensitive or in locations where there are many attempts at spirit communication. It is not out of the question that if Mr. Cady's spirit is restless, he could migrate over to the mansion.

Mary A. Cady

Mary Cady was Sybil Hutton's aunt and played a direct role in the Houghton family and also had a role in the August 1, 1914 automobile accident. Mary was one of the eleven children born to Alanson and Jane Bradford Cady. The large family was raised in a home that stood at the corner of Church and Pleasant Streets, now home to the Houghton Mansion and Masonic Temple. In fact, the hill that Pleasant Street ascends was known as Cady Hill, because of the proximity to the Cady residence. Mary's siblings include her sisters, Elizabeth Mary Cady Brown, Frances Augusta Cady Winton, Stella Harriet Cady Williams and Caroline Virginia Cady. Mary's brothers were: Arthur Daniel Cady, Edwin Bradford Cady, Hiram Torrey (H.T.) Cady, Henry Alanson Cady, William Garner (W.G) Cady, and Edwin Bradford Cady II.

Her father Alanson Cady was a First Selectmen for North Adams and established the first foundry in North Adams. Alanson also became prominent in the real estate market in the rapidly developing city. The Cady property was expansive covering much of what is now Pleasant, Wall, Cherry and Holbrook Streets.

When Mary was young she was educated in the local public schools. Upon graduation she attended Vassar College in Poughkeepsie, New York. At the time Vassar was an all-women liberal arts college. Mary graduated Vassar College in 1879. Throughout her life Mary was passionate about furthering her education and reading literature. She was well-known throughout the community for her vast wealth of knowledge. She appeared frequently for talks regarding a wide range of topics, especially with events that were contemporary for the times.

Mary was well-traveled, and in fact, was a chaperone for all of the surviving Houghton daughters when they studied abroad in Europe. When she returned, she would often give talks regarding their experiences in Europe and regarding the various cultures they encountered. Mary's talks were widely anticipated events. Mary was also deeply religious and for many years taught religious education to children at the First Congregation Church in North Adams.

Mary also was very interested in the many charitable organizations in North Adams. She worked tirelessly on an organization that was the precursor of the North Adams Community Chest. Since she was so active in many religious and women's organizations, she saw the redundancy of many of these organizations and sought out a way to have them run more efficiently. The result that Mary proposed was the Associated Charities of North Adams. The new association coordinated all the various groups and their efforts and weeded out the redundancies so that the valuable resources were more effectively used. Like most of the people that are profiled in this book, Mary was very interested in the affairs of both the North Adams Public Library and the North Adams Hospital and she spent considerable time and effort with those two institutions.

While Mary was very contemporary, she considered herself very much against the woman's right to vote. She did however, change her tune and her first ballot was against the fourth term of President Franklin D. Roosevelt.

As I mentioned Mary A. Cady did have a role in the tragedy that unfolded on August 1, 1914. When her niece Sybil and her husband Robert joined the Houghtons on that fateful trip, it was Mary who was babysitting Sybil's son. The last memory Mary had of her niece was when she hugged and kissed her two-year old son goodbye and the Houghton automobile pulled away from the mansion.

As Mary was playing with little Robert, the phone rang and it was news of the terrible accident and the passing of Sybil. In the chaos that ensued, did she tell Robert Jr. about his mother's death? That answer is unknown. Through all her grief, she pleaded with neighbors to watch little Robert so she can help out any way she could. Mary rushed over to the Houghton Mansion to be with Cordelia as the news was trickling in about the fate of her daughter and husband. When the tragedy became more evident, together Mary and Cordelia were contacting as many relatives as possible.

Mary died on Tuesday morning, December 28, 1948 in her home on Cherry Street. Mary was the last of her siblings and she found eternal peace at the age of ninety-three.

11. Houghton Mansion

> The mansion is alive, not like you and I, but is alive with living history.

I introduced you to the lives of the Houghton family and to those that have made an impact on Houghton Mansion, now it is time to introduce you to the stately mansion that has garnered so much interest. The old home has a pulse, but instead of the sound of a heart pumping blood through a body; it is the sounds of footsteps, doors opening and closing and even of phantom pianos. Instead of red blood cells circulating through the body delivering needed oxygen; it is the energy of its previous residents providing the mansion with its life.

The mansion is indeed alive. Not only does it contain spirits of those that once walked the hallways, but the mansion absorbed energy of an era gone by. If you step into the stately home, you too may feel her mood. Some days, she will be calm, but others, she will be in a rage.

If the walls do talk, think of the stories they can tell. She will no doubt talk about the happy times and the darkest hours. She was built as a grand monument to a family's importance to the community. She welcomed the wealthiest of residents into her rooms. She saw fanciful card parties put on by Houghton's daughters. She saw elegant fundraisers held on her beautifully manicured lawn and gardens. She witnessed a man help shape a community. She played host to grandchildren running around her hallways and in her lawn. All of those cherished memories left an imprint in the stone, wood and plaster.

The home even witnessed a President stop in front of her, as President McKinley stopped to view a marching band in his honor. Decorative buntings and flags adorned her exterior to welcome a standing President. She stood tall and proud as the procession moved past.

She also mourned. Several grandchildren, gone far too young – the poor babies never had a chance to live life. Her next door neighbor suddenly grew bleak when the sound of laughter and joy were ripped from those walls when the second bright star was extinguished. Countless times, Houghton's family; brothers, sisters, nieces and nephews were mourned. Each and every tragedy the walls, the foundation, the very fabric of its existence absorbed each and every mourning of a loved one.

On that beautiful and serene morning of August 1, 1914, the mansion witnessed five people get into an automobile. When the car pulled away from the covered carport, the mansion would never be the same. The walls, the floors, the roof could not protect those that graced it. Those five human beings who went on a pleasure ride would never be the same. Only one of the car's occupants would live past August. Two of its inhabitants would lay in its parlor, waiting for burial. A third took his life on the property. The home across the street welcomed the mourning members of another victim.

The matriarch of the home remained as did the sadness and the loneliness. When the matriarch's own health began to fade, the mansion sobbed once again. Once again a loved resident waited for burial in the parlor. A new family moved into the hallways, but the grandchildren were grown. There was a sense of familiarity for the mansion as these new residents spent considerable time within her walls previously. That new family would move out, leaving the mansion without a family of its own.

The mansion would be converted to another use. She was glad to serve an important capacity to the community again. Not even two fires could extinguish her existence. She witnessed the fall of Arnold Print Works and later Sprague Electric, throwing the community into high unemployment and difficult times. She witnessed many of her neighboring homes sell to other owners or converted to other uses. But the mansion stood tall, holding onto all of her cherished memories and unfathomable sadness. She has seen plenty, and she does tell her story. It is only a matter of whether people are really listening to what she has to say. The mansion is alive, not like you and I, but is alive with living history.

The Houghton Mansion is located at 172 Church Street in North Adams, Massachusetts. When Houghton decided to build his new residence, he selected Church Street because it was the most prominent real estate in North Adams at that time. Many of the wealthiest and most prominent families built their stately residences on this street. Even today, you can drive down the road and still see some of these stately homes that still stand as a testament to the families who built them.

Before Houghton built his mansion on the land, the land once held the residence of another wealthy industrialist. William Blackinton built his residence on the spot where Houghton Mansion currently sits. Several years before Houghton purchased the land and built his mansion, the Blackinton residence was taken apart and rebuilt on 126 and 128 East Brooklyn Street and used as a tenement house.

The home was built in an area that was once known as Cady Hill. The slope in the vicinity of Pleasant Street was informally named Cady Hill as the residence of Alanson and Jane (Bradford) Cady was located in the spot of the current Houghton Mansion and Masonic temple. The family of Alanson and Jane Cady consisted of eleven offspring, many of whom were important to both the history of North Adams and in our narrative of the Houghton family.

In order to connect the property to the stable and land owned by Albert C. Houghton, a sliver of land was purchased from three other property owners.

Henry Neill Wilson – The Father of the Mansion

The discussion regarding the mansion should not begin without discussing the architect Albert C. Houghton hired to design the mansion. Mr. Houghton selected H. Neill Wilson then from Pittsfield, Massachusetts to design his home. Mr. Wilson was no small-town architect, he designed some of the largest, most luxurious "cottages" in the Berkshires and many examples of his work are on the National Register of Historic Places.

Henry Wilson was born in Glendale, Ohio on May 1, 1855. His father, James Keys Wilson was a renowned architect in Cincinnati, Ohio. In 1873, Henry started working for his father's architectural firm, Walter and Wilson. He worked under direct tutelage of his father for seven years. In fact, his first project was the Glendale Town Hall, which is listed on the National Register of Historic Places. Henry was lured to Minneapolis in 1879 when a considerable building boom was under way. At this time, it was important to Henry to prove to himself that he could be a success on his own.

In 1885, Henry moved to Pittsfield, Massachusetts where he spent the bulk of his life and his career. He remained there until his death in 1926. He married Olivia Lovell.

His portfolio was impressive. In Wilson, Ohio the Rookwood Pottery building that he designed still stands. He also designed the Glendale Lyceum, which was constructed in 1891. It was his work in Massachusetts, however, that earned him his claim to fame. His Berkshire homes were so splendid that they were actually the subject of a book.

One of his more famous homes was Shadowbrook in Lenox, Massachusetts – the residence where Andrew Carnegie lived and died. Shadowbrook was destroyed by a fire in 1956 and it was rebuilt, however, not to the same standards as the original.

In Pittsfield, several of his designs are listed on the National Register of Historic Places such as the Pilgrim Memorial Church and the William Russell Allen House. Other projects included the Wollison-Shipton Building, the W.P. Burbank House, and the Berkshire County Home for the Aged Women. He also redesigned the Red Lion Inn in Stockbridge after a devastating fire necessitated major work. The Red Lion Inn was originally constructed in 1773. In 1897, a fire that started in the pastry kitchen devastated the structure. He designed the eighty-room building, but separated the kitchen into a separate structure so that the inn would not have a repeat incident.

In North Adams, Wilson's designs can be seen with the Hoosac Savings Bank Building and of course, Houghton Mansion. The list goes on and on, but I highlighted the more significant accomplishments. Several of his designs were featured in the architectural digests that were published at that time. My point being that Mr. Houghton did not trust some schlub for the design of his residence, he went out and hired the best available.

As if his designs were not impressive enough, Wilson had also invented and patented fire-proof flooring and operated a company to manufacture his product in Kentucky.

After he designed Houghton's new mansion, he was hired by W.G. Cady, Sybil's father, to design his new residence on Church Street, across the street from the Houghton Mansion. In order to accommodate the new residence, the Cady's old home was dismantled and moved to a new location on Porter Street so the new home could be built on-site. The first part of the old Cady house to move was the ell section of the house. When the ell was placed, the main part of the house was dismantled and moved and connected to the ell. While the new Cady residence was being constructed, the Cady family moved into a house at the corner of Cherry and Pleasant Streets while construction was ongoing. The design was completed and constructed started in July of 1895.

The Mansion Claims a Life

Houghton Mansion has seen its share of family tragedy, but before the Houghton family moved in, a life was taken during the construction of the home. In the afternoon of Thursday, May 16, 1895, an Irish immigrant by the name of Daniel Ringwood was working alone near a derrick pole. The other workers were unaware of what exactly Ringwood was doing. As they were working there was a substantial noise which made them stop working. They discovered that the sound of the noise was a derrick pole crashing to the ground. They also discovered Daniel Ringwood lying unconscious nearby. The derrick pole had struck him on the head and he was in grave condition. He was taken to the North Adams Hospital immediately, but he never regained consciousness. Daniel Ringwood was pronounced dead at five in the afternoon at the age of fifty-six years old. Daniel left behind his wife and three surviving children.

As a result of the accident a formal inquest was held over the death of Ringwood. Judge Thayer presided over the inquest and a total of three witnesses testified. That day, it appeared that Ringwood was digging near the derrick pole and that there was insufficient soil to hold the pole. The pole was not a structural piece of the mansion, but one used for construction. According to the witnesses, there was no known reason as to why Ringwood was digging near the pole. They claimed that he was neither supposed to nor ordered to.

The funeral for Daniel Ringwood was held at Saint Francis Church. His body was then taken to Schuylerville, New York where he was laid to rest in the Cemetery of the Visitation Blessed Virgin Mary. Daniel Ringwood had a life insurance policy with the Metropolitan Insurance Company. When he died, his widow received that payout, a sum of only two hundred dollars.

Like every person in the book, Daniel Ringwood's life should be told. He was not just an extra behind the scenes; he had a family, with his own struggles. While Ringwood is not a part of the Houghton family, he is part of the Houghton Mansion. His blood was spilled on the site of the mansion, and thus he is forever part of it.

Daniel Ringwood was born in 1839 in Ireland to Daniel and Anne (Savage) Ringwood. While he was still living in Ireland he married Ellen Conners. They immigrated to the United States and settled in New York. While they lived in Schuylerville, New York, Ellen gave birth to a daughter Agnes. The family would then move to Fort Miller, New York where the family grew with the additions of John, Daniel, and Nellie.

On September 12, 1887, tragedy struck the Ringwood family as John Ringwood passed away as a result of typhoid fever. He was only nineteen years old at the time of his death. Typhoid fever is a bacterial disease that is commonly transmitted through ingestion of water or food contaminated by fecal matter of someone who had the disease. The illness can also be spread by insects that feed on fecal matter from inflicted persons. The disease was more common in this era as public sanitation was a bit more problematic than it is now.

After the death of her husband, Ellen Ringwood opened up her home to boarders in order to support her family. Ellen could neither read nor write, but her children could since they attended the local schools. Sadly, tragedy once again struck the Ringwood family. On December 24, 1903, Daniel Jr. passed away at the age of twenty-nine in his mother's home which at the time was located on Center Street in North Adams. Like his father, he was a laborer, specializing in carpentry. Daniel's cause of death as listed on his death certificate was tubercular phthisis with a contributory of progressive cardial asthenia. In other words, he contracted tuberculosis and the impacts of this terrible disease damaged his heart. His body was buried in the same cemetery as his father in Schuylerville, New York.

The three men in the Ringwood family all died tragically. The patriarch perished in a construction accident, and it seems only he knows what exactly he was doing to cause his death. His two sons died at young ages from diseases that ravaged their bodies. The women in the Ringwood family, however, lived long lives.

Houghton Mansion Opens

Houghton Mansion is a colonial structure that was constructed with a wood frame. The original dimensions of the house were one hundred feet long by forty feet. There was also a wing that was sixty feet by forty feet. The original color of the mansion was a light gray color. The roof was tiled and the chimneys were made of stone. The architect of the home combined Old English and Spanish styling. In the front of the house was a broad flight of steps comprised of granite. When entering the house from the front, one enters a broad veranda which was forty feet long and fourteen feet wide.

The main hall on the first floor was painted white, with touches of green and silver. One of the distinguishing characters of the home is the elaborate main staircase that was inspired by French architecture. The large beveled glass window was designed to allow prismatic colors throughout the mansion providing for a very elaborate effect.

Opposite the staircase on the first floor was a nook that had a marble mosaic floor. Within this area was a large floor to ceiling mantle with a shelf that displayed antique silver pieces. The hallway was furnished with antique black oak English furniture which was very ornate with intricate carvings.

To the right of the nook, if you entered through the front door, was a parlor with the dimensions of 35-feet by 45-feet. The walls were painted white with gold accents. The moldings in the parlor were of yellow and gold. The fireplace in the parlor was white onyx that had a gold frame and irons. At either end of the fireplace where intricate onyx pedestals with antique bronze statues. The furniture, carpets and draperies were carefully selected to be rich and luxurious. From this parlor, there were two doors which led to the covered porch – with heat.

The main library, located to the left of the main hall is eighteen by thirty feet in dimension. It was designed in the Empire style with mahogany and accents of gold. The room was originally furnished in dark mahogany furniture and the walls had red and gold tapestry.

Immediately opposite the entrance to the hall was the dining room. The walls were covered with wainscoting that was six feet high. The wainscoting contained very detailed carvings. The room was furnished in a light mahogany. Exposed wooden beams were located on the ceiling as well as a paneled ceiling which was decorated with oil colors and relief designs for additional pizazz.

The kitchen was very modern and spacious due to the Houghton's propensity to throw lavish parties both socially and to benefit the various causes they supported. The kitchen was outfitted with tile, glass and aluminum. There was a dumbwaiter located in the kitchen that extended from the basement all the way to the third floor. The second floor and third floor of the mansion were divided into bedrooms that were arranged almost as individual suites. The second floor was devoted to the Houghton family and the third floor consisted of rooms for their hired help.

The heating system consisted of a boiler and hot water radiator system. The plumbing was modern for the times. The sun porch on the south side was heated by steam and also contained a stone on the backside of the parlor's fireplace for additional comfort in cooler months.

The landscaping around the mansion was breathtaking with various walks, terraces and several elaborate gardens. The head groundskeeper for the property was Henry Lane. Not only was he responsible for the formal gardens, but he also worked the greenhouse on the property. This greenhouse provided fruits and vegetables for the Houghton family as well as flowers that would adorn the mansion as well as for special events, such as functions at the mansion as well as family events such as weddings. Mr. Lane was well-regarded in the area for his green thumb and vision in making the Houghton property a sight to behold.

When the mansion was opened, the very first social event was put on by Susan Houghton. Susan was the hostess of a whist party in which eight tables played whist. Whist is a card game that was the foundation of the game bridge. Unlike bridge, there is no bidding in the game of whist. Like bridge, the game is two teams of two people. The winners, in which both a female and male team were named, received a prize of china. The mansion would go on to see many whist parties thrown by the Houghton daughters. The mansion would see many extravagant parties. The announcements of engagement of daughters Susan and Alice Houghton occurred during special events held at the mansion.

While Houghton Mansion was an extravagant home, many would be surprised that this residence was not the full-time home of the Houghton family. The family would often spend considerable time in the winter in apartments in New York City. One of the residences often used by the Houghton family was the Buckingham Hotel in Manhattan.

The Buckingham Hotel was opened in 1876 and was located at the corner of Fifth Avenue and Fiftieth Street. This was no ordinary hotel. The hotel boasted of suites with parlors, private bedrooms with fireplaces, a washroom, and a separate toilet room that was advertised as being separate in order to prevent the escape of noxious gases into the living quarters. The most elegant of the suites were priced to begin at sixty-five dollars per week. It is safe to assume that the Houghtons stayed in the more luxurious suites in the hotel.

The Buckingham's door shut in June of 1922 and was demolished when Horace Saks and Bernard Gimbel were looking to create an upscale store. This store opened on September 15, 1924; its name? Saks Fifth Avenue. Even as early as 1898, Albert Houghton and family moved to New York City around December 1 and remained there until the spring returning to North Adams around mid to late April.

The family lived in New York City in the winters as Albert C. Houghton moved his Arnold Print Works office to the city from North Adams so he could be close to the commodities market. The trip at the time was far too difficult to be completed on a regular basis, especially in the winters. Houghton would return to North Adams only when business of Arnold Print Works required his presence.

Meanwhile, for fifteen years the various Masonic chapters used the sixth floor of the Kimbell building. It was becoming clear that the current arrangement was highly inadequate for the needs of the Masons. On April 1, 1927 the Masons agreed to purchase the mansion and a portion of the Houghton estate from the Gallups for a very nominal price.

The North Adams Masonic Association, Inc. was formed from the smaller Masonic bodies of the city in order to purchase and construct a larger temple that could be used. The proposed lodge was to be utilized by the following bodies: Lafayette Lodge, which was instituted in 1847; Greylock Lodge, which was instituted in 1871; Composite Chapter, Royal Arch Masons, instituted in 1872; Hamilton Council, R. and S.M., instituted in 1920; St. Paul Commandery, Knights Templar, instituted in 1882; and the Naomi Chapter of the Eastern Star, instituted in 1885.

An architectural firm from Springfield, Massachusetts by the name of McClintock & Craig was hired to design the temple. The design was no small feat as it needed to serve the needs of approximately nine hundred members. Harvey A. Gallup, the brother of William Arthur Gallup was involved in the Greylock Lodge. It is interesting to note because prior to the sale of the mansion to the Masons, William and Florence Gallup owned the property. Edward S. Wilkinson Jr. was also a member of the Greylock Lodge.

On Tuesday, August 2, 1927 a meeting was called by the full board of trustees and the motion to purchase the Houghton property was overwhelmingly approved. This vote authorized the trustees to enter into formal negotiations to buy the property. The mansion was sold for what was considered a nominal price. Altogether the purchase of the mansion and construction of the temple was estimated at one hundred thousand dollars.

On Thursday, August 4, 1927 the paperwork was officially completed which transferred the ownership of Houghton Mansion to the five Masonic orders that were to call the residence home. At this point, the new owners did not have plans on how the mansion would fit their needs as that was to wait until the next month when the five organizations held formal meetings to ratify the property transaction. While the Houghton estate belonged to the various Masonic chapters, it was clear that the existing space at the

Kimbell Building needed to be retained for at least another year while the Mansion underwent renovations.

The preliminary idea was that the front portion of the mansion would not be altered, but the construction of a building at the rear of the structure was needed. This addition included a lodge room on the second floor and a banquet hall on the main floor. The lawns on the south and east side of the mansion was proposed to remain as it was.

The remaining parcel of land from the Houghton estate that was not sold to the Masons was sold by the Gallups to Morris Gold of North Adams on January 18, 1928. This parcel of land is significant as it contained a large stable on it. Yes, the same stable in which John Widders committed suicide. This parcel of land was assessed a value of $10,000 at that time and was located just south of what is now Arnold Place. Mr. Gold saw an opportunity to develop this parcel of land and devised a rather significant development on it. Mr. Gold's plan included the construction of a three-story, twelve-family apartment complex at an estimated cost of $75,000 to build with an associated nine-car garage. The stable would be remodeled into a two-family structure.

Mr. Gold's original plan was denied by North Adams as it was decided that the plans did not comply with city zoning ordinances. The city Engineer H. L. Ashley denied the permit and the North Adams Board of Appeals upheld that decision by refusing to grant a variance to building ordinances. A revised plan was granted a permit application in March of that same year that called for the former Houghton stable to be remodeled into a two-tenement residence. As part of the permit approval, two ends of the building were removed and the former barn was reduced in size.

On February 1, 1928 over twelve hundred Masons and their families attended an open house at the Houghton Mansion. The open house consisted of a tour led by the board of directors. This was the first time since the various Masonic lodges purchased the mansion that the doors of the mansion were open for its members to enter.

After the open house, a week-long campaign was launched in order to secure the funding needed to purchase the mansion as well as convert it into a temple. The goal of the campaign was one-hundred thousand dollars.

Just five days into the weeklong campaign, the drive exceeded the goal raising a total of $102,800.

The Temple is Built

For the design of the temple, the Springfield architectural and engineering firm of McClintock & Craig was hired. McClintock & Craig was founded by Edward Hubbard McClintock and Charles H. Craig. Craig had a connection to North Adams since his wife Mae Irving Craig hailed from the city. The firm was chosen because they had experience designing large structures. A sample of the firm's other work includes the Springfield Masonic Temple, several buildings at the Eastern State Exposition grounds, several buildings at Smith College, and several large power plants and other industrial buildings. The firm was responsible for alterations in the original residence as well as the design of the large Masonic temple that was constructed.

The square and compasses adorns the front entrance of the Houghton Mansion.

On May 29, 1928 the ground was broken for the construction of the Masonic temple. Constructing the temple was general contractors J.R. Hampson and Company of Pittsfield, Massachusetts. In addition to the temple, this firm was responsible for the construction of the Lasell Gymnasium at Williams College, First Methodist Church of North Adams, the Hoosac Savings Bank of North Adams, as well as the Williamstown High School. As part of the construction process, cornerstone ceremonies were held on July 31, 1928.

Heating and ventilation of the temple was performed by The Holyoke Valve and Hydrant Company. A North Adams electrician, Robert R. Costine was contracted to perform the electrical work. The floor of the lodge which was very expensive and very detailed was put together by Linomosiac Company which was based in New York City.

The exterior of the mansion was largely unchanged when the temple was built, except in the rear of the building where the temple was added. The interior of the residence had some minor alterations, especially to allow access to the new temple addition. In addition, the roof on the back of the mansion had to be altered to match the flat roof of the temple addition.

The lodge was constructed on the rear of the Houghton residence. This photograph shows the scale of the structure in relation to the mansion.

Lodge Dedication Ceremony

The Masonic temple was opened with a dedication ceremony on April 5, 1929. The ceremony was a lavish affair fitting the awe-inspiring mansion and newly constructed temple. Many dignitaries took part in the ceremony which began at 3:45 in the afternoon including the Massachusetts Grandmaster of the Masons, Herbert W. Dean. About three hundred people were present during the ceremony. Prior to the ceremony Horace Snape, the organist of the local fraternity played a prelude.

The ceremony began with the reception of the Grandmaster who was presented by Robert A. Fairbanks, master of the Greylock Lodge. The ceremony then included an offer of prayer by Reverend John C. Breaker. Edward H. McClintock the head of the architectural firm McClintock and Craig, which designed the new temple and oversaw its construction, presented the working tools of the craft. Charles H. Craig surrendered the working tools as part of the ceremony.

Engelbert M. Schmidt, Master of the Lafayette Lodge gave an address to the Grandmaster. The officers were then given a tour of the building which was followed by the ceremonial dedication to Freemasonry. The Grand Chaplain then provided an invocation which was followed by a proclamation by the Grand Marshall. Following this the Masonic Choir sang the anthem "Send out Thy Light" while Horace Snape accompanied on the organ.

At the end of the ceremony, Grandmaster Dean addressed the assembled Masons. The presentation of gifts was the final part of the program. The two gifts that were presented was the James E. Hunter Memorial organ, given by James D. Hunter of North Adams whose father was a past master of the Greylock Lodge. The other gifts consisted of a bible, square and compass, known to Masons as the Three Great Lights. The Three Great Lights were a gift of the Past Matron' and Patrons' Association of Naomi Chapter, Order of the Eastern Star, and they were presented by Harold E. Byam, Vice President of that association.

The Portrait of Albert Charles Houghton

If you have the opportunity to enter the mansion, one prominent feature that you sure will notice is the large portrait of Albert C. Houghton that hangs in the former library on the first floor. The oil painting was painted by Paul Kirk Middlebrook Thomas and was commissioned to be a life-size painting. The three-quarter length portrait is still on display. The painting was completed from a photograph of Albert C. Houghton. The painting was placed within a highly detailed and carved frame that is gold in color.

The portrait of A.C. Houghton still hangs in a prominent location of the mansion. His image adorns the grand home had built for his family.

The portrait was a gift by Houghton's daughter Florence Gallup to the Masons. The portrait was hung on Friday April 5, 1929 amid the ceremonies that dedicated the mansion. According to Florence's wishes the portrait will remain in a place of honor as long as the Masons utilize the property.

As well as the portrait, Mrs. Gallup sent over several large bouquets of talisman roses and blue delphinium as part of the festivities of the temple's dedication.

Pipe Organ

Another feature of the property is the pipe organ you can see from within the lodge. The walls of Houghton Mansion do talk, the noise coming from spirits of those who walked the hallways. However, the Mansion also has something else that fills up the voids with sound. A sound that can rumble through the home and temple, that of course being the organ. The pipe organ, manufactured by the Skinner Organ Company, was purchased in January of 1928 by James D. Hunter. The organ was purchased as a memorial to his father, James G. Hunter who was a charter member of the Greylock lodge of Masons and a member of the Composite Chapter, Royal Arch Masons, and Knight Templars.

James E. Hunter was born in Galashiels, Scotland on January 14, 1830. His family relocated to North Adams in 1838. He became a Mason in 1871, a member of the Greylock Lodge. He passed away in North Adams on January 19, 1919.

The organ and its associated pipes were installed in a room on the west end of the lodge room. The pipes can be accessed through the third floor of the original Houghton residence. While the pipes were located on the west end of the lodge, the console in which the organ was played was located on the east side of the lodge. Between the keys and the pipes were heavy cables that were placed within the walls.

When the pipe organ was installed, employees of the Skinner Organ Company were simultaneously installing one of their pipe organs in the Methodist Episcopal Church in North Adams. Installing the organ was no easy task taking three installers more than three weeks. For those that are not familiar with the inner-workings of a pipe organ, a rather significant one could have tens of thousands of parts with several miles of wiring.

Ernest M. Skinner, who founded the Skinner Organ Company, was one of the preeminent American organ builders in that era. Many of the organs that were produced by the Skinner Organ Company would grace cathedrals and the finest music venues as Skinner was considered a pioneer in the industry.

The organ was presented during the opening dedication ceremony by Hugh P. Drysdale, an attorney.

Fires Threaten the Historic Home

On Friday, May 25, 1934, workmen were repairing the roof of Houghton Mansion. The workmen were using a firepot while working on the roof. Either through a spark or a burning ember, part of the old roof caught on fire. The lodge room began to fill with smoke as the flames spread in the partition between the original structure and the new temple. The fire was small, but it was particularly stubborn as firemen had trouble getting to the source of the fire. The fire smoldered from ten in the morning, until about three in the afternoon. The firemen had to tear away part of the wall in order to extinguish the fire. Since the fire was stubborn, there was considerable smoke and water damage in the areas impacted. Some of the furnishings in some of the parlors were ruined by smoke and water damage.

On June 20, 1934, the city of North Adams approved the permit application to repair the damage that occurred as the result of this fire. The fire in 1934 was a minor event compared to what would come a bit later in the history. If it were not for the quick action of the North Adams Fire Department in 1960, the mansion may have just been a footnote in the history of the region and out of our collective awareness.

Wednesday, April 20, 1960 started like any other school morning for twelve year old Sanford Plumb. Plumb was a student at the Pine Cobble School in Williamstown. Plumb's family lived on East Main Street, but he would walk down Pleasant Street towards Church Street where he would get a ride to school. Unbeknownst to Plumb at the time as early as six in the morning several homes on Pleasant and Church Street were noticing the strong pungent smell of smoke, but could not determine the source. Several residents were inspecting their properties for fear that their own home was the source.

At approximately seven forty-five in the morning, as Sanford Plumb came upon Houghton Mansion he knew there was something wrong. So he immediately ran to the home that was adjacent the Mansion to the north. The home belonged to the Welch family and knocked on their door. When Plumb told Mrs. Neal Welch of the fire, she immediately contacted the North Adams Fire Department. Mrs. Welch was the granddaughter of William Arthur Gallup and his first wife, Harriet.

When the firefighters arrived on scene, the first who entered the building were hit by blistering hot air and dense smoke. They were quickly becoming overwhelmed by the conditions until enough windows were smashed so that the heat and smoke could be ventilated. The fire was limited to the northeast corner of the original mansion. The fire spread quickly and burned through the first and second floors also impacting the third floor, which is now called Widders' room, even though he may have lived above the stables. Several of the firefighters became concerned when the floor beneath their feet became unstable, several yelling out the windows in a truly chaotic scene.

As a result of the fire, the first and second floors were burned through leaving only unstable flooring near the walls. The quick moving fire moved within the partitions, which made fighting the fire a bit trickier, as it was in 1934.

A fire in 1960 caused tremendous damage in this section of the Houghton Mansion. The fire smoldered in the basement and when fully engulfed, the flames reached the third floor.

The fire was finally under control around nine in the morning, a little more than an hour after fire fighters arrived. By ten in the morning, the fire was completely extinguished, but the damage became apparent. On the first floor, the kitchen and butler's pantry were called a total loss. The back staircase was also heavily damaged. On the second floor, the recreational room, which was located directly above the kitchen, was also a total loss. Adjacent rooms on either floor suffered from smoke and water damage.

While the dense smoke infiltrated the entire mansion and temple, the spread of the fire was slowed due to the fact that the night prior, the rooms of the mansion were locked up tight for the night. This slowed some of the progress of the flames. The cause of the fire was not immediately known. In the afternoon, the fire officials began their investigation to discover the source of the fire.

While in the basement, the cause was discovered. It was thought that the fire was the result of spontaneous ignition of cheesecloth that was soaked in linseed oil. The cloth and oil were being used to clean the mahogany woodwork within the temple. These rags were being stored in the basement immediately below the kitchen. The rags smoldered for some time before igniting and resulting in flames that burnt upwards through the first and second floors in that vicinity of the mansion. The damage was so extensive that the lodge was not used until September 13, 1960, just shy of five months after the fire.

Historic Nomination

In 1982, the row of mansions on Church Street in which Houghton Mansion is a prominent feature was nominated for the National Register of Historic Places. The original nomination included 56 buildings on 20 acres of land. The homes were all built in the nineteenth century.

The plaque on historic Houghton Mansion.

In 1983, Houghton Mansion was included in the Church Street Historic District on the National Register of Historic Places. The final area involved includes East Main Street from Church Street to Pleasant Street and Church Street from Summer Street to Elmwood Avenue.

12. Walking Amongst the Shadows: Houghton Mansion

You may have noticed the inscription of the Houghton family monument that was placed at the beginning of this book. "Until the day break and the shadows flee away". I am astounded with the prophetic words and how true these words ring. For those that are unfamiliar with these words, this is contained in the Bible in the Song of Solomon. The mansion has its share of shadows that move in the night, when the day does break, these shadows seem to take respite only to return as the day ages into night. Could these shadows be of Albert, Mary or John – or perhaps, can there be others?

I realize that many people love the spine-tingling tales of a haunted house, so I cannot write about the Houghtons or of the mansion without discussing our experiences there. Personally, I cannot put down a really good book of real paranormal experiences, so this section will be dedicated to the living walls of the mansion. The first part of this book introduced you to the family and all those that have made an impact on the history of the mansion. You were introduced to the life stories of those whose energy can still be felt in the house. If you feel a sense of sorrow or dread, there is good reason for this. The mansion has seen its share of tragedy. The spirits of people you may encounter have gone through extraordinary joy and sorrow – unfortunately, there was too much sorrow. The home was opulent, their fortunes were vast, but like us, they have feelings and those feelings were tested by enormous tragedy they faced.

I felt it was important to tell their life story – albeit a brief synopsis of each – so these spirits are seen for what they are – human beings. It is far too easy to enter a haunted location with an enthusiasm and a quest for adventure. Some lose touch that these entities are people, just without the physical vessel the soul was attached to. They are not there for our amusement, they remain behind because something is holding them back, and they should be treated with respect.

As of this writing, we visited the mansion three times to conduct a paranormal investigation. On all of our investigations, our team consisted of my wife Christiana and me as well as our friends Vanessa and Chris. The first investigation occurred on November 13 – 14, 2010; the second, October 8 – 9, 2011. The third investigation occurred when I completed the book. This section will be broken down into the first two investigations.

Before I begin to discuss the investigations, I will first discuss some of the more common claims of experiences at the mansion.

As one can expect, the tragedy associated with the car accident has left its mark on the mansion. I believe strongly that there is residual energy within the mansion, as well as the strong possibility that the spirits of Albert and Mary Houghton as well as John Widders remain. A spirit of a little girl is also widely reported as being very active in the mansion. Interestingly enough, the large Masonic temple is said to be haunted by past members.

The little girl who has been dubbed "Laura" is said to frequent the area of the hallway outside of Albert Houghton's library, and the hallway leading to the kitchen and basement. She is also reported to play in the basement. She is most often seen as a shadow figure, and is known to play with women's hair or jewelry. She will also touch people lightly. Every once in a while she can be heard giggling or appear as a full-bodied apparition.

Albert C. Houghton is often reported as pacing the second floor hallway or keeping an eye on his mansion and visitors to his home. He is quite often seen as a shadow figure. Mary Houghton is often reported to be very active within a room that has long since been claimed to be her bedroom. Many in her bedroom report EVPs, strange lights and apparitions. Unsuspecting visitors have also been surprised to hear furniture in her room creaking as if someone has just sat down in an empty chair.

The claims in relation to John Widders are very intriguing. Neighbors have reported several times that a room on the third floor is lit up when there are no visitors; the odd thing about that claim is that there is no operational light in the room. Many have also experienced seeing a faint light heading up the stairs and hallway leading to the room. Apparitions and shadow figures have also been reported in this room.

However, the most common claim is that visitors to the room can be quickly overcome with an overwhelming sense of grief or sadness, especially to those that are sensitive to the paranormal. The interesting thing about this claim is that Widders was said to live on the upper floor of the stables on the property rather than inside the mansion itself. For this project, I will refer to this room on the third floor as "Widders' room" as this is where many believe his energy is located.

Interestingly enough, there are also claims of past Masons who can be found within the temple. They are seen as shadows moving, and can be heard by many as whispers and voices. The spirits are very active, quite often knocking back upon request.

The mansion and temple have many claims of activity with the most common being doors that open and close on their own, the sounds of footsteps and disembodied voices and the sense of being touched. Many have also reported feeling that they were continually followed or watched as they walk in Houghton Mansion.

With all these claims, we were excited for the opportunity to visit the mansion and experience some of the claims. We were also eager to come up with alternative explanations for some of the activity. What we found at the mansion backs up many of the claims that have been made. As for researching and providing alternative explanations, i.e., "debunking", sadly it was difficult to disprove many of the claims, meaning that spirits are present and not where they belong in a higher spiritual realm.

The First Investigation

Our first visit to Houghton Mansion was on the night of Saturday, November 13, 2010 into the following morning. It was my first visit to North Adams, Massachusetts, and I will be honest and admit that before the mansion and the Houghton family piqued my interest, the only locations in the Berkshires known to me were ski areas. Of course being the first time driving in the area and it being after sunset, we took the accidental scenic tour by missing several turns. Once we found ourselves on the right path, the significance and the splendor of the mansion struck us.

We pulled under the covered car port and parked the car towards the rear of the mansion. The first thing that struck me was the sheer size of the temple addition on the back of the mansion. The mansion itself was what I would call the traditional New England mansion while the large addition looked out of place with its surroundings.

After we unloaded our cars and walked in the mansion, we met Nick, a lodge member, in the former library. We were about to begin the tour of the mansion but in the meantime we were reviewing some evidence that was previously gathered by other paranormal investigators. I was standing behind my wife Christiana, who was standing completely still, when she suddenly looked back towards me suspiciously as if I had done something wrong. For those that do not know me, I will admit that I can be a bit of a prankster, so it is not unusual for me to receive this type of glance. But I had done nothing wrong – or more accurately, I do not believe I did anything wrong.

I noticed Christiana's glance and she asked me if I had been touching her hair. Being innocent – this time – I responded that I was innocent of all charges. Not only was I innocent, but I was several feet away from her, eager to be turned loose in the mansion. Christiana checked all around her head to make sure there was nothing her hair could have caught on. Only a few minutes later into the tour

A photograph of the fireplace in the library. It was within this room several years ago that we were introduced to Houghton Mansion. It was also here where I began the journey that led to this project.

Nick informed us that women's hair is often manipulated in this section of the mansion and Christiana quickly realized that this same experience just happened to her. We were not aware of this claim before this happened, so we can reasonably rule out overblowing a natural sensation because she was not expecting this type of activity.

One important thing to remember as a paranormal investigator is to always be skeptical. Never take an experience and automatically associate it with being paranormal in nature. It is important that we keep an open mind to all possibilities and rule out other explanations first before we can conclude that it was paranormal in nature.

Christiana became excited as this was her first experience being touched by a spirit. It was thought that the spirit that was responsible is the spirit of a little girl who frequents the first floor and basement of the mansion. We had not yet begun our active investigation and activity was already picking up. We were all excited as to the possibilities of what can happen that night.

I have to sidetrack and talk about this girl's spirit. Clearly, we were not the first group to investigate the mansion, and we are not the last group. Many have come before us and many have come after us. One such group that visited just happens to have a television show that is broadcast on a major national cable network. Now typically I do not like to criticize or critique other groups, but this group clearly overreacts to make their show more interesting. They were lucky enough to capture what sounded like a disembodied voice of a little girl giggle while the EMF meter registered a spike at that exact moment. Clearly, to me that is impressive evidence. However the main investigator, in a voiceover, asked the audience if that giggle came from a demonic little girl. Okay, he lost me on that one. I understand that they need to keep their audience intrigued and glued to the edge of their seat, but a demonic little girl? Really? For those that saw this particular program, I just want to assure you that at that time there was no demonic little girl present at Houghton Mansion.

I will now get off my soapbox and return you to your regularly scheduled account. After Christiana felt someone play with her hair, the group was led to the Houghton family plot located within Southview Cemetery. The first thing we see in the large family memorial was the monument with the inscription I introduced you to earlier in this book. We then saw the graves of Laura, Mary, Albert, and Cordelia. Within a short distance, still within the family plot was a solitary stone with the name of John Widders. We did not conduct an investigation at the cemetery, as we were more likely to connect with the family at the mansion. After silently paying respects to the family and being respectful of those who were departed, we returned to the mansion to continue our tour and to start our investigation.

After spending some time on the first floor, we ascended the main staircase to the landing on the second floor. Chris was standing with his back towards the staircase, when he felt a bone-chilling cold blast of air go through his body as if a paranormal entity passed through him. While we did not have immediate access to our temperature sensors to record this temperature variation, it is important to note that this staircase would host several other experiences throughout the night.

You may be asking yourself why cold spots are prevalent when spirits are around. The prevailing thought is that cold spots are a sign of a presence of a spirit because the spirit is tapping into whatever energy is available in able to manifest. Typically they can drain batteries or even utilize energy from us, but they also tap into energy from the environment. Since heat is a form of energy, they can utilize that energy leaving what we experience as a cold spot.

The main staircase where Chris felt a rush of cold air move through him. These stairs become noisy at night when the sound of footsteps can be heard traversing up and down.

After Chris experienced the cold spot, we continued our tour of rooms that are considered Mary and Albert's bedroom. Nothing occurred in either location during our tour. Then we entered the Mason temple which provided for some interesting evidence. During the tour, I was carrying a hand-held digital recorder for two reasons: to have documentation of the claims during our tour, and to record any possible paranormal evidence during the tour. One thing I can count on is that paranormal events can happen at any time, so it is better to be prepared whenever you can.

One of my biggest regrets as an

investigator is an occasion where I did not have a digital recorder recording during a walkthrough. We were at a location where there were footsteps behind us; they were so loud that I turned around to expect a member of the living world, only to find absolutely no one.

While we were in the temple, there were two very intimidating electronic voice phenomena (EVP's) we recorded. Being an EVP, we did not immediately hear them, only when we were reviewing data in the days following the investigation did we hear them. If we heard them at that time, the investigation would have taken a different feeling. Just to give a bit of a background, the difference between an EVP and a disembodied voice is easy; an EVP is one you do not hear at the time since it is in a different frequency than our ears can process, while a disembodied voice is one that you can hear with your own ears. You will see both terms in this section, so a little background is helpful.

A little background will also help set up the EVPs we captured in the temple. I will admit, I was a bit excited to investigate the Houghton Mansion. I did some initial research in an attempt to better associate myself with the spirits rumored to be present. Looking back, I feel my heart was not in the right place at that time, and I think that may have been evident to the spirits present. I may have had a "kid in the candy store" look on my face in the temple. Someone made sure to wipe that goofy smile off of my face.

While the group was standing in the lodge, there was a very loud, intimidating scream captured. When I first heard it while reviewing the digital data, I immediately ripped my ear buds out and walked away from the computer. I am not joking when I say that every hair was sticking up on the back of my neck. I paced back and forth, trying to process what I had just heard. I returned to my computer to replay what I thought I just heard, I was hoping that I heard some sort of interference from outside, maybe a television in the background.

Sure enough, my suspicions were valid; I heard the scream again and again as I replayed that segment of the audio. Seeing that no one tagged it, I have no choice but to say that this was not heard at the time. When investigating, if there is a noise we hear, we tag by stating out loud "dog barking", "people walking by", etc. There was nothing but what I could best describe as a primal scream. Without knowing the true intent of the scream, I cannot state that this was something that was meant to intimidate us. We try to keep an even keel while investigating; we cannot assign intent to anything, as only the spirit can know its true intent.

Not long after the scream, we captured a very clear EVP telling us simply "Get out of my house." Again, since this was a true EVP, we were blissfully unaware that there was a spirit that was not too keen with us intruding in his home. I will admit that this is speculation, but I think we may have made contact with Albert C. Houghton and he was not clearly impressed by us – or specifically me in particular. I am thinking it was Mr. Houghton because the voice was clearly a male and he referred to the location as *his* house. The only males that technically owned the mansion were Albert Charles Houghton, followed by his son-in-law William Arthur Gallup. Since Albert is long-rumored to be present, by process of elimination, we are fairly comfortable that it was Albert C. Houghton removing the welcome mat.

Of course, since this was an EVP, we did not realize that someone was very unhappy with us being there, so naturally we continued on our tour of the mansion. After we investigated the temple, we continued to the back room of the second floor. Shortly after the group entered the room I started to feel the impacts of a spirit trying to coerce me out. Again, I must interject with some background. I am not the stereotypical spirit medium who can talk to spirits, but I am very sensitive to the paranormal world. I can feel their presence, I can sense their mood, and I can have feelings placed onto me from their world. I also had images and phrases given to me while writing this book. Since the spirits sense I am somewhat open to them, I tend to get harassed more than the rest in our group.

While we were standing in the room and Nick was discussing some of the claims in this room, I felt an intense pressure within the right side of my head to the point where I was losing my balance. While I was trying to listen to Nick, I started to lose focus and could not concentrate on what he was saying. After a bit of time, this feeling which I would best describe as someone placing my brain in a vice subsided.

Moments later, this pressure started again and once again I began to lose my balance. Again I was attempting to listen to Nick, but as I was focused on him, I noticed Nick looking at me wondering what the hell was going on. Again I braced myself by placing my hands on a chair in front of me.

This time Nick stopped talking and was looking at me like "what the hell did this guy drink?" I then admitted that I had an intense pressure in my head as if someone was squeezing it. Immediately after a loud bang was heard in the adjacent bathroom and I ran into the room to see if this can be explained or see if something happened. At this point in time, nothing was obvious as to the source of the sound, but later on it was evident that it was changing pressure in the old plumbing that was causing this noise.

As for the feeling in my head that I experienced twice, later in the evening we used our electromagnetic field meter to rule out high EMFs from electrical systems as the reason I felt the pressure and lost balance. We found no fields of impactful electromagnetic energy to blame that feeling on. The feeling in my head was noteworthy at the time, but after reviewing all of the evidence and putting the pieces together, the feeling took on more significance. While putting the timeline together, the link between the scream, the "get out" and this feeling was clear. We were not welcome, and it was an attempt to get us to leave. It did not work, however, and we continued on. Even after his displeasure was known, we returned a second time the next year.

Again, I cannot definitively state what the true intent on the "get out" and the brain squeeze was, but I have a theory as to why this spirit was not exactly enthused by our presence. When we first entered the mansion, we walked in with the thought of an exciting evening. This was not an investigation at a private home with a client needing relief from paranormal entities, but a group bonding exercise where we can have a bit more fun and try out new things. We failed to take into account the old adage we abide by - that the spirits there are like us, just without their physical vessels. At the time I had done research on what happens there and regarding the accident itself. I did not have the time to dig too deeply into the family's history or become familiar with them. Did Albert Houghton feel like I was somehow disrespecting him and did not want me in his house? I feel more certain that this could be why he was not too keen with me. This was completely rectified for the second investigation and at that time, it was almost a welcoming feeling for me – for the most part, but I will get into that later.

Our tour continued to the third floor where we ascended the staircase that the servants would have used. During the tour, not much happened on the third floor. Sure, it had a creepy feel, but was that real or was that just our own feelings as the claims were being discussed? After touring the third floor, we descended the staircase and headed into the basement. When we first entered the basement, Vanessa felt a bone-chilling cold on her leg. The basement is one of the locations where the little girl is regularly reported, so was this the cold spot related to the little girl's spirit? I can tell you it was not *the* demonic little girl.

The tour was now over and we went back to the first floor to grab our equipment and split into two teams since the mansion and temple are sizable. We split into two teams to cover more ground in the mansion and to increase the odds that we were able to capture something truly extraordinary.

Christiana and I started our investigation in the basement. For those of you that had not yet had the opportunity to tour the mansion, the basement is a maze of hallways and rooms. In the pitch black, it is creepy since you do not know when you turn the corner whether or not you will see an apparition before you. It is a location where you feel that you are being watched and even followed. In the basement, there is also the old boiler which looks like it jumped straight out of a classic horror movie into reality. To me, this seemed like the perfect place to start a paranormal investigation.

Since most of the activity in the basement is thought to be associated with a little girl, who better to draw her out than the parents of two little girls? Whenever we investigate we try to earn the trust of the spirits – especially when it involves the spirits of children. We try to treat the spirits as if they were living, so approaching a little girl who tends to be playful and mischievous, we decided to act a little silly to earn her trust and to get her to open up. What better way to open than

When did we warp onto a set of a horror movie? The old boiler within the basement just screams "spooky".

to show a child that you are not afraid to make a fool out of yourself? We sang "Ring around the Rosey" and pretended to play hide and seek, in which I admit, a spirit has an unfair advantage.

Since there are numerous claims that the little girl could be heard giggling, I thought it would be an ideal time to really make a fool out of myself and laugh in an outlandish way. It worked on my own children, so why not? We were walking around in the basement playing hide and seek and I let out this really goofy laugh to see if I would get a reaction. What we did get was an EVP of what sounds like a child going "psssst". Since we were actively playing hide and seek with an otherwise invisible opponent, there is a chance that the child was playing along with us.

After I was thoroughly done making a fool out of myself, we decided to sit down and let the child come to us. We felt that we may have earned her trust at that point, so we sat down in an area that contained balls and dolls others have left for the child.

I need to veer off the path a bit and discuss dolls. Dolls are creepy enough already, but when you have a doll staring at you in the dark in a haunted location, they take on a different level of creepy. Say you move your flashlight, and the light glances across the doll, that porcelain or plastic face is enough to keep you up at nights. On one of our investigations outside of the mansion we were investigating the claims of a child spirit who liked to move a doll. We set up a camcorder on the doll to see if it would move. It did not, but the mental anguish was in the fact that I had to review three hours of close-up footage of a doll. If our investigative group offered benefits, I could have really used a comprehensive employee assistance program after that!

Anyway, returning back to the basement at Houghton Mansion. We sat down staring at the toys on the floor because we were asking the little girl to move a toy. I thought I heard some movement in the basement so I pulled my attention away from the toys and was looking around the room. Christiana swore up and down that the ball was beginning to shimmy as if someone was attempting to move it. She had her flashlight on it at the time, so I doubt it was a trick of the eye in a darkened location. By the time she mentioned it and I looked at it, the movement had stopped. This is what we call a personal experience, since we do not have any evidence to back up this claim.

Thinking that a spirit may have been present, I placed two electromagnetic field detectors on the ground next to the ball. I went into my usual speech informing the spirits that the device would not harm them but can be used as a tool to let us know that they are around since we could not see them. One of the meters is designed to light up and make a sound whenever it detected an abnormal change in the electromagnetic field. After I asked a spirit to make the meter light up and make a sound, it did. The entire time we had digital recorders in order to capture any EVPs as well.

Since it seemed there was an intelligent paranormal entity, a spirit, that seemed to be cooperating, we decided to place a flashlight on the floor and demonstrated how to turn it on and off. We then asked for the little girl to play with the flashlight. Three times within quick succession, the flashlight turned on and off on request.

Immediately after the flashlight turned off the third time, I felt an unexplained bone-chilling cold pass through my body. I will admit, it was autumn and we were sitting in an unheated basement. Yes it was cold, but this was a different cold than the ambient temperature, this was a rush of cold air that chilled me to my core. On the audio, I was heard quickly start to shiver or whimper because of the cold burst of air. There was no air movement down there, so we could rule out the experience as being a draft. I mentioned the chill of air and asked Christiana if she noticed the temperature dropping. At that point she mentioned that she did not notice anything out of the ordinary. As soon as she finished that statement, I heard her react a bit as she too experienced the same feeling that I had previously. It was either the power of suggestion, or the spirit saying "Oh yeah, well how about now?"

When the activity in the basement settled down, Christiana and I returned to the first floor to change batteries in some of the equipment and to start in a different area. I decided to spend a couple of minutes in the kitchen by myself to perform a quick EVP session. When I walked into the room, I heard a disembodied female voice from the back corner of the kitchen. What was said was not clear, but I do know at that point the digital recorder was not on, so I failed to record a bit of impressive evidence. However, that voice did stick in my memory, and I would hear it later on in the evening. I was able to rule out Christiana and Vanessa as they were in other parts of the mansion and their voice would not have carried over to where the voice was heard. In fact, I had not heard a peep from either for some time before or after that incident. If only I had my recorder on!

After I turned on the digital voice recorder however, there was an audible sound in the kitchen. Remember, I was the only one in the kitchen at this time. It sounded like someone banging on a pot. It is easy to quickly dismiss as a sound of plumbing, but the sound came from an area of the kitchen where there was no plumbing, believe me I looked. The kitchen was also the source of some interesting sounds when we returned for our second investigation, but I will discuss that later.

Later in the evening, Vanessa and Chris were also in the kitchen investigating and they had some odd occurrences there as well. They were using an ovilus to communicate. For those that are unaware what an ovilus is, it is an electronic speech synthesis device that theory suggests spirits can manipulate electromagnetic energy in a way to make the programmed device speak. I was a huge skeptic on the validity of this device. While we do sometimes receive gibberish and random words, we also have been able to receive rapid succession of words that still gives me the chills. I am becoming less of a skeptic, but one must always be open-minded to the chance that some words may be the result of chance.

Vanessa was holding a K2 meter and checking for changes in the electromagnetic field. The ovilus then spoke two words, "green" and "light". Not impressive until you realize that the K2 meter was currently omitting a green light and the only two words spoken was green and light. Was this a coincidence? We do not have complete evidence stating one way or the other, but interesting, nonetheless.

After the ovilus stated "green" and "light", both Chris and Vanessa were positioned in the kitchen so that they could look down the hallway where the little girl's spirit is typically reported. Much to their amazement, they saw a shadow move quickly. Several minutes later, Vanessa again spotted what appeared to be a shadow near the door that leads to the basement. Immediately after the shadow was seen, they heard a strange scratching sound on the walls near them. The digital recorder was able to record this scratching sound. Typically when we hear reports of scratching sounds, we assume rodents in the wall. However, the interesting point about this was the timing of the scratching to the moving shadows as well as the fact that I did not record any similar noises when I left a digital recorder near this spot. Since we were able to review the scratching on audio, it also sounded different than a typical mouse in a wall.

While this was going on, Christiana and I were in the room that is claimed to be Mary Houghton's bedroom. We spent a considerable amount of time in her room trying to get her to communicate with us. Unlike other rooms at the mansion, there was a calm and peaceful feeling to the room. Christiana was sitting in a chair while I was standing up in a position which allowed me to look out into the hallway while seeing the entirety of Mary's room. When I looked at Christiana, I saw a bright yellow light appear out of nowhere by her right shoulder and make a quick exit. There were no passing cars at the time, no one was nearby with any flashlights, and this light was similar to other odd lights we have experienced in other legitimately haunted locations.

Not long after the yellow light, I turned my attention to the hallway outside of Mary's room. Much to my surprise I saw a shadow appear in the hallway near the temple and move towards Mr. Houghton's bedroom. What was interesting about this shadow was that it was not on a wall, the floor or anything. It was a free-floating black mass or partial shadow figure moving. I immediately chased after it and watched the shadow disappear by the entrance of Mr. Houghton's bedroom. One of the claims at the mansion is that Albert C. Houghton is regularly seen in the hallway pacing back and forth curious as to what people are doing in his house.

After Chris radioed me wondering about the light, which was my flashlight, and the noise caused by my madman sprint, Christiana and I decided it was time to investigate the temple. Vanessa and Chris then went into Mary's room to investigate. They had similar experiences in Mary's room. They were able to capture an EVP that simply said "Chris". There is no way to confirm whether they were calling out to one of our investigators or some other person.

While using the ovilus in Mary's room a full sentence shot out in a rapid succession. What is amazing about this is that the device typically spits out a word every once in a while, but a full sentence came out in a couple of seconds. This was the first time I witnessed a device act this way. The sentence came out so quick that it was impossible to tell what exactly was being said at that time, and reviewing audio later is a bit questionable as the last word was drowned out by the sound of a loud muffler on the street. Of course as luck would have it, that final word was the most important. According to the recordings the ovilus stated one of two things. One interpretation was "It is all very (inaudible)" or "It is all Mary's (inaudible)." Because of the generated voice, it was also difficult to determine whether the word was "very" or "Mary".

Vanessa continued to conduct an EVP session in Mary's room and was able to capture a very faint EVP from a female in the room when she mentioned "some people have luck with you being in here." Later on, Vanessa also spotted a similar shadow moving in the hallway towards Mr. Houghton's bedroom. Remember how I mentioned that I saw a light in Mary's bedroom? Later in the evening, when Chris and Vanessa were in Mr. Houghton's bedroom, Vanessa saw a light flickering in Mary's room when the room was empty. It could not have been light from a passing car as the bedrooms both have windows facing the same street and there was no passing car – a car would also be heard on audio at that time.

Later in the investigation Christiana and I went into Mr. Houghton's bedroom and at the time things seemed very quiet; I did not have the sense that anything was occurring. The only experience I had so far in this room was the shadow I chased down into the room. I introduced myself again. I thought I could get a reaction out of Mr. Houghton by asking a slightly pointed question. I do not think it was provoking, but just wanted his take on a simple statement. I casually mentioned that I just came from Mary's bedroom. I then asked him what he thought about the notion of a gentleman being in Mary's bedroom at that time of night. I must have struck a nerve as immediately after I asked that, I felt a slight electrical charge that felt like a charged cobweb form around my left ear and neck.

This is a common experience in legitimately haunted locations. While this was a familiar feeling, I had to investigate to make sure that there were no actual cobwebs or something that could rule out this experience. After nothing was found, I firmly believed that my line of questioning elicited a response from Mr. Houghton

After the room quieted down, I was trying to get a feel for the room's layout and trying to envision what the room must have looked like back in the day. I wondered how big Houghton's closet was and went to see for myself. I had trouble opening a door because of settling and warping and I gave up. When reviewing the digital recorder at a later date, there was an

EVP corresponding with that time that sounded like a slow deep chuckle as in "serves you right, twerp." Shortly after that a faint EVP was recorded, it was a male stating "get out of here".

We investigated the temple several times during the first investigation, as two separate teams and as a larger group. To tell you the truth, the most impressive experiences during both investigations occurred in the temple. I will stick to describing the first investigation for now, but we have repetitive themes in the temple between the two separate investigations.

During the tour of the temple, we were blissfully unaware of one of the creepiest EVPs we ever recorded, the scream. In fact, the sound of the scream is similar to what I would expect to come from the painting "The Scream". When we entered the temple, we were all oblivious at that point to what we had captured earlier that evening. I will be honest to say that if we did hear that scream, we would have entered anyway – we are tough like that!

Vanessa and Chris were the first team investigating the temple while we were in the basement playing peek-a-boo with a spirit. The perceived veils of secrecy of the Masonic traditions make the temple that much more intriguing and exciting. Vanessa was asking about those rituals and asked "Is it a secret?" when on her digital recorder was a faint male EVP that simply responded "yes".

During the tour of the night, we were taken behind the temple in the series of staircases and hallways behind the temple. Unfortunately, access was closed off for our second investigation as that was one area I was itching to investigate. During the first investigation, however, Vanessa and Chris were walking towards the door that lead to the area behind the temple when to their surprise, the door's latch or knob was being manipulated. No one else was at this location at the time and there was no way for another person to accomplish this without being spotted or heard. This was captured on their digital recorder. Listening to their audio, you can clearly hear the door being manipulated and both of them stop dead in their tracks when they realized what was going on.

When Vanessa and Chris left the temple, Christiana and I moved in. Christiana was sitting down in a chair on the side of the lodge and I was standing in the middle of the spacious lodge. I thought I heard her talking to me so I walked closer to her. Then I realized that she was not talking to me, but there were a series of whispers coming from behind her and louder voices to the side of her. Christiana was sitting motionless and not saying a word. Typically when we hear voices, we call out to each other to verify. Since Christiana was sitting still I was not sure if I was the only one hearing the commotion. I asked her if she was hearing the whispers and voices that were coming from all around her, and she said "Oh yeah!"

One of the reports that we were told on our tour is that spirits in the lodge will respond back to your knocks. Typically I loathe the knocking routine, it is a bit dated. With the new technology, there are more impressive responses. But for some reason, they love to knock in the temple. I decided to play along and sure enough there was knocking response. There were also very loud bangs from the temple. I radioed the other team asking if the sounds were coming from them since they were in Mary's room at the time. They responded that they heard them to and they were not coming from them.

But the most impressive portion of the whole evening was when all four of us descended upon the temple and investigated as a larger group. More people translates into more energy for the spirits to tap into and they did not disappoint.

Christiana and I were sitting in the front of the lodge and Vanessa and Chris were sitting in the seats on a side of the lodge. The room was extraordinarily quiet at that point so I asked for a spirit to make a noise that we all could hear. As I was saying this, there was a loud knock from within the lodge. It was so loud it stopped me mid-sentence. Chris then verified that he heard the knock. Then much to our surprise all of a sudden a loud and clear piano note was played.

Christiana was sitting right next to where the sound came from. At this location there were a couple keyboards. I immediately thought maybe a piece of ceiling fell on a key. Chris and I both investigated the area. I mentioned my theory and then I started to press the keys. Then I realized, they were electric – and off. I also believed the circuit breaker was off. Chris and I were then a bit confused and I said "they're electric". Both Vanessa and Christiana were adamant that they heard a piano key. We were not arguing that, believe me, I heard it clear as day too. Then to prove my point I started to press the keys over and over so that they could hear me depress the keys. When I demonstrated that the keyboards could not be the source of the noise the only response I received back from Christiana was an "oh shit".

Something like that gives us investigators a rush. Prior to that the room seemed to quiet down, and we started to lose some steam. Believe me when I say the musical note woke us up and gave us a jolt like no caffeine can. The best part is we had two recorders on capturing one of my favorite bits of evidence. I say one of my favorites because no offense to the phantom pianist, but my favorite is a toss-up between two we captured at Shanley Hotel in New York. There is one that says to me jokingly "I'll kill you, you freak." Then there's one that responds to a "hello" from us with a surprised and slightly scared "There's someone right there!" as if we were the ones haunting her. So the piano is number three on my countdown of audio evidence.

The lodge seemed to quiet down after the piano key so we took a break to recharge ourselves. When we returned to the lodge for more, I placed my digital voice recorder in the middle of the room and walked back to a seat along the edge. At one point Vanessa was asking a question and there was a brief chuckle recorded on the recorder that was not attributed to any of us. A short time after the chuckle, a door slammed within the lodge. We all went our separate ways to determine if the door was the result of some other cause. We found no evidence of human tampering to explain a door slamming.

Besides the basement, in my opinion the third floor is the location in the mansion that just feels plain old creepy. Whenever I was up there, it seemed as if I was never alone. I am confident that we were able to capture evidence to prove that we were never alone up there.

When we were investigating the third floor, I had my digital recorder operating in my hand. As we were walking through the rooms in the middle of the third floor, I was talking and there was a voice that was saying something – unfortunately since they were talking at the same time as me, we could not decipher what was being said. Shortly after that there was a second EVP, this one was clear, it was a male saying "...interesting." There was a word before that, but it was difficult to decipher. Immediately after that voice, there was another EVP captured, again it was difficult as the voices were appearing as we were walking and talking. This third EVP consisted of two words, the first was clearly "super", and the second word began with a "sp" sound.

We all spent time in the room that is called John Widders' bedroom. Of course, if you did not jump past the historical information to the "spooky" tales, you already learned that Widders was not Widders after all. I will refer to him as John or "Widders" to clear up any confusion if you skipped ahead. To add to the confusion, Widders may not have lived within the actual mansion itself. Just to avoid confusion, I will call it his bedroom since that is what it is often referred to as.

Early in the evening, Christiana and I were sitting in John's room. It was quiet for us that evening. The light that entered the windows from ambient lighting outside lit up the room a little bit. I was sitting in a chair against the wall with a window facing opposite the hallway. I was sitting with my legs crossed. Because of the light entering the window, the white of my sneakers was glaring. At one point the room started to feel a little different, like we were not alone. Suddenly the room seemed to grow darker, like darkness was enveloping me. The bright white of my sneakers was gone now, even though the light remained from outside. I literally could not see my sneakers that were just feet from my eyes. This would not be the first nor will it be the last where darkness envelops us on an investigation.

At one point in the investigation, a digital recorder and a camcorder were left in John's bedroom. All investigators were on the first floor at this time and there was a very loud bang from within John's bedroom or immediately in the hallway adjacent the room. I was able to sync up the other digital recorders to verify that everyone with a pulse was on the first floor at that time and the bang was not caused by us. In fact, the bang was audible as a faint sound from the first floor and several of us reacted to that sound questioning what exactly that was. Was it definitely paranormal in nature? I have no evidence to verify either way, just an interesting event. When we returned to retrieve the equipment, we noticed nothing out-of-place that would account for the noise.

As part of our investigation we left digital recorders running while we were attempting to sleep at the mansion. We placed one recorder within the temple and another recorder in the hallway where the little girl is often seen. The active part of the investigation ended after three-thirty in the morning, but that does not mean the spirits were done for the night. In fact, they only seemed to get going at that time. As we were trying to sleep there were constant sounds of footsteps and whispers that were not attributed to anyone who was alive.

The mansion contains not only shadows, but amazing lights. When I heard a voice by the base of the stairs, I saw the most amazing bright white light.

It was about one-half hour after we turned in for the night when I heard a familiar voice. Remember previously when I talked about the female voice in the kitchen, well I heard it again. I was not yet asleep or close to sleep. This time the voice was at the base of the main staircase. I picked my head up and saw the most amazing bright white light at the base on the stairs. It was undulating in appearance, and it was quite the sight. This is something paranormal investigators live for! I mentioned to Christiana that there was someone standing at the bottom of the stairs. Christiana was half-asleep at this time and sternly retorted to "go to sleep". I may have responded with some sort of incoherent babble such as "ha-ba, but, da, ders a ahh, a ba". Then the light disappeared. A few hours later I filled her in on what she missed (then she was jealous).

Maybe an hour after that I was awoken by the sound of footsteps. These footsteps were right in front of us and they got louder and louder. These footsteps then went into the room, right next to where we were sleeping. I picked my head up and opened my eyes, expecting to see someone grabbing a cold slice of pizza for an early morning snack, but there was no one there. The sounds of the footsteps then began to pace back and forth by the top of our air mattress where our heads were, the entire time my eyes were wide open expecting to see who exactly was pacing. The footsteps then stopped.

Several times during the night, we all heard footsteps up and down the stairs, around the rooms, opening and shutting doors but a quick check showed we were all within eyesight, still as can be. The mansion was alive!

We had our digital recorders going so these sounds were captured on audio. One thing to remember is when someone was awake and moving about, you can hear them on audio. If someone, besides a spirit opened a door, you would hear their footsteps for some time before and after a door opened or shut. Some noises were recorded with no other discernible noises for several minutes before or after questionable noises. If it was someone pulling a fast one on us, I would shake their hand for their dedication as it is difficult to take a footstep, wait thirty minutes, before taking that next step.

We warily woke up before eight in the morning, one thing that strengthens a group is that we have all seen each other with bed-head and pass no judgments. A group needs to be strong and close-knit as you will find yourself in some possible dangerous situations and you need someone to watch your back as you do the same. We packed up our equipment that was left running and said our goodbyes.

While reviewing the evidence that was captured while we were sleeping, we were able to record a number of interesting things. The recorder that was left in the lodge seemed to have recorded some odd noises, while the recorder left on the first floor captured a few voices. In the lodge, while everyone was asleep there was the sound of a door within the lodge slamming shut. There were no footsteps before or after this sound, so we can rule out anyone who was living. The infamous piano was also heard again, this time two notes were played. On the first floor we captured some whispered conversations that sounded like they were near the kitchen. There was a couple of "hey"s thrown in there for good measure too.

The Second Investigation

We had the pleasure to return to Houghton Mansion to investigate on Saturday, October 8, 2011 into the morning of October 9. This time we returned armed with new information, and new trigger objects in order to illicit better responses. During the first investigation, I found out rather quickly that we were unwanted visitors in the mansion. This time, it appears that we were a bit more welcomed. I truly believe that the level of research I conducted gave the Houghton spirits a sense that we truly cared about their welfare rather than just looking for an interesting evening.

Prior to investigating, I uncovered the bit of history regarding Daniel Ringwood, the construction worker that was killed during the construction of the mansion. I was a bit excited to find this information, not because there was a fatality, that is never great news, but because we could have possibly uncovered a reason for some of the reported activity at the mansion. This information seemed lost in the passage of time, and he was generally forgotten. My theory was that Daniel Ringwood, if he was present would have been overly excited that someone remembered him and was seeking him out. Over time, his spirit could have degraded as he would have felt largely ignored. We all need validation – even spirits.

I am not saying that just because a person dies tragically that automatically means their spirit is trapped. There are many factors as to why a spirit becomes trapped or chooses to remain. When we look at a location's past, we tend to look for these incidents because that raises the odds that a spirit is there. Nothing is guaranteed in this field. I look at hauntings as risk factors and odds, not a given. My initial thought was that hopefully he had moved on, but it was exciting because if he was there and forgotten, maybe the recognition would set him free.

We spent some time trying to call out to Daniel, and I think we did not make any contact with him. It was not a disappointment however, as I would rather not make contact with a spirit as that means he or she possibly passed to where they truly belong. I find the spirits we do encounter as tragic figures as they really do deserve to be at peace. I would rather have a quiet investigation meaning that everyone is where they belong, but the world is not perfect and as such there is the need for individuals and groups who try to contact those trapped souls.

For the second investigation of Houghton Mansion, we tried something a bit different. For the first investigation we split into two teams. This worked out because we were able to cover more ground, but we noticed that activity at the mansion seemed to have picked up with a larger group. It probably had more to do with the fact that there was much more energy for the spirits to tap into. But to make up for the loss in coverage, I strategically planned coverage, to the minute, of active locations by infrared motion-sensor camcorders and other recording devices in areas we were not covering with our eyes and ears. I walked in with complicated charts and a plan of attack. It seemed like I was a war general instead of an investigator. I think part of the over planning was the fact that I was a bit eager to return. The first thing we did when we entered the mansion was to place motion sensor infrared camcorders in the basement and in John Widders' room.

We started the investigation by trying something a bit different in a location where we did not record any activity during our first investigation. The ballroom located on the first floor and immediately below the temple was very quiet, almost too quiet during our first investigation. I had the thought to try out the Singapore Experiment in the ballroom to see if that could trigger paranormal activity. The Singapore Experiment is also known as the Theory of Familiarization. The ballroom is located in what used to be the back of the Houghton Mansion. It was thought that there were formal gardens in this location and the site of regular charitable gatherings held when the Houghton family resided there.

The Singapore Experiment is basically a methodical approach in order to recreate an environment of a specific era in an attempt to stimulate paranormal activity. The belief is that spirits can become more active if they recognize something from their history. For this experiment I used four original recordings of music from 1910 through 1914. I had loaded the music onto a digital recorder and placed it in the center of the ballroom. The music was played and we sat down on the steps leading to the ballroom.

Interesting enough, activity did pick up in the ballroom during this experiment. Was it just a coincidence or did we pull in activity with the music? It is impossible to formulate an answer one way or another, as there is simply no way to prove that this activity would still occur without the stimulation. It is however, noteworthy that someone's energy became active when the music was played.

I was holding my MEL meter, which measures not only electromagnetic energy, but it simultaneously also measures the temperature. I was holding this device in my hands as I was sitting on the steps. We had placed digital recorders further into the room. As the music first started to play, I was able to detect and record an abnormal spike in the electromagnetic field on the steps leading into the room as if someone was entering through the doors and steps. The reading then decreased then lowered back to the baseline level.

The ballroom located directly under the lodge. By playing music from the era, we may have lured a spirit into the space curious as to what we were doing. Using stimuli from a particular era is called the Singapore Experiment or the Theory of Familiarization.

I then stood up and walked towards the center of the room where the music was playing. I was able to locate the abnormal EMF readings and it was moving towards where the recorder was playing the original recordings of period music. This abnormal spike stayed centered in the room for some time before it started to move again, I was following it until I lost track of its location. When the fourth song finished playing, I turned off the music and we began a session with a spirit box. A spirit box is a radio that has been programmed to flip through frequencies at a rapid pace. The theory is that spirits can utilize the white noise and speak through the device. Generally radio broadcasts come in as snippets as the tuner rapidly changes frequencies, but longer words, phrases and sentences can span many frequencies, meaning they are not the result of broadcasts.

What we received on the spirit box was two requests for us to leave. A little warning to the spirits: that hardly works on us, especially when we travel a couple hours to be there, so we trooped on. We tried the flashlight trick with some success. It turned on when we asked and turned off again on request. Then it stopped. We finally stated that we would leave if someone turned on the flashlight. Sure enough, as soon as we finished that statement the flashlight turned on. We then thought we would add a bit of validation as we then asked it to turn it off immediately if that was a cue for us to leave. Again the flashlight responded immediately by turning off. Since we offered to leave and made a promise, we honored our words and left the ballroom.

After we left the ballroom, we immediately headed towards the temple. The temple proved to be incredibly active during our previous investigation so we were eager to reenter that space. For this investigation, the temple not only reproduced its level of activity, but there was a marked increase and some truly amazing things were occurring at this location.

The biggest difference for the second investigation was there was an incredible amount of movement within the temple. Throughout the entire evening, there was constant movement in the walkway besides the temple, the area with the arches. Not only was there movement, but the constant sound of rustling or even the sound of fabric moving, suggesting clothing. In a bit of a spoiler, this location also provided us with a bit of shock later in the evening. Within the temple there were also several instances of sparklers. Sparklers are common in locations with paranormal activity, they are small, but incredibly bright twinkling lights. They are called sparklers because they somewhat resemble pyrotechnic sparklers that we all enjoy on July 4th.

We tried to perform a spirit box session in the lodge as well as EVP sessions, but the spirits were less cooperative in using these forms of communications this time around. We tried the flashlight trick, but again the spirits seemed uncooperative. We knew they were there; we were seeing and hearing continual movement. Since our "modern" forms of communication were not working as planned, we decided to do the corny "Shave and a Haircut" bit. Personally, I know things are not going well during an investigation when I pull out the last resort of requesting them to knock to make a noise. But for some reason, the spirits in the temple just love to respond that way. I think it is easy for them, but it does not provide us with much information to go on. Try that at your next business meeting, instead of providing a substantive answer, just knock on the table – you will not get far in promotional opportunities. We go into investigations with an expectation to find answers. When the spirits are playing coy, well you have to swallow your pride and do what you have to do.

I would be ecstatic if I get a long-winded EVP stating, "Hi, I am John. There are others here. I am here because I feel regret that I did not make amends with my son. Tell him that I love him and I can move on." But in the lodge we get a knock saying "Yes, I'm here." Not incredibly deep or profound, but I have no control over that.

When I start the "Shave and a Haircut" bit, I skip the final two knocks. Sure enough immediately after my knocking there was two knocks that came from within the lodge where there were no investigators. After this reply, we were able to get someone to knock several times on request. When this was going on, Vanessa and I kept an eye in the alcoves where we continually noticed the movement. Because of this movement, I decided I would move to that end of the temple closest to the movement.

The hallway on the other side of the arches was a hotbed of activity. There was constant movement of shadows, unexplained light anomalies and the sound of walking. Our equipment was also tampered with in this location.

As I was sitting there, I kept an eye in the alcove area. At this point not only was I seeing the shadows moving, but I heard footsteps with the movement and also the light sound of what appeared to be fabric moving. Then all of a sudden, a piano note was heard, again. However, the piano was quieter and seemed like it was emanating from a different part of the temple than the year prior. Again, we were lucky enough to capture this as audio evidence.

Because of all the movement we were seeing in the alcove area I thought it would be wise to move the motion sensor infrared camcorder that we left in John Widders' room to the alcove area in an attempt to capture the movement on video. When I retrieved the camcorder I stopped by the staircase by Widders' room as I thought I had heard something. I then continued my trek back down to the temple. I opened the door and Christiana and Vanessa both confronted me and looked disappointed and said "Oh, it's just you." Being slightly confused I said "Well, okay…Nice to see you too." Well I was not aware, but this turned out to be one of those recordings that I need to keep for entertainment purposes.

When I was reviewing the evidence days later, I was listening to the digital recorder that Christiana was holding. As I was upstairs, Christiana and Vanessa moved to the area in the hallway where we kept seeing the movement. At the point where I retrieved the camcorder, Christiana asks the spirits to make a noise to let them know that they are present.

Unaware of what was transpiring a floor below, I began my trek out of Widders' room. My footsteps were very loud and heard by both investigators and on audio. It appeared to be a direct response to their request. Then as I mentioned, I stopped walking once I got to the stairs because I thought I had heard something. During this pause, Christiana and Vanessa were asking if each other heard the footsteps. Then Christiana asks "Can you do that again?" Again, I am unaware of what is happening below me, so I start to go down the stairs, and quite frankly gravity and momentum kicked in and I was flying down the stairs and into the lodge.

So, when Christiana asked for the spirits to do that again, I came barreling down the stairs like a bull. The footsteps were coming louder and faster and right towards them. As you know, timing is everything. After a few choice words as they realize that something is charging at them, the door swings open and lo and behold it was just little ole me. I could not have timed it any more perfectly if it were intentional. Now I know why I received the welcome that I did. At some point every one of us will scare the living hell out of each other – it is only natural in the field we are in. Albeit this certainly was not a paranormal encounter, but amusing nonetheless.

After taking years off the lifespan of my fellow investigators, I placed the infrared camcorder in the alcove area and set it to record any movement. I connected it to a monitor so I could make sure that the coverage was perfect, and then I removed the monitor. I have self-diagnosed myself with a bit of OCD, so before we left I double checked that the power light was on and the device was working. We then went downstairs to replace batteries in other equipment, change data cards, and gather trigger objects to be used in Albert Houghton's bedroom.

About a couple hours later, I went to check in on the camcorder that we left in the alcove area of the temple. The red light to indicate power and the other light indicating there was data on the card were both dark. Not unusual as I figured the battery had run out of charge. I took the camcorder and brought it to "command central" to recharge the device. When I brought it down and into the light I plugged it in to an outlet to recharge, then I noticed something peculiar. The camcorder did not stop working because it ran out of power. The camcorder stopped working because the switch was physically turned to the "off" position. I thought that this was odd, because I know for a fact it was running when we left it because the lights were on denoting power and data on the card.

It was also odd, because we were investigating in an area that we should have seen and heard if someone went into the temple and turned it off. If someone did sneak by, the camcorder would have captured whoever the culprit was. But as it turns out, that is not the end of this story, more on that later.

The four of us went to Mr. Houghton's bedroom carrying some props to see if activity would be enhanced. I created props which consisted of photographs and documents that I had adhered to cardboard. Originally I was looking for an inexpensive toy or model Pierce Arrow, but I could not find one in time. In the center of the room we placed on a chair a KII meter, a photo of an undamaged Pierce Arrow car and a copy of Albert's death certificate.

We then sat around the chair near the center of the room to start an EVP session followed by a spirit box session. Vanessa directed a comment to Albert Houghton saying, "It's not every day you get to see a copy of your own death certificate" and almost immediately the KII was registering a very high fluctuation in the electromagnetic field, almost as if Albert himself was standing over his death certificate, reading it over. At that point the photo of the car accident was not placed on the chair yet. When I had it in my hand and was placing it on the chair, the MEL meter I had in my hand recorded the highest field fluctuation of the whole evening.

Shortly after, I saw a sparkler near the chair with all of the props, the way we were positioned, this sparkler was blocked by the props to the other investigators. But as I was mentioning I was seeing a sparkler, Christiana reported at that same exact moment a significant hit on the KII meter. I love it when a personal experience can be backed up with actual data.

Having done some research on the Houghton family, I had much more information to use as trigger questions. Most of the EVP session was quiet, until I asked one particular question. I addressed Albert Houghton specifically and asked if he was still present at the mansion because of the fact that everything he worked so hard for was now gone. On the digital recorder, there was an EVP that sounded like someone defeated saying "yes". Mind you, this does not mean just his business, his family too was gone. If other members have entered the light, he may be feeling a bit of isolation from his loved ones too.

Back in the first investigation, I seemed to get a response when I grabbed Mr. Houghton's attention when I asked how he felt about a gentleman in Mary's bedroom late at night. I had felt the static-like cobwebs around my head. This time, I turned towards a different topic – politics. Since Mr. Houghton was heavily involved in politics and was widely respected by both political parties, I thought I would use this topic to illicit a response.

It would appear that with all the chairs in A.C. Houghton's room, he attracts a very large audience.

I began to talk to Mr. Houghton, or rather out loud to a seemingly empty space, about the state of politics in the country at this time. I mentioned what a dysfunctional mess local, state and federal politics have become. I asked him if he would even recognize the political process he was once heavily involved in. Pretty heady stuff compared to the "Shave and a Haircut" piece I was doing an hour or so earlier. Rather than ask insignificant things, I thought a bit of intelligent Sunday morning talking-head topics would rather suit Mr. Houghton. When I was in this discussion, I felt the static cobwebs form near me in response to the conversational stimuli. After that experience, Mr. Houghton's room was quiet – well, until later that night. After that heavy political discussion, I felt the energy of the group was drained, so it was break time!

I went down into the basement, alone, to retrieve the infrared camcorder and planned to place it in the second floor hallway. To those that have not spent time in the basement, I will admit, it is a creepy place to be. It is even creepier with no light, and creepiest with no light and all alone. Well, I should not say alone, because there is the feeling of someone who is following you, watching every move you make. With the maze-like quality, your mind plays tricks on you imagining what is waiting for you when you turn that next corner, what is peeking out at you from behind the walls. I picked up the camcorder and we did capture some very odd things, I'll discuss later. I also picked up the digital voice recorder that we left in the basement on a metal chair.

I can share one bit of evidence that came from that digital recorder: while all of us were in the temple on the second floor, there was a sound of a bang on a metal chair in the vicinity of the recorder. While looking at the timestamp and looking at the precise moment on our other equipment, I can verify our location being the temple and that no one made a noise that would have produced that recording in the basement.

At that time the pizza and wings had arrived, and my stomach let me know to head on up. As I said, that basement can mess with your mind, and as I was heading towards the stairs, suddenly I could not find them. My pace picked up and I was walking through the various corridors. My heart rate seemed to pick up and it felt like my heart was finding a new home in my throat. I was by that damned spooky boiler again. Didn't I just pass that already? Finally I found the stairs and went upstairs trying to look composed. I placed the camcorder in the hallway of the second floor to capture any activity there.

After some pizza and wings to refuel, and to create those wonderful moments when your stomach talks to you and spoils any legitimate EVPs hours after eating a feast such as that, we decided to go to the basement to investigate. At first it was Vanessa, Chris, Christiana and I in the basement. We sat in a circle in an area where there were several toys left for the little girl, including those blasted dolls I discussed previously. Before I took my seat, I placed three electromagnetic field meters around the room in a perimeter in order to alert us where a spirit would enter.

As in the previous year, I started by telling corny kid-friendly jokes, silly songs and games in an attempt to establish trust and to draw the attention of any child who may be around. At one point Christiana heard movement down the hallway in an area of the basement.

I was holding a handheld camcorder and had it focused on flashlights and other devices I had set up on the floor in the middle of our circle. For some reason the camcorder kept turning off while I was recording. I just placed in a charged battery and it had a full charge, so something may have been manipulating my equipment. The camcorder was actively recording, so it was not a power-saving feature, it just kept turning off. Not to spoil the surprise, but based on everything else that went on that night, I am not shocked that someone was manipulating the camcorder.

For props, I brought a game of jacks. I figured that jacks were an appropriate game for a child that age and from the timeframe in which she lived. I also had an EMF meter with me as well. I held up the bag with the jacks and I made the offer that I would let the girl play with them on one condition – if she played along with us. There are two things that can make children listen – the promise of toys and ice cream. As soon as I mentioned the game of jacks, the EMF meter I had placed on the chair next to me registered a significant change in the electromagnetic field.

Since it appeared that a spirit may have been with us, I turned on the spirit box in order to communicate. While the spirit associated with the basement is presumed to be a little girl, we were surprised that during our spirit box session, what appears to be the voice of a little boy provided us with the name Phillip. It is not uncommon that other spirits are lured to locations that play host to many investigations, like a beacon, so this may be a spirit that had been drawn to this location versus one that is attached to the property. It is also quite possible that Phillip could have been unknowingly attached to one of us, through another investigation or through a distant relation that we are unaware of.

As I mentioned earlier, there were many pieces of equipment that were located on the floor in front on us. As our attention was elsewhere, Christiana calls out that she just witnessed a milky white light swirling over the equipment in a figure-8 pattern of movement. These types of faint lights can often be seen during some investigations, so I was not overly surprised. We were lucky enough to record a similar light just a few minutes later. When Christiana mentioned the light, I again focused the camcorder onto the floor right in front of me where the light was witnessed swirling over the equipment.

At this point in time Nick and several other members came downstairs and joined us in the basement. They sat down and I felt that it was time to have a bit of fun. Being somewhat of a practical joker, and knowing that the little girl has a tendency to be a bit mischievous, I was egging her on to try something a bit fun. Whenever I say "Wanna have some fun?" during an investigation, I can feel the wrath of dirty glances from team members even in the pitch black darkness – they know what we are in for.

The stairway that leads to the basement of Houghton Mansion. While in the basement, many will feel like they are never alone. As you walk amongst the darkness, you will feel that someone is following you, peeking out from around corners to see what you are doing. There is also a little girl who is reportedly very active in the basement.

I told the little girl how funny it would be if she touched one of us to make us jump. Again, I felt the reservation from the group, but hey, if you are investigating for spirits, you have to expect to be touched. We're relatively young, we can withstand a bit of heart racing. When I am older, I will do more subtle techniques such as – oh, I don't know – "can you knock so I can hear you" or "turn on this flashlight". I warned her not to touch me as I am very difficult to startle and used to being touched or grabbed by unseen hands. I am too even-keel and calm during an investigation to jump out of my chair. That is why I chuckle whenever we get contacted by producers, we are far too calm and do not overreact (overact?) to bring in high ratings. We also do not call a little girl's spirit a "demonic little girl".

Although I will admit, this investigation is the first, and so far, the only time I had to remove myself from a possible paranormal situation. This happened in John's bedroom and I will get to that a bit later. Don't you hate these teasers? It is like watching television and you see a teaser for a news story that is on too late to watch that says "You are probably drinking this right now, learn about how this drink can potentially kill you. It's real and it's dangerous. That's at eleven." But I have to keep you reading, don't I?

I was playful in the basement suggesting that the girl touch certain members of the team. Nothing was happening though. After four minutes of me pleading for her to have a bit of fun, I relented and told her that she could tug on my shirt. Immediately after I said this, I felt a tugging on my right pant leg. I told the group that someone tugged on my pant leg and immediately after Nick, who was sitting immediately on my right, jumped out of his chair and exclaimed "Holy shit". He was wearing shorts and he felt something brush against his left leg. That was a validating experience because we were both affected by whoever was between us.

But the absolute best part of this experience was that I had my camcorder trained on the floor in front of me, focused on all of the equipment on the floor. On the video recording, I mentioned my pant leg being tugged. Then a pale white light is seen moving from me towards Nick. As soon as the light whizzes by Nick, he immediately reacts by jumping out of his chair. When I showed this particular clip to Christiana, she stated that the pale light was similar to what she saw swirling around the equipment.

Well that had to make the spirit happy, as she did get the reaction that she was promised. This may have opened her up a bit. I was pleading with her to try that on other members of the group so they too can experience that. A couple of minutes later, I asked the girl if she could tug on my pant leg again. Again, I felt a tugging sensation on my jeans below my knee. However, before I had a chance to mention this, Nick mentions that he felt the static cobweb feelings by us. Afterward I told the group that someone was tugging my pant leg a second time. As this was going on, a freshly changed and fully-charged battery on the camcorder powered down. This battery drain is also very common and it is thought that spirits drain the power in order to manifest.

I felt as if this spirit was now extremely comfortable with the group and he or she was responding to my requests. So again I tried to get her to make someone else react. Again, I felt the tension build in the room as if the others were thinking I was an evil bastard. I told her that she can do better than that. Then to my surprise on my left knee I felt a hand rubbing my knee and shin. This stroking of my knee and shin lasted for about twenty seconds, but it felt like an eternity. As I was trying to focus my concentration on what was happening I found it was nearly impossible to effectively communicate with everyone else. The sensation was varying in intensity and when I would start to talk, it would pick up and I would stop talking so I can focus on the situation at hand. This provided another light moment as listening to the recording I could see how my lack of concise or coherent communication created a situation.

I casually mentioned that I felt a stroking sensation, then I stopped talking because I was trying to place whatever mental faculties I had into analyzing the situation, looking for alternative answers and just processing the experience. But before I could specify that the stroking was at my knee, people's minds were in the gutter. Perhaps stroking was a poor choice of a word to use, lesson learned.

After I asked the little girl to touch someone besides myself, another investigator felt a hand on her shin. Moments later, I felt the static cobwebs around my hair and neckline.

Things were definitely picking up in the basement so I again started a spirit box session. We received another name in the basement, "Chris". It was during our first investigation in Mary's room that Vanessa and Chris were able to record an EVP of the name Chris. To this day, I cannot answer if this is a spirit named Chris or were these two incidents because we had an investigator named Chris. On several other investigations, we'll get my name "Dave" and this is probably the spirits letting us know that they are aware of our presence. We also believe that it takes considerable energy for them to "speak" words to us so it is much easier for them to say single-syllable names.

When the basement seemed to quiet down, we decided it was time to sit in John's room. In 2010, the room was relatively quiet for us, besides the stereotypical "get out" and the darkness which seemed to come out of nowhere. But for the second investigation, the room took on a whole new feeling. I am not entirely sure if this was coincidence or if it was due to the fact that we brought some trigger items to his room.

After replacing all the depleted batteries and grabbing the props, which included mounted death certificates of John Widders, Mary and Albert Houghton and Sybil. I also brought photographs of the accident scene, an undamaged Pierce-Arrow and a photograph of John Widders standing with Mary's horse. We placed all of these items in the middle of the room to illicit a reaction.

I began a rather intense EVP session. For those that do not know me, I was very respectful to Mr. Widders; I realize the pain he still feels so I was being sensitive to that fact. I began talking about the day of the accident and the passengers in the car. As I was sitting I felt an oppressive heaviness start to surround me. I started to talk about Sybil and the little boy that lost his mother. At this point this heaviness was getting very severe. I felt a very strong sense of dread and regret. These feelings did not seem to be my own feelings. This is not the first time a spirit transferred their emotion on me – but it was by far the worst. At this point I had difficulty breathing, my throat felt very tight. When I listened to the audio after the investigation, I could hear that my breathing was fast, shallow, and labored.

I started to talk about Mary and Mr. Houghton through the difficulty breathing. The thoughts, the emotions were getting far too strong and too severe. It was clear that these were not my emotions. Because I was fearful of how strong these feelings would get, I decided to immediately remove myself from the situation. I shot up out of the chair, with all the equipment I had sitting on my lap crashing to the floor. I started to pace in the room then paced the hallway. I did not want to know what was coming next. The emotion was clearly not mine, and since I received a firsthand experience of the pain and torment John must live with, I did not want it to escalate.

After a few moments, I returned back to my seat, picked up my equipment and changed the topic to something lighter. I was discussing working and knowing with the Houghton family, thinking that positive memories at this point would be better than the avenue we just came from. To me, the atmosphere of the room changed immediately. It had gone from feeling that I was being crushed by a ton of bricks to a normal room – well, except this room is haunted.

At various points during the investigation in John's room, we were hearing noises in the hallway leading up to his room. At one point there were very loud footsteps heading towards the room. When I looked at the doorway, I saw a black mass start to materialize at the bottom one-third of the doorway. It dissipated fairly quickly however.

We were still trying to keep the EVP session a bit lighter after my run-in, so we were discussing the servants that worked at the mansion that also lived on the third floor. I thought by bringing up familiar names, we would more likely get some sort of meaningful reaction. When bringing up names of former servants, there was a reply; a male voice that simply said "get out". In life the man known as John Widders was colorful and friendly, although his spirit is resigned and not very welcoming. Not that I blame him, with all the misery and guilt he shoulders, he has the added burden of being poked and prodded regularly by some who want to provoke him.

At another point I clearly heard more footsteps in the hall, since I was closest to the door. Then there was a louder noise in the hallway that everyone heard. I decided I was going to investigate. I walked towards the door and I heard the sound of shuffling fabric in the hallway. The best way I can describe it was the sound of someone walking, minus the footsteps on the floor. The sound was loud and clear and right in front of me. I followed it down the hallway where it disappeared in the room with the lockers.

The third floor hallway leading into the space that is often called "Widders' room". During our investigations, we would hear footsteps in this hallway, odd lights and we would feel a strong sense of dread. The staircase to the left also has an oppressive feel to it.

After I returned to John's room, we turned on the spirit box. When we started more lines of questioning, including the accident, there was a stern response. It clearly stated "Don't push", a stern warning for us to move on. We did move on – to Mary's room.

We were in Mary's room around 2:20 in the morning. I had on my complicated chart that we were to be there around that time, so we could be there at the time when another group was able to record an EVP of a woman yelling "oh God". One of my goals was to see if that was residual energy and occurred at the similar time. This time, however, the room was quiet, too quiet if you ask me. The room was very peaceful, a complete 180-degree turn from the feeling in John's room. If I had not had so many coffees from the box of joe, I could have comfortably slept in Mary's room. Instead the box of coffee had me shaking like a small Chihuahua in a snowstorm.

While Mary's room was quiet, I kept hearing faint footsteps and the floor creaking in the hallway immediately outside of Mary's room. Was this Mary uneasy about the group in her room or was Mr. Houghton pacing the hallways as he reportedly does often. I cannot answer that question for sure, but we were able to capture some of these noises on the voice recorder.

It was around three in the morning when we decided to wrap it up in Mary's room. The atmosphere in Mary's room put us a man down as Chris wanted to call it a night. However, I was too caffeinated and far too excited to even think about sleep. I could barely close my eyes to blink! So Christiana, Vanessa and I went back into the temple for what I now term "The Main Event!" The exclamation point is mandatory, it is not an exaggeration. While everyone else was in Dreamland, the three of us experienced some truly amazing events that would soon play itself out in the temple and in John's room.

The three of us sat in the east side of the temple. At first there were subtle noises and movement. Then all Hell broke loose later on in the early morning. As soon as we took our seats, a door leading to the lodge shut and then there were footsteps immediately after that. I then verbally called a meeting in order and directed all Masons to file in. Shortly after that, all three of us were seeing flashes of light in the corner by the alcoves where we saw all the movement earlier in the investigation. Then after the flashes of light, the sound of footsteps could be heard in that same area.

Although we were sitting in this vast, open space – in complete darkness – I was feeling very claustrophobic, like the room was closing in on me. It felt as if there were a number of people invading my personal space. I can get like this in a crowd where everyone is pushing or nudging you even though you cannot go anywhere faster than the throng of people in front of you. I may have been feeling the energy of some spirits that were

When I sat in the seat in the middle, I felt as if many people were rushing towards me and crowding my personal space. We learned several years later that others have experienced this peculiar feeling as well.

closing in on me. Before I had a chance to mention this to Christiana and Vanessa, "The Main Event!" started. We learned in 2014 that this feeling is common when women sit in the chair I was sitting in. While I can honestly tell you I am not a woman, I had this experience several years before knowing it is a common experience.

The noises within the temple were getting louder and more frequent. At some points it sounded as if someone was stomping or jumping on the roof. The sound was hard to pinpoint as it was echoing off all the walls in the vast space. At some points it seemed like the roof was going to cave in over our heads. We recorded dozens of bangs and several slightly naughty words by us. Upon further inspection I had a thought. I had this feeling that the noises were coming from within the mansion and the sound was carrying into the attached temple. I told Christiana and Vanessa that I was going to try to duplicate the noises and to verify whether or not that was the sounds we were hearing.

I left the temple and headed up to the third floor using the main staircase. I started to walk heavily on the floor and I opened and closed doors as I would come to them. Then I walked into John's room, which at this point just felt oppressive, and I opened and shut the door. I could not wait to get away from the third floor as the atmosphere was really charged.

When reviewing the sounds I intentionally made and compared them to the sounds we were hearing and recorded, there were differences. The sounds that I made on the third floor of the mansion did carry over to the temple. Without knowing what door was being slammed or the area the banging and footsteps was coming from, it was not possible to make the same exact sound. I also have a different weight and mass than whatever was making the noise so again it would be very difficult to replicate the sounds exactly. My takeaway from all of this is was that it was possible that all this noise came from the third floor of the original mansion.

Shortly after that, we all heard a very loud noise again, so I left the temple again. I crept along the hallway to check to see if anyone was awake and responsible for the entire ruckus. No one was conscious on the second floor. Then I crept down to the first floor, again, everyone was out cold. I am not sure how anyone could sleep through that noise. I returned to the temple and took my seat. We sat there in awe listening to the chorus of loud bangs, doors slamming and various unexplained noises. The three of us sat speechless with the unfolding events.

Vanessa then witnessed a shadow move upwards by the door to Mr. Houghton's bedroom. She described it as a black ball that literally moved straight up. Then immediately after that, I heard the door that leads to Mr. Houghton's bedroom shut. I decided to take the digital recorder that I had in my hand and place it on a chair closest to that door.

When I was returning to the front of the temple, I heard a noise behind me and to my right. This is the location of the door that we heard close and the black mass that Vanessa saw. I immediately stopped walking and I was about to turn around when Vanessa asked me if I was carrying anything with a red light. After I stated that I was not carrying anything but my flashlight (which was off), she said that towards the left of me (my right) there was a red light, the very same area where I heard the door shut, the shadow, and more recently the noise that stopped me dead in my tracks. On our audio, the noise is heard, as well as my footsteps that stopped immediately after.

I again took my seat and there were more loud bangs and doors slamming. I had about enough of it at this point; I could swear that someone was messing with us. I decided that I was going to investigate again. As I opened and closed the first set of doors out of the temple, I had a voice talk right into my left ear. What was said, I could not decipher because I was not expecting a voice and my focus of attention was elsewhere. I was relieved however, because I always carried my recorder with me. But wait, I left the recorder on the chair in the temple in order to pick up any sounds by the other door. To this day I am still kicking myself in the rear as I missed out on a whopper of a piece of evidence. The voice was male, and it was clear as day that it was a sentence.

This time I went up the stairs that the servants must have used and the ones closest to John's room. I cannot state enough that the overall mood of that staircase was different. There was a powerful feeling of dread, anger, and sorrow – a real myriad of negative emotion. Every step I took it seemed to get stronger and stronger. I was preparing myself for a potential face-to-face encounter with a frenzied John Widders. I walked the hallways of the third floor and listened for any evidence of tampering. Not that anyone there would do that – they have a top-notch operation, but I have to rule out everything else first.

The odd thing is that when I went to the third floor to investigate, the noises stopped. I went to investigate three times and it was quiet. If these noises were the result of residual energy, the activity would have continued when I investigated. So I believe the noises were the result of intelligent energy rather than residual noises. When all of these noises were occurring was around the time when a restless and guilt-ridden Widders finally had enough and decided to end it all. This was about the time he went to the stables to end his life. To this day, I wonder if the trigger objects or the line of questioning upset him that night. If I was the cause of this, I am deeply sorry as I meant no harm.

The noises settled down after four in the morning, so we decided to turn in for whatever darkness was left. But of course I cannot let a great opportunity pass me by, so before I went to sleep I booby-trapped the mansion with all kinds of equipment to capture any possible paranormal activity. So after setting up all the equipment, my head hit the inflatable air mattress mere minutes before the sun came over the horizon.

Christiana and I set up camp in the former parlor, directly under Albert C. Houghton's bedroom. This was the same location as the previous investigation. As I was trying to sleep, I heard pacing on the floor directly above us, in Mr. Houghton's bedroom. The equipment that I had scattered across the mansion backed up the thought that no one slipped by to make these noises. If it were an actual person, you would hear doors open and shut and their footsteps. The old floors make noise when you walk across them – it would be a feat to sneak by. I had trouble closing my eyes because I was waiting for those footsteps to come down the stairs and pace behind us like the first investigation.

Before I closed my eyes, I thought I would do something a bit unorthodox. I invited Mary Houghton to contact me by way of a dream visitation. On a previous investigation, I had the unwanted experience of being visited in my dreamtime slumber by a spirit. It was an extremely accurate and vivid replay of the earlier encounter, the markings of a true dream visitation, and it was an experience that I would rather have avoided. This time, in the sake of seeking answers I was inviting Mary to pop in and give me an idea of why she is still at the mansion. Not much has been documented regarding the life of Mary, except for the car accident and the rumors that persists regarding her life. So I tried to open up my mind to allow for her, or even Mr. Houghton to appear and chat. I did not invite John Widders to the party, because based on my experience in his room earlier that evening; I didn't need his unstable emotions invading my psyche.

Unfortunately, I woke up with no memory of anything interesting. I realize that Mary was from a different era; maybe asking her to visit me in my dreams on a second investigation was too forward. Maybe I had a psychic slap to my cheek for being rude. It would have been interesting to be able to interact that way, but alas, it was not meant to be.

What I did wake up with, however, was an idea. For some reason there was new and strong urgency to write a book about the mansion and the lives that called her home. It felt like I had to write about the family and the struggles they faced and the lives they lived. I realized at the time that I barely scratched the surface bringing their story to light. I had to do more. Where this thought came from, I do not know. Could it have been planted as I had opened myself for a dream visitation? Could this idea finally let the members get the validation they may have been seeking in order for them to feel free to move on in their spiritual journey?

When we woke up, bed-head and all, we started to gather all of the equipment that was scattered throughout the mansion. The motion-sensor infrared camcorders were plugged into operational outlets and the lights were blinking letting me know that there was data stored on the memory cards. I mention this as you will later find out that we were sabotaged. I was giddy with anticipation on what was on those memory cards.

We began our journey back home. As I was driving down the state routes and interstate highways, all I could think about was the possibilities of what we captured on those memory cards. The movement in the temple, seeing who or what physically turned off the camcorder switch. The digital voice recorders left throughout the mansion, what sounds did they pick up while we were asleep?

All the possibilities were prancing around in my head like I was a child on Christmas Eve. Did we finally capture that Holy Grail of evidence? Do we have any information from our EVP sessions that finally answer deep questions? How the hell do I start writing a book? All of these thoughts and questions were swirling in my sleep-deprived head. How we got home, I have no clue. Oh, and we picked up the kids? Funny I don't recall. There were no dents in the car, no police chasing us, no broken arms or limbs, so I guess I drove okay.

So as soon as we got home, I giddily put one of the memory cards into a computer to get a sneak peak at what was there. Nothing. The card was blank. Then I put the other card in, again, empty. Suddenly, my euphoria was replaced by devastation.

Now I must spend a couple of moments disputing the easy diagnosis. The motion-sensor infrared cameras write immediately to the memory card. Say if power was disrupted, the current fifteen-second clip would not be written but all other data would be preserved. To physically erase a card, you have to go into the menu and choose a bunch of options with the obligatory "hey knucklehead, you sure you want to do this?" prompt. The monitor was also put away so it would have been very difficult to navigate the menus without a monitor. This was no user error, they make these things idiot-proof. While there, someone not living was manipulating the equipment I had, turning off the switch on one, my handheld camcorder was being manipulated as I was holding it. To me, it seems like some secrets were meant to be kept secrets. Was there a secretive spirit who with their energy wiped the cards clean? I learned during our visit in 2014 that this happened to another group, so this made me feel a bit better that we were not the only lucky ones.

The good news is several months later using software I was able to recover data on one of the cards. I was not disappointed. The other card, however, is useless. The one card I could not recover was the one that was in the device in Widders' room, the temple, and by the main staircase. All that data – gone forever. But what I did recover from the other card is interesting.

When I had the camcorder in the basement, there was an odd voice. At the time everyone was in the temple and our voices did not carry down to the basement. I have hours of video footage and audio from digital recorders proving our voices did not carry into the basement from the temple. The voice sounds female and it sounds like it is saying "Doctor McCrean" or "Doctor McClean" or a name similar. After conducting extensive research, the closest resemblance we found was that John Widders had relatives with the name of "McLean".

Also in the basement we captured a giggle from a little girl. Not a demonic little girl, mind you, but a typical little girl who likes to play games. I cannot prove that this giggle is from the little girl who is often active in the basement, the odds are high though. Was this the same spirit who was having some fun with us later that evening? We can never know for sure.

The more interesting video clips, however, came from the time we had this camcorder adjacent the kitchen entrance facing the hallway with the stairs to the basement. It seems there was a very active spirit from 4:50 to just before seven in the morning. There was no way a person who was living could have done these without being seen. The camcorder was positioned so that there was no way someone can sneak by it. Even if someone had the ability to scale the ceiling, the ceiling was in view too. The only people who knew this camcorder was set up were Christiana and I, everyone else was asleep when we planted the traps. So if anyone was trying to be funny they would have been caught unsuspecting of our video presence.

The first thing that can be heard is the sound of a noise in the kitchen. This noise was a bit interesting as it sounds like a cabinet door being shut. About fifteen minutes later, we recorded the sound of something heavy being dragged across a floor. Almost twenty minutes later there were more sounds of something heavy being dragged and a few seconds after that the sounds of what sounds like someone rummaging through a cabinet or drawer.

The most interesting is that a light in the kitchen was turned on and then off several minutes later. Again, there was no way someone could have sneaked by the camcorder without being seen. Even if someone did, their footsteps would have been captured on audio placed throughout the area. As if whatever was rearranging furniture was not happy, a few minutes later more dragging of a heavy object could be heard. Then the last bit, a strange rhythmic banging that we could rule out being the plumbing or heating systems. While we did not capture the Holy Grail, a full-bodied apparition, we did capture some truly odd phenomenon.

For a second time, Houghton Mansion surely did not disappoint.

13. Why They Remain

There is a lot of information out there regarding the haunting of Houghton Mansion with several different theories as to why the departed did not enter the light. Some theories seem reasonable, while others seem far-fetched. A word of caution, no one can state definitely why there are spirits who remain in the walls of Houghton Mansion. To date, I am confident that the spirits did not provide that one answer that we are all seeking.

Is the Houghton Mansion haunted? Based on the three nights our group spent there, I would say that there is definitely some energy present. I believe that there are both intelligent spirits and residual energy present within the walls. Will the haunting of Houghton Mansion end if the Houghtons or Widders move on into the light? I believe that as a result of continuous investigations, more spirits will be drawn to the mansion, hoping that they too can be validated. It is also a fear of mine that the investigations may also invite a darker energy that can cause havoc on visitors as well as any spirits that remain in the mansion.

To my knowledge we only received one response when we asked for a name at the mansion and that was what sounded like a little boy named Phillip. No one volunteered their names as being Albert C. Houghton, Mary Cordelia Houghton, John Widders or Winters. I can infer from responses gathered that Albert is a strong possibility for being present as we were told to "get out of my house", and we were receiving EVPs when we were addressing Albert about his life. We were also getting experiences when we discussed anything that he would have held near and dear.

Since information from the spirits is often very vague, I can only take stabs at an explanation as to why they may remain. I have thought of a few scenarios. The truth is, there is no main reason the spirits may remain, and it is more likely a combination of many different factors. Life is not cut-and-dry, it is complicated and as such there is never really a simple reason why a spirit may choose to remain. Below are my thoughts regarding possibilities. These are not meant to sound as if they are an end-all discussion, but merely an opening of discussion as to the simple main question – "Why?"

Laura

One of the most widely reported spirits present at Houghton Mansion is a little girl who is thought to be very active in the basement as well as parts of the first floor. This spirit is generally referred to as Laura, although I am unaware how this name was assigned to this energy. We tried many times to verify what this girl's name may be. I must caution you, just because we did not capture a voice identifying herself as "Laura" does not mean I am insinuating otherwise – I just like to have my own evidence before I come to a conclusion.

Many times a spirit is assigned a name for several reasons. Some spirits are given a name by the living because "it seems to fit". Other times people assume there is a spirit present because there was a specific event, such as a tragic death at a location. Even if someone were to get a name either as an EVP or on a spirit box, I would be cautious as that name may have come from a spirit that is only there temporarily as a result of an investigation pulling in energy. It is even possible they could be providing a false name, or saying the name of someone who is living to validate their awareness of our realm.

Without knowing exactly what her true identity is, it is nearly impossible for anyone to assign an explanation as to why she remains walking on the first floor and lurking in the shadows within a dark and spooky basement. Some people hear the name "Laura" and they automatically assume that this spirit is the first-born child of Albert and Cordelia Houghton. I would be confident in stating that the little girl is not Laura Cordelia Houghton. One reason is that Laura passed away in 1871, decades before the land was associated with the Houghton family. The Houghtons at the time of Laura's passing were living in Stamford, Vermont. There are also reports from several people who claimed to have seen the spirit of the little girl within the basement. Those lucky enough to see her describe her as being anywhere from six to eleven years old, far too old to be Laura as she passed when she was three years old. Now it could be possible that spirits can project as being older, as spirits can sometimes appear younger or more intimidating.

We were lucky enough to capture two EVPs (electronic voice phenomena) from within the basement that appeared to be from a little girl. Again, the EVPs seem to come from a girl that sounded considerably older than a three-year old.

Then exactly who is this little girl? There are many possibilities as to why this little girl remains. I will touch on some of the more likely explanations. It is possible that this girl's spirit is attached to the land or structure and that her family lived at this location before the Houghtons, Blackintons and Cadys took ownership of the land.

It is entirely possible that the spirit of this girl became attached to the structure because she felt comfortable in this location. We have seen a scenario in another investigation where a little girl moved into a private residence because she felt comfortable around the family. This is known to happen and the spirit can either be comfortable with the family dynamic or of a certain individual. A spirit can move to a location with strangers where there is a familiarity to their own life. If that is the case, maybe after the person she connected with moved on, she somehow remained.

As we will discuss later, maybe this little girl was pulled in with all the paranormal investigations. Spirits often feel isolated and jump at the chance to have some interaction. Put yourself in the shoes of a spirit, if you lived alone in a house and no one calls or no one stops by to visit, what happens to the first person you see? You talk their ear off. While they try to get away, you follow them chasing after their vehicle until you realize that you are out of your comfort zone – you become frightened and confused, so you remain hoping that someone will help you find your way. This can happen to a spirit.

The girl's energy may have been attached to an object that was brought into the mansion. While this seems strange, it does happen. This is the phenomenon where someone goes antiquing and finds out that they brought home much more than an armoire.

I will go even further down the depths of scenarios. This is thought to happen, but can be somewhat rare. Some believe a spirit, especially one that is particularly strong and has knowledge of how to do incredible things, can appear in a form they wish to be seen. Sometimes a truly harmless spirit that just wants to be left alone can take on an ominous form, just so people would leave them alone.

What if the little girl is actually Mary or another spirit associated with the family that wants to be seen in happier times? I bring this up because some have documented this as happening. Whether it is true or not, we may never know. I theorize below about Mary prior to her death and a small part of me wonders if this little girl is a manifestation of Mary who wishes to be seen in happier and simpler times. Maybe she wants to go back to have a chance to have fun. Growing up a Houghton in the spotlight must have put enormous pressure on a little girl to live up to high standards. What if Mary wants to be a kid again if she felt that she was prevented from having a carefree childhood?

What if Mary was happiest as a child? A lifetime of potential ahead, lofty goals and dreams that sadly never came to fruition. As Mary got older, she must have realized that her dreams may never come true. Instead of appearing as a moping adult, maybe she wants to be seen as a mischievous little girl with the promise of hopes and dreams gleaning in her eyes?

One thing I learned as a paranormal investigator is to never throw out a possibility until you at least look into it. These things have a way of surprising closed-minded people. If you keep an open mind you are less likely to be shocked and more accepting of what others may find preposterous. And just in case you were wondering, no – I did not eat lead paint chips as a child, I do not wear a foil hat, and while I may have fallen off of a few things, I never fell off of my rocker. Do I think it is Mary? No, but it could be a remote possibility.

Mary Houghton

A tragic death does not automatically mean that a spirit will fail to cross over into the light. I believe that for the most part, someone who experiences a death as tragic as Mary's will move on into the light in a relatively short timeframe. So why is Mary thought to be walking the halls of Houghton Mansion a century after her death?

As I mentioned earlier, I cannot state whether Mary is actually at the mansion. I had no one walk up to us saying "Hi, I'm Mary Houghton". But I also cannot state definitively that she is not in the mansion. How does one prove that a spirit does not exist? Do I think her presence is likely? Yes, I think it is possible that Mary has not yet found peace and comfort.

The experience that I was able to have first-hand which makes me think it is possible for Mary to be present was the disembodied female voice that I heard twice in 2011. I heard a woman speak in the kitchen when no one was present, then hours later I heard the same exact voice at the base of the main staircase on the first floor. This second time, the voice was accompanied by a very bright light.

It is a stretch to claim that this voice was indeed attributed to Mary. The truth is that it could have been the voice of another spirit that is either tied to the location or was drawn in as a result of either our investigation or the series of investigations that take place within the mansion. The female presence could be another member of the Houghton family since Mary was not the only female to live in the household. One possibility that I cannot get out of my head is the idea that Cordelia may be present to try to guide her husband and Mary towards the light.

I believe that since very little information is known about Mary, people feel the need to concoct stories about her to give her an identity. Because we do not know the absolute reason she would remain behind, our imaginations begin to create her life story. One common rumor why Mary possibly remains behind is because her secret lover John Widders refuses to pass into the light. Granted, that makes for an interesting storyline, one in which you would typically see in a soap opera. I hold a theory near and dear in my heart that life is often more mundane than soap operas.

I mentioned earlier that I do not give the Mary and Widders romance much thought. Frankly this is because I believe it is not true. I have no evidence stating my position, just as those that believe it do not have any facts supporting their theory. For me, personally, I think the pairing up of Mary Houghton and John Widders is highly unlikely for several reasons.

First and foremost, there was a tremendous difference in economic standing. For the most part, people tend to gravitate towards others that are similar to them. As unusual as it is today, it was much more infrequent in Mary's era. The Houghton family married within their social and economic status - that is not debatable. While John Widders was a respected family employee, I cannot fathom Albert C. Houghton approving of such a relationship, but I could be wrong.

As such I cannot see Mary, "Daddy's little girl" risking scorn and alienation from her father for a man twice her age. Would John Widders, a loyal employee risk alienation from his long-time employer and someone he highly regarded? Would John be interested romantically in a woman he witnessed growing up from a small child? Would Mary be interested in someone who has been with the family so long that he must have seemed like an uncle or cousin, or simply what he was – hired help?

I may be completely off, but I have several thoughts that have popped into my mind I would be more than willing to accept versus the soap opera love story. Instead of Mary remaining behind because of John's refusal to move on, maybe she is remaining behind to be with her father. In life, Mary sacrificed her future so that she could take care of her ailing father. Instead of meeting a husband and having a family of her own, she nurtured her father when he needed it. It could be that this dedication to her father remains to this very day. Albert C. Houghton fails to move on, and the doting daughter remains as well, either trying to help him focus on getting to the other side or trying to care for him in the state that he is currently in. It certainly supports the theory that people maintain their personalities even after death.

Can the situation of Mary giving up her dreams of finding her Prince Charming and having children create an issue of regret? It sure could. If Mary sacrificed so much to help in the care of her ill father, I would assume that she had a very strong motherly instinct within the fabric of her soul. Toward the end of her life, she could have started to regret the fact that she had no children or husband of her own to care for. Maybe this feeling of regret is so strong that when she died she lost focus on crossing over and fails to see the light because she is too focused on her feelings of losing out on the blessed miracle of motherhood and all the joys it brings. Yes, I do have children so stop snickering, most of the time it is a blessing.

Her last few days of her life were spent with her childhood friend Sybil and Sybil's two-year old son. Obviously, the sight of her friend doting over a toddler would have made Mary wonder what could have been. Since I believe that Mary had this motherly-instinct ingrained inside of her, this scene must have been difficult for her to bear. On the day of the accident, Mary also saw Sybil with her husband and it would have been very natural human reaction for Mary to be a bit jealous.

By not having a family, Mary could feel unfulfilled, like she could have done more with her life. Is there a feeling of resentment that she, under her own power, may have let go of her dreams? If she started to feel resentment towards her plight maybe a strong feeling of guilt set in as she realized her resentment towards her father. This guilt alone could possibly make her lose her focus onto moving on.

Can Mary be saddled with all the grief the family lived through? That again is possible. As we discovered throughout this narrative, there are many instances where loved ones were lost tragically. Mary lost a sister, and several nieces and nephews. To be killed tragically could have been that final straw, the one where her grief became too severe to be able to let go and find eternal peace, love and comfort.

Maybe Mary is remaining behind at the mansion because that is where she is the most comfortable. Besides her time spent in Europe, she seemed to be closest to her family most times. She knew no other existence. She never really moved away from home, never got to start her own household, her own family, that existence is the only one she knows. Could she be used to or prefer the isolation of her current existence? Maybe she is fearful to move into the light and start a new phase of existence because she is used to the one she is in now.

There is also a theory in which a spirit that has already crossed over into the light may be able to return and then get so wrapped up in whatever brought them back that they become trapped. Could this have happened to Mary? Could she have returned to help her father cross over and then get so caught up in that cause, that she lost her way? It is also possible that Mary already passed into the light and returns in an attempt to move on her father and John Widders. Maybe she already passed and what we experience is her residual energy.

Maybe she is trying to help John Widders cross. With John, I am thinking they have a plutonic relationship where she generally cares for his well-being and is trying to help him through his regret and guilt over her own death. It could be that Mary feels that her death is responsible for John's grief and his failure to pass on. As we discovered, John was a long-time employee of the Houghton family and as such he may have been treated as part of the family. Maybe Mary is not at peace because she feels responsible for John's current degraded condition.

Personally, I believe the reason that Mary remains behind is a combination of the reasons above, and possibly even more reasons that only Mary knows. As part of our human nature, we want simplified answers, but we are complex. I mentioned that life is more mundane than a soap opera, but we are also more complicated than having just one answer.

I do not get the sense of Mary being the tragic figure. When we felt that we may have been around energy in her room, the atmosphere in the room seemed to be peaceful and calm. We did not experience the traits of a haunting where a spirit is tormented. Her room seemed to have a warm feeling to it. Quite often when I come into contact with a spirit who is not in a great frame of mind, I can get antsy and start to pace as I can feel their energy. Mary's room is one of the few in the mansion where I feel at ease and that I can sit down and almost fall asleep from the comfortable and quiet space, even when there was activity.

Some groups have presented evidence from Mary's room that is contrary to this peaceful and calm feeling. Who am I to question how the atmosphere was in the room when they went? For all I know, our experiences were out of the ordinary and Mary is typically a nervous wreck. But I also think that a possibility for these episodes of traumatic screams or crying could be something different – residual energy.

If Mary does indeed remain, we may never know the reason or reasons why. Regardless the reason, I truly believe that Mary is best served moving to the light and enjoying a reunion with her loved ones and an everlasting existence of unconditional peace, love, and comfort.

Albert C. Houghton

Albert C. Houghton was a tyrant! Did I grab your attention? Mr. Houghton was not really a tyrant; in fact he was described as a deeply compassionate man who was very interested in the welfare of his family, his workers and his community. If he was a tyrant, it was only to himself. Albert C. Houghton is a man who in his own eyes could always do better and achieve more for his adopted community. For him, the sky really was the limit and failure was out of the question because too many people depended on his success. There was always a cause to fight and a problem to solve. He did not sit idly by while the world passed him by. If his spirit lingers at the mansion, it is probably because he felt there was still so much left unfinished and he still had a job to do.

Out of any intelligent responses we had the pleasure to capture at Houghton Mansion, the one that was most significant came from the bedroom of Mr. Houghton. As I was addressing him during an EVP session I asked him if he remains because of the fact that everything he worked so hard for is now gone. The response we received was a solemn, if not resigned "yes". His vast business empire that fueled the regional economy is gone. His vision of a metropolis fueled by a strong manufacturing base is gone. Most importantly, his pride and his joy, his family members, are also gone.

Albert C. Houghton seemed to be an extreme Type-A personality, which I believe has a substantial higher risk of remaining behind when their physical vessels perish. His business empire, which provided a high quality of living for his family, was also incredibly important to the community as thousands of them were employees of his own companies. He sought a vibrant community, and with the death of his beloved Arnold Print Works, he may feel that he let down his community.

How much responsibility did Albert C. Houghton feel when his business empire faced financial difficulty in 1907? As you recall, he lost his daughter Alice the year previously. Did he feel that his business judgment was impaired when he took the bold move of procuring an extraordinarily large amount of raw material before a financial scandal nearly wiped out the national economy? Because of that decision and an unexpected recession and drop in the prices of cotton, his company was in serious trouble, jeopardizing the employment of thousands. It was impossible to foresee the

1907 economic troubles, but in Albert's mind, did he feel an unfair share of the blame? Does he think that the past financial situation hurt the company decades later when it was forced to close? It can be an anchor.

Is Albert Houghton remaining behind because he feels that the community cannot move forward without him? Would crossing over into that light be an admission of defeat? He could be so consumed on this realm that he fails to see where he truly needs to go.

Could Albert C. Houghton be held back by regret? Both Cordelia and Albert had a nagging feeling about the roadway where the car accident occurred. They knew it was very dangerous, but Houghton plowed ahead without reconsidering the route. Being a paranormal investigator, I cannot help but wonder if a degree of premonition by Cordelia and/or Albert occurred and he is now regretting not listening to that nagging feeling.

By ignoring his intuition, his little girl was taken from him. Place yourself in his shoes. Whenever something bad happens in our lives, we often think about the "what-ifs". Some of us can be consumed by these questions. Albert witnessed first-hand the death of a young wife and mother. He inevitably thought of their child who would grow up without knowing his mother. He witnessed his daughter's excruciating pain as she was dying, and there was nothing he could do. He buried his daughter, another child taken far too soon. Then he had to bear the suicide of his trusted employee who was consumed by grief.

As Houghton lie dying, maybe he thought of little Robert, not having his mother's kisses or hugs. I am sure he heard the hysterical cries of Robert Hutton as he stayed with the lifeless body of his wife. Who knows what images flashed through his mind from the accident scene? He saw Mary's casket. John's casket. Sybil's casket.

"What if… we did not go?

"What if… we took another route?

Hindsight is 20/20, but it is these questions that can linger in our minds and make us go mad. Could it be Albert Houghton did not move on because he feels responsible for the deaths of everyone from that day? It was Albert who convinced John Widders that he could drive a car, even though John was very uncomfortable with the idea.

Is he consumed with guilt that his daughter Mary did not live the life of her sisters who found love and gave birth to children? As parents, we are supposed to take care of our children, not vice versa. Did he see his daughter Mary with two-year old Robert Hutton Jr. in the days leading up to the accident and saw the image of "what-if"?

"What if... my health had not failed, would she be holding her own toddler right now?"

"What if... I was firm and begged her to not worry about me? I'll be fine."

Can Albert C. Houghton choose not to leave his beloved home because his home is a symbol of his past importance to the community? He did build himself up from the son of a humble farming family to a very influential businessman and community leader. That prominence is now gone and is he afraid that once he enters that light, he would just be a mere footnote in the history of the community he loved? By him moving on, does that admit failure as he is walking away without a spirited fight?

"What if... the community needs me?"

"What if... no one remembers me?"

It could also be that while Albert C. Houghton was slipping out of his life, he realized just how quick life truly is. While he placed an emphasis on his family, his time and attention were pulled in many different directions. There were of course his many business interests, his political interests, his involvement in charities, the banking interests, the rail interests, the educational interests, being a Mayor. Where exactly did that leave for time with his wife and children? As he buried his youngest child, and third overall, did he regret not spending more time with his own children?

"What if... I spent more time with my kids?"

Cordelia Houghton

Some may be surprised that I am discussing Cordelia as she is hardly mentioned as being a possibility for any of the activity that is experienced within Houghton Mansion. Although she is not discussed as a central figure in the tragic car accident that took place on August 1, 1914, she lost her youngest child and her husband as a result of his injuries sustained in the wreck. Cordelia experienced the death of four people in a short amount of time, including John Widders, the family employee and Sybil Hutton, a friend of the family.

Cordelia also had to experience all the heartbreak that we have discussed throughout this book. It was not Albert C. Houghton alone who had to deal with all the tragedy throughout the years. It baffles me that more do not at least consider the possibility that Cordelia may have left residual energy or is responsible for some of the activity.

Cordelia was the matriarch of the family. While much is made of Albert Houghton's business and community work, people often forget Cordelia's role. She was a strong influence in Houghton's life, a true partner. While Albert was busy running a business and a community, it was Cordelia who would raise the family. Cordelia was also the matriarch of Houghton Mansion. When one would enter the mansion, she would welcome their visitors and make them feel comfortable.

I think back to the woman's voice I heard at the bottom of the main staircase. When I heard this voice, I looked at the source of the sound and there was an amazing bright light where the voice came from. I wonder if this may be Cordelia making her presence known from within the light. Why then would she appear to us?

When spirits are trapped, there are often other spirits that are present that attempt to help their loved ones cross into the light on the other side. When we attempt to move spirits on in private residences, we often call on those spirits within the light to help us with their loved ones. They are often there already however, trying to help. What happens is that the trapped spirit can become so focused on this realm or so focused on whatever anchor is binding them here that they fail to recognize or even see that their loved ones are trying to help. We often try to break that focus and ask spirits to concentrate on the voice or face of their loved ones. The theory is that this change of focus with the help of their loved ones can literally help them "see the light".

Could this amazing light have been Cordelia letting herself be seen in an attempt to show us that Albert is truly not alone and that she is there attempting to get Albert and Mary to pass on? I believe it is a strong possibility.

Cordelia may have also left her impact on the mansion inadvertently. She may have left residual energy at the mansion. As you discovered, the Houghton family faced a number of hardships during their lives, she was a mother, a grandmother, an aunt, a sister. When we looked at their lives, remember that each event could have left an imprint on the mansion that can be experienced to this very day.

It is possible that the energy from Cordelia is present from within the light, trying her best to bring her family back together in Heaven. As she was the matriarch and responsible for raising her family, her energy may not feel complete until everyone she loves is at peace and comfort. As investigators continually enter her home, she may be trying to get their attention, letting them know that she is indeed present and is trying to save her family. Here's hoping they reunite sooner rather than later. I believe we have more to do with that than we think.

On an interesting note, I went to a medium for the first time in my life, and the topic of this project was brought up without giving any details of the subject matter or any other detail. The medium I saw was able to describe Houghton Mansion to a tee. She then described Cordelia as being a strong presence in the mansion, not as a trapped spirit, but as one who entered the light. Cordelia watches people come and go in her old home and she is still the matriarch of the home. She may even be the spirit responsible for planting the seed which led to this particular project. I hope and pray that I was able to achieve what she wanted me to.

John Widders

Whenever I say or write his name, I feel that I should put an asterisk besides his name. This is because in truth, he is John Winters. Since everyone knows him as John Widders, for the sake of this effort, I will refer to him as that.

The common thought is that John Widders' spirit is still present at Houghton Mansion because of the guilt he has over the death of Sybil Hutton and Mary Houghton. Some believe that he remains because of his suicide and the fear of judgment he believes will be incurred upon his soul as retribution for the taking of his own life. Quite often those who committed suicide are a bit fearful of what lies on the other side. These tormented souls are especially reluctant to take that next step into unconditional peace.

I believe that it is more than likely that John has not passed into the other side because his spirit is trapped in his death state and relives the same emotional torment that he experienced prior to his suicide over and over again. He may feel that he has already been judged and that his punishment is largely deserved, although we usually judge ourselves most harshly.

When investigating, I try to place myself in the shoes of whatever spirit we attempt to encounter. In John's case I have trouble fully understanding the amount of guilt and grief that his spirit is enduring. While he was legally cleared in any wrongdoing in regards to the deaths of Sybil and Mary, he has already judged himself as being solely responsible for their deaths. Life can be so cruel in that, within a split second, a happy leisurely drive can turn into a tragic nightmare that John Widders is forced to relive.

When I place myself in his shoes, I see and hear some truly horrifying images and sounds. Imagine coming across a scene in a roadway in which you change course to avoid an obstacle. That moment you realize that something is terribly wrong; the automobile starts to tumble down the embankment. You are tossed from the vehicle, but you hear the sounds of the automobile crashing down the embankment, the screams of those as they are tossed about.

When you come to and realize what just happened, you see a husband running to his dead or dying wife. You hear his cries, you see him hold her. You may even see her, badly crushed as the result of an automobile rolling over her. You see the wrecked car with a young woman slumped in the rear seat. You see an employer who treated you like family, badly hurt, but trying to attend to his daughter. If you ran to the car, you immediately see the aftermath of the accident with Mary's badly broken and bloodied face.

You hear the voices of the workmen, who you originally tried to avoid, running down the embankment seeing the tragedy first-hand. You watch helplessly as time seems to be at a standstill while Mary's condition deteriorates. You still hear the sobbing of a husband, you think of their child. Finally hours later, you are within the property of the family. You hear the reaction when it is discovered that Mary passed away. You now hear the sobs of her family. You may even have caught a glimpse of her lifeless body depending on when she was returned to her home.

Your friends arrive and try to console you, but there is no hope. There's no way I can continue you think to yourself. What have I done? You reach a point where you think that ending it all is far less painful than to deal with the situation at hand. Those moments before you pull that trigger, those are the thoughts that your spirit will grab hold of.

Now take all of those emotions, and add on the fact that you have been isolated for nearly a century. All those that you cared about are no longer there. We all have a necessity to socialize, some more than others. Picture this need to communicate, but there is a huge disconnect, people cannot not effectively see or hear you. After a while even the strongest wills can be broken. Then add to that the fact that strangers are constantly walking in and making you relive that terrible moment. Some may even try to provoke you by accusing you of blame – your own worst fear. You become bitter on top of all the other emotions you felt.

Think about all these emotions, and then think about what John Widders went through as a child. A childhood that he thought was so bad that he changed his name and began to invent stories. Imagine learning that your father left your family. Any child has a thought "Is it my fault?" Then your mother, the woman who gave birth to you, the woman who nurtured you no longer wants you. At that point you are too young to understand that your mother could not afford to raise a family by herself. You then find yourself being taken care of by strangers. When your mother was remarried, she did not beckon for you; you were left alone in what you felt were conditions you should not endure. How can you forgive someone so easily who did this to you? How can you forgive yourself for taking your own life? How can you forgive yourself for the accident that changed so many lives? Why won't these people leave me be with my own thoughts?

This could be what John Widders endures each and every hour of each and every day. While it sounds bad, we can only guess at what he is feeling, we are not in his shoes.

When his mother passed away, is she a spirit that is trying to get her son into the light? She knows what was in her heart when she gave her son up, but to John Widders, did he turn his back on her like he perceives she did to him?

Did John Widders see that light and fear what was going to happen to him since he committed suicide? Did he feel that he would somehow be judged for the deaths of Sybil and Mary? Was he so inconsolable that he already judged himself and feels that this is his punishment? Did he give up on the dream of unconditional love, comfort and peace that one experiences in the light?

One theory that I just cannot get out of my head, is not so much why he remains, but why he is so grief stricken. As you may recall John's father abandoned the family not long after John's birth. His own mother, who could not afford to take care of the family, sent John to his uncle who placed him under the care of Shakers in New York. When John's mother was remarried, she did not send for him, instead leaving him in the care of strangers. John had no sense of family growing up – it was not until John met Albert C. Houghton that John experienced what family is all about.

Both Albert and Cordelia Houghton were taught from an early age that family is the most important part of one's existence. As such, the Houghtons took care of their family. John being a trusted employee was like part of the family. He witnessed the Houghton children grow up and have their own families. When John needed a place to stay, it was Houghton who welcomed him to live within the family's property. The Houghton family gave John something he never had – a sense of family. The strongest indication was that the Houghton family gave John a spot in the family plot after he died. In death, he became one of them, the family for which he worked for decades; he will now eternally be with them in burial.

John Widders had built himself a sizable estate. He had been for decades someone who dealt with horses – that was his specialty. When Widders continued to work for the Houghton family, times were changing. Instead of horses with their own level of intelligence John was tasked with learning to drive a cold piece of steel, one without thought. Could Widders have thought that he was becoming an antique and unable to keep up with advances? Pride is a powerful feeling, and one inherently needs to feel useful. With John Widders very uncomfortable with an automobile, did he think about retirement? He did build up a sizable nest egg to live off of. I assume that he quickly dismissed retirement because the Houghton's provided him that sense of family he was seeking his entire life and if he retired he would be abandoning his family.

But in the sake of keeping his job and being close to the closest thing he had to a family dynamic he chose to deal with his discomfort of modern technology and learn to drive a car. As he replayed the accident in his head I wonder if this thought came into his head, "I have no place in the modern world for I am a relic." This idea may come to mind to someone outpaced by technology. We see it often in industries where older workers feel intimidated by younger counterparts whose ideas, on the surface, seem fresher. But for Widders, that decision to continue on led to a terrible accident that saw his "family" torn apart.

I cannot get into the head of John Widders, when I visited, I felt what think was just a small fraction of the pain and torment he is still feeling. It was evident that John loved the family and was touched that the Houghton family treated him so well – especially when his real family did not. They gave him a home; they gave him a healthy dose of what a family should be. The pain and torment is strong because John shouldered the blame for destroying the family that provided him something he was seeking his entire life – a sense of belonging. And now John cannot forgive himself for what happened, he believes the blood is on his hands. For John Widders, he was his own judge, jury and executioner.

Daniel Ringwood

Even though we found no evidence of the spirit of Daniel Ringwood, I cannot state for certain that his spirit is not there based on only two investigations. His tragic death while constructing the mansion could have left some residual energy – whether or not that residual energy is still active is also at question. Residual energy will replay itself out. Some residual hauntings can be very quick to very lengthy lasting for decades and even centuries.

If Daniel's spirit is truly restless, there is no guarantee that he would be present at the site of his death. Some spirits will gravitate towards locations that meant something significant – a favorite spot, a childhood home or their own home, just to name a few. If I died at work, and can move about, the last place I would be is at work – especially if that is where I met my end.

My hope is that he was not present at the mansion and that he found that light and moved on. His tie to the mansion was forgotten with the passage of time, and the theory was that if he was indeed present and was largely ignored for well over a century, I thought he would be very eager to communicate when someone called out for him. Since that did not happen, part of me wants to believe that he did move on.

I do not necessarily buy into the theory that all cases of tragic death automatically means that a spirit is trapped. A spirit becomes trapped when they have emotional anchors holding them back. I also do not buy that when one dies instantly, they do not realize they are dead. I admit, this does happen, but it is extremely rare and is typically experienced by those spirits that may have been a bit delusional in their final moments. Most spirits know they are dead. After all, many of them saw their own lifeless body before them.

Henry A. Cady

Henry A. Cady is an interesting possibility for some of the activity at Houghton Mansion that I cannot discount at this point. Of course, his energy may not be present and this discussion is all a stretch. Henry, of course, as we learned earlier was Sybil's uncle. Henry has several risk factors that we look at as we consider a location's history and the possibility of paranormal activity. I am discussing Henry because sometimes we can walk into a location with a preconceived notion of who may be present and then walk away surprised that there was in fact someone else responsible for the activity since spirits can be coy and not give their identity

Henry Cady does have a connection with the land that the Houghton Mansion and the Masonic lodge currently sit on. As a child, Henry and his family called the property home. It is unclear if the house was located on the foundation that Houghton Mansion was built on. Sometimes a spirit can go back to a location that had a significant meaning to them. It is not out of the question that Henry's energy went back to his former childhood property as that may have been a source of happy memories that his soul desperately wants to connect with.

While he has a link to the property, there are a few other factors which raise a red flag when I looked into his history. As with John Widders, Henry A. Cady committed suicide and as discussed previously, someone who commits suicide has a much higher risk factor for remaining behind. What also stands out is where he committed suicide, just across the street from the Houghton Mansion in the home of W.G. Cady, Sybil's father.

The factor that really raises the red flag for me was the state of Henry's mind before he committed suicide. In his younger years he was a very proud and intelligent person. As his health started to deteriorate, he had to retire which caused him to become depressed because he really disliked being idle. He seemed to be exhibiting signs of mental deterioration in his final years of his life. This could have been the impacts of either dementia or Alzheimer's disease. As we know now, by not stimulating the mind, the mind's deterioration can be more rapid.

In the years before his death, he became very restless and started to act erratically. He started to discuss how there was a vast conspiracy against the Cady family, and his family became very concerned regarding this mental health. Finally it got to be too much, so Henry committed suicide. Unlike John Widders, his death would not have been instantaneous. Henry slit his own throat with a safety razor. I cannot imagine the thoughts that crossed his mind in the timeframe between when he sliced his throat and when he died. Unlike a bullet to the head, there is time to second-guess what was just done.

So why would I think his energy has a legitimate chance of being active within the mansion? First of all, he committed suicide and as discussed with Widders there is sometimes a hesitancy to enter the light because of fear of judgment. But I think the more likely reason was the state of Henry's mind before he committed suicide.

One interesting phenomenon that can happen as a result of someone living with dementia is something that I do not think would be at the mansion, but would occur in the home he spent his final years. It has nothing to do with a spirit or soul, but of energy that is released by someone with such a disease. We discussed residual energy and residual haunts earlier, this is a bit different, but the concept is similar. People with strong mental disease or degenerative diseases can release a great deal of strong and negative energy. This energy can remain over time and attract or manifest an entity that can utilize this negative energy for its own gain. I know it sounds a bit kooky, but hear me out.

Have you ever been in a situation where there has been a fight in a room, you may not even have known about it at the time. You walk into the location and the air seems thick, there seems to be some sort of residual tension in the air. You knew something just happened, but you don't know what. This is what I mean by negative energy filling a space. With someone who is battling mental illness, this repeats itself over and over again, so this energy can multiply and cause some really odd paranormal events – potentially dangerous. This is one of the reasons why abandoned asylums lure in trespassers; they know these locations are breeding grounds for paranormal events – although they may not understand exactly why.

These asylums are also ripe for activity for another reason, and this also relates to Henry, and this is why I think there is a possibility that he is present. Those with serious mental disorders are tormented in life. When they die, this continues. Spirits remain the same in death as they were in life, their condition does not improve as soon as they die. I do not want to sound grim; I believe their mental illness disappears once they enter the light. There is nothing but unconditional love, peace and comfort within the light and any ailment is automatically gone.

People who have serious mental issues can have a real difficulty entering the light. If they had delusions when alive, this remains in death until they cross over. In fact, their spirits can degrade rather easily because they were already mentally fragile, and death and isolation are far from ideal as is. Their already tormented souls become even more tormented when they become isolated. They can fail to recognize their exit – the light. They can even fail to think logically. Their energy can become very frenzied and degrade even further.

What is the worst that can happen? In rather dramatic cases, a spirit can degrade so much that they enter what is called the death-state. This is where their spirit relives those agonizing moments of their final moments over and over again. Whatever emotional duress they experience will replay and it is relentless, they seldom can find release in a timely manner in a state such as this. Someone in a death-state fails to recognize anything else going on around them; all they experience is great emotional strain, the likes of which I would not wish upon anyone. This death-state can occur in normally stable spirits, which is a concern of mine with the other spirits in the mansion and why I hope others show respect to the spirits present.

If the spirit of Henry is indeed still present, there is a good chance he may be at the mansion or appear from time to time. Paranormal investigations seem to lure nearby spirits into a location. Once they are there, they can leave after a short amount of time or they may choose to remain or could become trapped at that location. If Henry is nearby, he may sense an open invitation to communicate. If he does remain, he needs help and may be hoping to get a little assistance from those seeking to talk with the dead. His spirit may not be in the best of condition.

So when I think back to that creepy scream that we recorded in the temple, I cannot help but think, could that have been Henry? That scream was almost primal; it seemed to be full of strong negative emotion. It is a scream that continues to give me goose bumps when I replay the clip, even several years after the fact. Maybe the reports of a cranky spirit are true, but instead of cranky I would call it deeply troubled and in the need of help.

While I admit, it is only a possibility that his energy remains, I hope and pray that I am way off base and that Henry has found that light and that any impact of his mental health has been erased and he is enjoying his eternal comfort.

Houghton Mansion

Will Houghton Mansion ever quiet down? I do not believe it will under the present circumstances. There may be a time when Albert, Mary and John finally do find their way and enter the light, but when that happens, I think there will still be activity there. The players may change, but the game will stay the same. This also is not taking into account that some of the activity at the mansion is residual, meaning it will play itself out for many more years to come, with or without the intelligent spirits of the Houghton family members.

Some of you may not be aware what residual energy is. Truth is, it is a very difficult concept to grasp, even for those who consider themselves experts in this field. Residual energy is basically an imprint of an event or energy that replays itself throughout a period of time that can last for seconds to centuries and beyond. Residual energy has no intelligent features, meaning there is no logic, no awareness and no interaction. This is where it gets difficult. You may be asking yourself how energy can be imprinted.

If you think back to old recording media such as magnetic audio and video tapes, they all contain natural elements that are able to record information when a process oxidizes these elements. Since these elements are natural, they too exist in nature and thus things such as stone, wood and metal can have these elements that record this energy. If you ask me to explain oxidation of elements, you turned to the wrong person.

In locations where there are paranormal investigations, it is common to see an increase of activity. This is because those restless spirits that need to be heard will sense this open channel to communicate. They see it as an open invitation; as such more spirits may flock in. They are drawn to these locations as a beacon.

Unfortunately, with the increase of activity as a result of paranormal investigations, there may be a drawback, an increase in activity as a result of malevolent spirits or other darker entities. As with what I call the "harmless spirits" these other entities also sense an open invitation and can make an appearance briefly or can remain creating some serious issues, especially if investigations are done incorrectly. This is a phenomenon that has been documented in the past, but is increasing in reports as more and more paranormal groups pop up and do not realize what impact they may have.

Either way, for the betterment of the mansion, the spirits inside and to other visitors, I ask that you do your best to assure that everyone can have a safe and pleasant time at the mansion.

14. A Word about Investigating Houghton Mansion

For those of you that are interested in stepping into the historic Houghton Mansion to conduct a paranormal investigation, I hope that you too will appreciate the human stories that are contained in this book. My only hope and request is that you respect the memories and the legacy of the family whose spirits are thought to still be present within the walls.

My intent is not to get up onto a soapbox and preach, but to ask you to respect the fragile condition of the spirits that may inhabit the mansion. My fear is that the spirits contained in the home and temple are degraded or face additional hardship as a result of those who may not realize the real harm that the living can inflict upon the dead. We often think about how spirits and paranormal energy impacts us; we rarely think about the reverse, how we impact them. The spirits that are thought to remain in the walls of the mansion faced tremendous tragedy while alive and they are only facing even more hardship as they remain in a location they should not be. They should be in a place of eternal peace and comfort, not stuck in a state of limbo.

For me, I have a serious internal struggle when it comes to investigating places such as Houghton Mansion. The investigation is different than if we were investigating a family home, in which we have been called to help someone. When we investigate a location such as Houghton Mansion, I feel a bit guilty as it seems we are taking advantage of someone whose condition is less than ideal. We are not providing the help that is needed, but honing our investigative abilities. My main objective when entering a place such as this is to find out why some spirits remain. Frustratingly enough, the spirits hardly ever provide this valuable information. We seek these deep answers so that we may be able to help many others – both the living and to the spirits we encounter.

As I mentioned earlier, something drove me to write this book. I pushed other projects aside because it felt like a seed was planted in my mind that this project must be done. The sense is strong that this project was the right thing to do and this is something I had to do. As I researched the family, I felt it was more important to the spirits at Houghton Mansion to look out for their best interests as well. I felt the need to humanize these spirits and to get others to think about how their actions can impact them.

Whether you intend to investigate Houghton Mansion or another haunted location, the following suggestions can help you and the spirits have a productive investigation.

- Introduce Yourself

I realize that this small step seems kind of odd. Why is this important? It forms a level of trust between you and the spirit. Think of it this way, are you more than likely to respond to a stranger who tries to engage a conversation with you or are you more likely to respond to someone who politely introduces themselves. In eras past, it was considered very rude and aggressive to strike up a conversation with someone without properly introducing yourself.

- Ease Their Concern

This is an important step which will also strengthen a level of trust. Many times we go into locations with all sorts of equipment, flashing lights and all. Think of it this way, if you were lying in bed and a bunch of people storm in carrying equipment you have never seen, would you not be scared? Establish that level of trust. Ensure the spirits that you are not seeking to harm them in any way. State your objective in that you would like to talk with them. Ask that they do not harm you as well. For many spirits, we dress differently than they are accustomed to and we speak a little differently as well. Please keep this in mind and avoid slang too as they may not know what the heck you are 'lol'-ing. That equipment with the flashing lights, bells and whistles – assure them that the devices will not harm them in any way.

- Be Polite

"Please" and "Thank You" go a long way when you communicate with the living. The truth is, it works on the spirits as well. Think of it this way, if a stranger walks up to you on the street and said to you "I demand that you give me the time" you may walk away thinking to yourself what a jackass that person was to speak to you like that. You may even call him a jackass to his face. You are more than likely to assist if someone asks you nicely.

It also helps to never demand. When you demand something, you may get it; unfortunately it may be from a malevolent spirit or darker entity that will be happy to mess with you.

- Never Provoke!

I placed the exclamation point because one trend that I have been seeing that causes me great concern is when individuals or groups provoke in order to obtain some sort of reaction to post on their website or on the social media outlets. Part of this provoke-first scenario is being played out because of the popularity of a certain television program where you often do not see the consequences to their actions.

The best advice I can give you is to treat spirits as you would like to be treated. The "Golden Rule" works great in paranormal investigations as well – it is a rule I wish we all can subscribe to in life, but humans are not perfect creatures. If you have a warped sense of humor and actually enjoy if a stranger walks up to you and starts harassing you, try this exercise. Treat the spirits as you would a muscle-bound stranger you meet on a sidewalk. Would you walk up to someone who can twist you into a pretzel and start insulting them? I would hope not. If you do, we may be talking to your spirit and we will try to find out why you did that.

There are several different reasons I do not think it is wise to intentionally provoke a spirit. One reason is that they can lash out at you. Did you ever have a bad day and someone set you over the edge? Sometimes our emotions can get to the best of us, this holds true for those in the spiritual realm. To top it off, they are generally precariously close to snapping as they are dealing with issues that many of us do not know. First of all, they are

274 | 14. A Word about Investigating Houghton Mansion

dead and yes, most are aware of that fact. The spirits also have to deal with the isolationism of being separated from their loved ones, the difficulty of communicating with the living, and finally whatever emotional baggage that is preventing them from moving on all acts as kindling to the fire of an emotional breakdown.

Provoking spirits can have several consequences. If you intentionally (or even unintentionally) provoke, a spirit may have enough of you and leave for a spell because they do not wish to deal with it. If you seek a response, they will be elsewhere, ruining your evening. The spirit can lash out at you, and they have an advantage over the living. With the case of the living, you can see a fist and have a chance to duck. With a spirit, you could get pushed, scratched or hit or other depending on how well they learned to use their energy to manipulate the environment. Provoke a malevolent, and well, you may be followed where they will have a bit of fun at your expense. The issue that concerns me the most is the scenario where a spirit is put into such a foul mood that they can lash out at not only you, but to any others they run into.

Generally, I think it is unwise to provoke in any situation, especially when others live there or when others visit. If you follow one guideline, I hope it is to be respectful. After all spirits are like you and I, they have thoughts and emotions, hopes and dreams, they can have good days and bad days. The only difference between spirits and the living is that the physical vessel containing all those emotions is no longer present.

- Be Careful What You Ask For

I do believe that paranormal activity in Houghton Mansion will only increase over time. With all the groups that are actively investigating, it is possible that a malevolent spirit or darker entity can arrive. Even a degraded "harmless" spirit can be drawn to the location. As such, when the night gets slow, avoid the lure (thanks to a certain television program) to make things interesting. If you asked to be pushed, kicked or scratched, it just might happen and you may get more than you bargain for. Also by doing this, you may pull in these types of entities that could lash out at future investigators and even the spirits that normally call the mansion home.

- Be Specific

It is known that paranormal investigations can draw other spirits in as they see an open invitation to communicate. While this is not a problem if the other entities drawn in are harmless, but other entities, such as malevolent spirits and darker entities can also see an open invitation and move in causing serious issues for the property owners, visiting paranormal investigators and the other spirits as well.

When investigating, whether it is Houghton Mansion or a private residence for a family looking for help, it always helps to play it safe. When looking to communicate with a spirit, be specific in your requests, call out individual names. State firmly that this is not considered an open invitation for anyone – or anything – else to communicate. State firmly that no one with harmful intent is permitted to enter the space.

If you are faithful, ask for protection. Even if you are not faithful, ask for protection - it never hurts!

- Close the Communication Session

As mentioned, paranormal investigations can lure spirits into a location. Therefore it is important that when you stop an individual session such as an EVP or spirit box session, you should state that you are ending the communication attempts and clearly state that whatever spirits may have communicated with you should return to where they came from. Otherwise there is a slight chance that they can be trapped within the location where you lured them.

Once trapped, that spirit can degrade rather quickly. Since they are in a location unfamiliar with them, they can lose whatever comfort factor they once had. They can become confused or start to get angry creating a situation that can be problematic to others.

- Know Your Limits!

Again, with the exclamation point? Yes.

There may be a time when you feel like you are in over your head. Do not be afraid to pull back when you feel you have reached your limits. I say this because in Houghton Mansion I had to remove myself from a situation for the very first time (and only time) during any of our investigations. This happened to me in the room that is often referred to as John Widders' room.

If you are a bit squeamish or faint of heart, another interest should be pursued. The vast majority of encounters are relatively subtle, but some things can be so severe that they startle even those of us who have seen it all. A face popping up right in front of you, imposing figures, or deeply disturbing images can and do happen. In my case, emotions were put on me that weren't my own and they became so intense and disturbing I knew I had to remove myself from that location. Most injuries that occur on paranormal investigations are when people carelessly flee. It is always best to remain calm and steady, if you cannot, you may want to consider another hobby.

- Trust Your Instinct

This goes hand-in-hand with knowing your limits. If something does not feel right to you – remove yourself from the situation. It is always better to be safe than sorry. Our bodies are equipped with an amazing defense mechanism, listen to that system. I often wonder if this little nagging voice that is put in our head is the work of spirit guides or guardian angels that are often around us. Either way, it is best if you learn to trust that voice.

- Remember the Power of Editing

If you are inexperienced with paranormal investigating it is important to read this. If you walk into Houghton Mansion or any other haunted location, you may expect that things are continuously happening. Those television shows are pretty exciting, but that is due to the magic of editing. Paranormal investigations are not as exciting as the television shows, as the majority of the time is edited out. Those few minutes of action occur over the course of many hours and sometimes several days. Even our description of our paranormal investigations has been edited. What you will not read are the many times we sat with nothing going on.

- Stay Positive

Spirits will pick up and thrive on positive energy and are more likely to communicate with you.

Conversely, if you had a bad day and if it is possible, stay home. If you have negative energy associated with you or another in your group, spirits will tend to avoid that negative person. Even worse, negative entities or malevolent spirits may tap into that energy and cause some real problems for the entire group.

- Keep an Open Mind

Spirits usually will not waste their time if someone in the group is too closed-minded and will absolutely refute everything. Spirits can sense who are open and those that just will not believe even if a spirit pops up in front of them and bops them on the nose. This closed-minded skeptic will also send out negative energy which will drive the spirits away, see above. It is incredibly difficult for spirits to manifest and to communicate with us; they will not waste their effort if they see no reward.

- Make Questioning About Them

Don't get too carried away asking them to do something to prove that they are there. They may get bored and go elsewhere. Ask questions about them, why they remain behind, etc. Make it less about you getting a knock and more about interaction. Make them excited to talk to you, rather than them thinking "Oh dear God, not the 'Shave and a Haircut' bit again!"

- Ask Simple Questions and Wait

Communication between the realms is difficult and expends an extraordinary amount of energy. Keep the questions simple and do not use compound questions and give ten seconds or more for a response. Questions with "yes" or "no" answers are good – and you can even use a knocking or flashlight response system. If you are seeking the philosophical answer that will knock your socks off, you will not get it, believe me, I tried.

- Not Everything is Paranormal

If something happens rule out any logical explanations first. It is far too easy to accept everything as being paranormal. When something happens, think logically and try to recreate the situation. It turns out that most paranormal claims are not paranormal at all, but very typical events.

- Just Say No to Orbs!!

Wow, two exclamation points. The vast majority of orbs are dust, moisture, pollen, reflections, bugs, etc. I believe there are times where energy can be captured on film as an orb – but they are very rare. Those photographs you see with orbs are dust or other particulates, nothing more. There is another television program that hypes up dust orbs and usually has amateurs getting excited about angry or evil orbs. Dust cannot be evil, cannot have intent, and cannot be the work of a spirit. When you walk into a location, you will inevitably stir up dust. Even the cleanest house will have dust, it is inevitable. Please, just say no to orbs.

- Enjoy and preserve the history.

Take out what you bring in; take nothing, but your fond memories. As with any historic structure, please take care of the old home so that generations that follow us can enter and appreciate living history.

When visitors arrive at the stately Houghton Mansion, who knows who may be watching to see who is approaching. Could it be the matriarch greeting her guests as she did a century prior? Could the restless spirits of Albert or Mary be pacing, worrying about what painful memories they will be forced to relive? If you visit, please show them the respect that they deserve and remain compassionate towards their plight.

Appendix A: Thank You and Farewell – One Final Investigation

I celebrated the end of writing this book by scheduling a final investigation of Houghton Mansion on the weekend of April 12 and 13, 2014. Not only did I intend to say farewell to the mansion, but I also wanted to say farewell and 'thank you' to the spirits contained within. I was also a bit selfish in that I wanted our team to be in the mansion first when much of this information was brought back to light.

While our two previous investigations are discussed in detail within this book, I will only briefly discuss what experiences we had when we visited the mansion for a third time. The spirits at the mansion were a bit quieter, but perhaps it was for the best as what we did get was more meaningful than footsteps, slamming doors and moving lights and shadows. I did hear a grunt in the stairs behind the lodge, which was a bit different than previous investigations.

As part of the finalization of the book, I decided to reread the draft. It was at this point that I realized that by coincidence we were going to be investigating the mansion on the 170th anniversary of Albert Houghton's birth. I thought that this was deserving of an unorthodox paranormal experiment by holding a small and informal celebration of his birthday. I did not know what to expect, but was pleasantly surprised at the reaction we received.

For our third investigation, the most meaningful experiences we received involved responses from the KII meter. It is important to note that the KII meter did not register unusual hits when we were walking through the mansion or when we were not talking. The meter only registered unusual fluctuations in the electromagnetic field when we were involved in meaningful communication. When we did take note of a KII hit, we would rephrase the statement or question using the suspected trigger word or phrase to eliminate coincidence. Quite often the KII would register another change when we did rephrase the statement or question, further validating it as an intelligent response.

Albert C. Houghton

The most rewarding aspect of this project was to bring new appreciation to the individuals that may walk the hallways of Houghton Mansion. It was extremely important to me to bring the stories to the light of everyone involved and I felt proud to research someone who was as dynamic as Albert Charles Houghton. As part of this process I came to respect him as a human being rather than just a spirit who haunts a former residence. While I admit that no human being is perfect, I found his life story both inspirational and bittersweet.

Years ago, when I first stepped foot into the mansion, I had very little knowledge of the man Albert C. Houghton was. This time I felt like I knew intimate details of his life that were not discussed in many decades. I was excited to see what type of reaction we would get from all this information. I also entered with the desire of letting the spirits tell their own story, by giving them a chance to respond. We performed both EVP and spirit box sessions giving Mr. Houghton that opportunity. As part of the process I gave him a summary of his life, as I understood it – his success, his failures, his joys and his sorrows.

One interesting personal experience we had in Albert Houghton's room was when Vanessa noticed that the door leading to the lodge from Albert's bedroom was swaying back and forth. I turned around in time to notice it swaying as well. There were no windows open or draft of any sort and all of us were sitting down, eliminating any natural explanation to this occurrence. There were also footsteps, odd lights, and movement spotted when we were in Albert's room, but I will stick to the more important topics.

The first KII hit we picked up was when I was talking to Mr. Houghton about how deep personal tragedy would always seem to be around the corner from his many successes. This is a theme that is explored throughout the book, and it was a bit validating to receive a response to this statement.

Another trigger word that received several hits on the KII was when I mentioned Stamford, Vermont – Albert's birthplace. Before we visited the mansion, Christiana and I visited Houghton Cemetery in Stamford and paid our respects to all of Albert's family that are buried there. When I discussed his loved ones, the KII would light up. This was especially true when I mentioned his oldest sibling Julia Brooks and the multiple tragedies that her family suffered. As expected, this was something that mattered to Albert as we seemed to get a response.

When I was talking to Albert regarding the difficult times he experienced in 1906-1908 when his business and personal lives seemed to be crashing in around him, we received more responses. I credited him with having the courage to fight through the turmoil. When I mentioned that I could not fathom how he survived it all and how strong he must have been to go through that dark period, the KII lit up.

The KII meter became very quiet and we did not register much in the way until I got to the end of his life and the fateful car accident. When I discussed the 'what-if' questions with him, the KII became active again, responding immediately after I asked him if he often thought "what if we did not take that route?"

The one trigger that obtained several responses was when I discussed the fact that his great-grandson, Hobart Thompson, lost his life serving in World War II. Each time we discussed this, the KII registered a significant reading. Even though this happened well after the death of Albert Houghton, the energy in the room responded each time this was brought up. Hobart was not even born yet when Albert died, but clearly he felt a connection to his descendant.

One of the most unorthodox paranormal experiments we had undertaken was celebrating the 170th birthday of Albert Houghton. I felt that if we somehow connected with Albert in a unique way, we may have a unique experience. If not, we ate cupcakes; it was a win-win. We were wrapping up our main session in Mr. Houghton's bedroom when we realized it was after midnight. I returned to his bedroom with cupcakes and we as a group wished him a happy birthday and lightened up the mood of the room.

Several minutes after having our cupcakes and bringing a little levity to an otherwise intense investigation, we returned to a spirit box session. Within a very short amount of time, about a minute and a half, there were several interesting words spoken. The first word "Houghton" was said twice. Immediately after the second "Houghton", what sounded like an "I'm here" was recorded. I then asked if he appreciated his birthday celebration, we received a response on the spirit box that simply stated "thank you." There was also an odd response from the spirit box that said "love you". Now I cannot state who this response came from, whether it was extreme appreciation for the effort to broadcast this family's legacy or whether this was one of our deceased loved ones who took an opportunity to connect with us.

When we were about to leave his bedroom I asked one more time if he enjoyed his birthday celebration. Immediately after I asked, the KII meter in the center of the room registered the highest prolonged reading during the entire investigation. It is quite possible that Albert really appreciated us recognizing his birthday, and more importantly, bringing his history to light.

For me, the most meaningful response occurred when I took my draft book and read my final paragraph of the section of Albert Houghton. When I read about my wish that Albert Houghton was remembered not as a ghost, but as a man, the KII again responded. This small token of a response was important to me as it validated my stated purpose for this project. I believe Albert Houghton is indeed grateful that someone cared enough to broadcast his story. I could not think of a more fitting birthday present for him.

Mary Houghton

On a personal level, reaching out to Mary's spirit was something that I highly anticipated. The life of Mary is one in which I wanted to portray adequately in this book. This was especially important since much of her life story was shrouded in mystery as she generally liked to avoid the spotlight. I was hoping and praying that I was able to connect with Mary on a higher level so that she could have a say in how her life story would be told.

For our group, Mary's room has always been quiet and peaceful with very little in the way of activity. For the third investigation, the room was still largely peaceful, but activity was the highest that I had experienced in her room. Most of this activity was very subtle, however.

One of the more common experiences we all had in Mary's room was the movement of light. We saw "sparklers", or bright light anomalies, throughout her room. The sparklers appeared many times around the KII meter and over a yellow rose we placed down in her room. Reportedly, Mary loved yellow roses, so we brought one for her. At one point Vanessa saw a pale white light moving from the center of the room towards her. Later in the evening I also saw a pale white light, very slowly rise from just above the yellow rose.

I pleaded for Mary to manifest in a form in the center of the room so that we can all see her. Shortly after I did this, I noticed energy near me, what I can best describe as an electrical charge. Then the temperature around me seemed to drop very quickly and I felt what seemed to be a gust or air move from my left to the right. What was interesting about this was that as I stated this, it was noted by others that the curtains near me were not moving indicating that a draft from the window was not responsible for this feeling. The window was on my right, adding more skepticism that a draft from the window was responsible.

Later in Mary's room I saw a distinct light by the fireplace, a mere few feet in front of me. Immediately after this I started to talk about Mary and the rumors that were told regarding her life. Since I do not believe in those rumors, I told Mary that I thought I addressed that topic adequately in this book. Immediately after I stated this, a metal chair that was five feet to my left sounded as if someone with a ringed finger banged on the chair. Our digital voice recorders picked up this sound rather clearly. Less than a minute later there was another unusual noise from this very same area, again we were able to record this noise. Was this Mary's way of letting me know that I addressed the topic to her satisfaction?

As with Mr. Houghton's room, Mary's room provided interesting reactions from the KII meter. One trigger that resulted in several hits involved France and when we spoke French to Mary. As we have learned, Mary spent time in Europe as part of her studies, as did all of her sisters. This love for Europe seems to carry over to this day and age.

The KII meter reacted when I discussed the deaths of her sister Alice and her nephew Edward. This was an extremely difficult period for the Houghton family and understandably we received responses when this tragic topic was discussed. I tried to lighten up the discussion by having

Mary focus on the good times of her life, but unfortunately we did not seem to get any interaction. It was a goal to have her think about something positive rather than get hassled by continual questions about her own demise.

The strongest KII reading occurred toward the end of our session with Mary. I was attempting to communicate with Mary that she had a chance to write her own story by providing me with some answers. I again mentioned that one of my goals was to dispel silly rumors. I told her that I was looking out for her best interests. At that point the strongest reading was picked up on the KII meter. Shortly after that, a sparkler was seen by the yellow rose. Both of these events make me believe that Mary is appreciative of our efforts. I take the light by the yellow rose as her way of letting me know that it was her energy at that time.

John Widders

Before we investigated the mansion, Christiana and I arrived at the mansion early in the afternoon to take some pictures of the exterior of the mansion. We were welcomed in for a chance to take pictures of the interior during the daytime. Appreciative of the hospitable offer, we could not say no. As soon as we entered Widders' room, I was overcome by an oppressive energy in the room. I felt surrounded by it and felt as if I was being squeezed from every direction. My breathing soon became very labored. Based on this welcome I had, I thought we were in for a long night at the mansion, especially since I believe I now know his real identity and a more damning account of the accident.

When we returned to investigate Widders' room, that oppressive energy was no longer there as the room seemed peaceful. It is possible that the energy was used up during the earlier part of the day and he needed more energy to manifest. The room, however, did provide some validation as we again received meaningful KII readings during important parts of our communications. I carried with me many props regarding John Widders' past and I placed them down as I discussed his life story.

These trigger objects included laminated photos of the accident scene, articles about his mother claiming his estate, and other mementos of his life sure to be of interest of him. It is important to note that the props were delicately used as I did not want to further degrade John's spirit or invite an attack on anyone in the room.

I will be brutally honest and say I was looking forward to starting off our investigation by asking "Is John Winters here?" which of course is his given name that he tried so hard to cover up. I really did not know what type of reaction I would get. Perhaps that may be why I faced oppressive energy early in the day – he might have known what I was up to. Of course, I was very sympathetic and very careful in that I was not provoking him.

The first KII hit that we recorded was when I pulled out a copy of the 1860 Census showing a four-year old John Winters and the Winters family. As I discussed his family further the KII was quiet. Perhaps he did not want to talk about them. He refused to talk about them when he was alive, so it only makes sense that he did not give us the satisfaction of a reply.

A few minutes later I saw a shadow move in the third floor hallway near the top of the stairs that are just outside of Widders' room. I was positioned so that I had a clear view into the third floor hallway, which had been a hotbed of activity in previous investigations. At this point in time I was talking about the accident – a topic that I believe he is very tired of hearing about.

I mentioned the new theory about Widders accidentally stepping onto the gas pedal instead of the brake pedal. I was being very gentle and trying to reassure him as well. I let him know that we all make mistakes and that we are all human. As I said this, we registered a reaction on the KII. I discussed what it must have been like to come back to the property and to hear the cries, again the KII lit.

Since John did not want to have anything to do with his family after his father abandoned them and his mother placed him into the care of others, I thought it was best to give him updates. I placed a death certificate of his sister Lydia on the floor and began to talk about her. Immediately when I did this, the KII registered another reaction.

One of the most poignant responses I received was when I tried to talk about the accident from a different perspective. We talked to him about not placing the blame on his shoulders. I talked about him being part of the family. I then told him that the family mourned for him too. Immediately after that statement, the KII reacted.

We also conducted a spirit box session as the end of our visit in Widders' room. Interestingly enough, one of the words that came through was the word "Houghton". Since I had a pile of props spread out across the floor, I asked Widders if he would like for me to put them away. Through the spirit box we received a "yes", so I listened to Widders' wish and put them away. Shortly after that, we asked him if he wanted us to leave his room. We left when we received a "think so".

Until Fate Beckons

While I stated that this was our final investigation of Houghton Mansion, fate may truly bring me back within the hallways of this living monument to the Houghton family. As the past residents left their imprint within the walls, floors and ceilings of the mansion, the mansion itself left an imprint on me. This strong imprint forced me to reassess my role as a paranormal investigator, an imprint that gave me a strong desire to learn about the shadows within Houghton Mansion.

Appendix B: Suggested Links

The Shadows Within

www.TheShadowsWithin.com

Facebook: www.facebook.com/WalkingAmongstTheShadows

Please visit our website to review information that was cut from the book. Information that was removed included the lives of Albert and Cordelia's siblings and their children. Also removed was the infamous Reed double-murder with some surprising twists.

You can also keep current of the latest news including upcoming releases from the author and the series.

Houghton Mansion: Tours, Events, Private Investigations

www.HoughtonMansionGhostTours.org

Lafayette Greylock Lodge, A.F. & A.M

www.Lafayette-Greylock.org

A Note of Thanks

First of all I cannot begin without thanking my wife Christiana for encouraging me to expand my wings and seek out the answers I had regarding the paranormal world. You put up with a lot of my talking, my theories and my late nights/early mornings. You also had to deal with editing duties, which I admit was a chore based on how wordy I can be. It's not easy doing what we do with full time jobs, a family and normal chores, but somehow we make it all work. My biggest thank you is of course to you.

For Vanessa and Chris: for your hard work, dedication and enthusiasm – and most importantly, your friendship. We had a bit of fun in the old mansion – looking forward to more adventures.

To my family which instilled in me a deep faith in God and the afterlife which keeps me open to see, hear and feel the miracles of life and to experience the mystifying experiences of spirits. I also like to thank you for my inquisitive spirit which always wants to learn something.

To the stewards of the Houghton Mansion for allowing people like me to witness for ourselves the paranormal community and for caring about the preservation of this treasure. You run a top-notch operation and should be proud.

A big heartfelt thanks goes to you – yes you reading this right now - for picking up this book and taking an interest in this subject. All these letters, words and punctuation marks mean nothing without a set of eyes to see them.

Finally, thank you to the Houghtons and John Widders for putting up with our antics. We truly hope that one day you find the peace and comfort you deserve. I hope that by bringing your story to light, you may find comfort in the acknowledgement of your lives and move on to your reward of everlasting comfort and peace. I also need to give a special thank you to Cordelia, who I believe led me to this project and helped along the way. May you finally reunite with your family and enjoy the peace and comfort of God's love.

Sources

Spear, W.F. *History of North Adams, Mass. 1749-1885.* North Adams: Hoosac Valley News Printing House, 1885.

Chapter 1 (Saturday, August 1, 1914)

"Miss Houghton and Mrs. Hutton Both Lose Lives." *The North Adams Transcript* 01 Aug 1914: 1, 2.

"Takes His Life as Result of Fatal Auto Accident." *The North Adams Transcript* 02 Aug 1914: 2.

"Albert C. Houghton, City's Leading Citizen Dies at Home at 3 o'clock This Afternoon." *The North Adams Transcript* 11 Aug 1914: 2.

"City's Activities Cease as a Final Tribute to A.C. Houghton's Memory." *The North Adams Transcript* 13 Aug 1914: 1, 5.

"Massachusetts, Deaths, 1841-1915," index and images, FamilySearch (https://familysearch.org/pal:/MM9.1.1/N4H4-GSQ : accessed 03 Dec 2013), Albert C Houghton, 1914.

Chapter 2 (Albert C. Houghton – His Story)

"Legislative Statistics." *Vermont Daily Transcript* 28 Oct 1868: 2. *Library of Congress, Chronicling America, Historic American Newspapers.* Web. 27 Dec 2013. <http://chroniclingamerica.loc.gov/>.

"New England News Items – Vermont." *The Springfield Daily Republican* 05 Feb 1869: 2. *The Republican Archives.* Web. 13 Nov 2011. <http://www.newslibrary.com/sites/un/>.

"The Destructive Fire at Stamford." *The Rutland Daily Globe* 15 Apr 1874: 2. *Library of Congress, Chronicling America, Historic American Newspapers.* Web. 29 Dec 2013. <http://chroniclingamerica.loc.gov/>.

"Heavy Failure at North Adams, Mass." *The Vermont Phoenix* 12 May 1876: 2. *Library of Congress, Chronicling America, Historic American Newspapers.* Web. 14 Jan 2014. <http://chroniclingamerica.loc.gov/>.

"The Big Failure at North Adams." *The New York Times* 25 May 1876. *The New York Times.* Web. 17 Feb 2013. <http://www.nytimes.com/>.

"A Stronghold No Longer. Democratic Hopes in Western Massachusetts." *The New York Times* 14 Oct 1888. *The New York Times.* Web. 17 Feb 2013. <http://www.nytimes.com/>.

"World's Fair Commissioners." *Fitchburg Sentinel* 23 May 1890: 1. *Genealogy, Family Trees & Family History Records at Ancestry.com.* Web. 10 Nov 2011. <http://www.ancestry.com/>.

"Three Gifts to a Hospital." *The New York Times* 12 Sep 1890. *The New York Times.* Web. 17 Feb 2013. <http://www.nytimes.com/>.

Houghton is a Hustler. Friends Besiege Headquarters of the Berkshire Candidate." *Boston Globe* 07 Apr 1892: 4. *Boston Globe Archives* Web. 30 Mar 2013. <https://secure.pqarchiver.com/boston/advancedsearch.html>.

"Delegates at Large." *Fitchburg Sentinel* 09 Apr 1892: 1. *Genealogy, Family Trees & Family History Records at Ancestry.com.* Web. 08 Oct 2012. <http://www.ancestry.com/>.

"On to Chicago." *Boston Globe 17* Jun 1892: 10. *Boston Globe Archives* Web. 03 Apr 2013. <https://secure.pqarchiver.com/boston/advancedsearch.html>.

"Wealthy Brewer Dead." *Boston Globe* 26 Sep 1892: 9. *Boston Globe Archives* Web. 30 Mar 2013. <https://secure.pqarchiver.com/boston/advancedsearch.html>.

"Beaver Mills Changes Hands." *Boston Globe* 23 Mar 1894: 8. *Boston Globe Archives* Web. 01 Apr 2013. <https://secure.pqarchiver.com/boston/advancedsearch.html>.

"New Mills! North Adams Industrial Good Fortune." *The North Adams Transcript* 06 Jul 1895: 1. *Genealogy, Family Trees & Family History Records at Ancestry.com.* Web. 06 Apr 2013. <http://www.ancestry.com/>.

"Mr. Houghton Chosen." *The North Adams Transcript* 25 Sep 1895: 1. *Genealogy, Family Trees & Family History Records at Ancestry.com.* Web. 08 Oct 2012. <http://www.ancestry.com/>.

"Another Good Word." *The North Adams Daily Transcript* 21 Nov 1895: 2. *Genealogy, Family Trees & Family History Records at Ancestry.com.* Web. 15 Mar 2013. <http://www.ancestry.com/>.

"The Ward Meetings." *The North Adams Daily Transcript* 22 Nov 1895: 2. *Genealogy, Family Trees & Family History Records at Ancestry.com.* Web. 15 Mar 2013. <http://www.ancestry.com/>.

"Albert C. Houghton to be North Adam's First Mayor – A Native of Vermont." *The Vermont Phoenix 29* Nov 1895: 2. *Library of Congress, Chronicling America, Historic American Newspapers.* Web. 09 Aug 2013. <http://chroniclingamerica.loc.gov/>.

"Convention! A. C. Houghton Nominated for Mayor." *The North Adams Transcript* 30 Nov 1895: 1. *Genealogy, Family Trees & Family History Records at Ancestry.com.* Web. 01 Aug 2013. <http://www.ancestry.com/>.

"Full Results." *The North Adams Transcript* 18 Dec. 1895: 1. *Genealogy, Family Trees & Family History Records at Ancestry.com.* Web. 01 Aug 2013. <http://www.ancestry.com/>.

"Leap-Year Festivity." *The North Adams Transcript* 03 Jan 1896: 1. *Genealogy, Family Trees & Family History Records at Ancestry.com.* Web. 09 Mar 2013. <http://www.ancestry.com/>.

"Mayor Houghton." *The North Adams Transcript* 04 Jan 1896: 2. *Genealogy, Family Trees & Family History Records at Ancestry.com.* Web. 02 Aug 2013. <http://www.ancestry.com/>.

"Another Appointment. C.T. Ralston to be Private Secretary of Mayor Houghton." *The North Adams Transcript* 07 Jan 1896: 1. *Genealogy, Family Trees & Family History Records at Ancestry.com.* Web. 02 Aug 2013. <http://www.ancestry.com/>.

"Magnificent Gift." *The North Adams Evening Transcript* 07 Apr 1896: 1. *Genealogy, Family Trees & Family History Records at Ancestry.com.* Web. 11 Feb 2013. <http://www.ancestry.com/>.

"Mr. Houghton's Gift to the City." *The North Adams Evening Transcript* 07 Apr 1896: 2. *Genealogy, Family Trees & Family History Records at Ancestry.com.* Web. 31 Jan 2013. <http://www.ancestry.com/>.

"Warren H. Cook." *The North Adams Transcript* 10 Apr 1896. *Explore Historical Newspaper Archives Online.* Web. 06 Nov 2013. <http://newspaperarchive.com/>.

"In Loving Memory of His Brother. Mayor Houghton's Gift to the City of North Adams, Mass." *The New York Times* 03 May 1896. *The New York Times.* Web. 31 Jan 2013. <http://www.nytimes.com/>.

"National Democratic Party Now Fully Organized, it Appears." *The New York Times* 17 Oct 1896. *The New York Times.* Web. 17 Feb 2013. <http://www.nytimes.com/>.

"Sketches of Mayors Elect." *Boston Globe 16 Dec* 1896: 3. *Boston Globe Archives* Web. 30 Mar 2013. <https://secure.pqarchiver.com/boston/advancedsearch.html>.

"The President and His Party's Welcome in Northern Berkshire." *The North Adams Transcript* 22 Sep 1897: 1. *Genealogy, Family Trees & Family History Records at Ancestry.com.* Web. 01 Aug 2013. <http://www.ancestry.com/>.

"Mayoralty Question. Mr. Houghton Says He Cannot Consent to Accept Renomination." *The North Adams Transcript* 09 Nov 1897: 2. *Genealogy, Family Trees & Family History Records at Ancestry.com.* Web. 02 Aug 2013. <http://www.ancestry.com/>.

"Mr. Hamer Talks. Consents to Tell a Transcript Reporter What Policy He Stands For." *The North Adams Transcript* 30 Oct 1897: 1, 2. *Genealogy, Family Trees & Family History Records at Ancestry.com.* Web. 08 Aug 2013. <http://www.ancestry.com/>.

"The Beaver Job." *The North Adams Transcript* 12 Nov 1897: 1. *Genealogy, Family Trees & Family History Records at Ancestry.com.* Web. 08 Aug 2013. <http://www.ancestry.com/>.

"Mr. Cady Withdraws. Mayor A. C. Houghton Will Not Accept the Mayoralty for Another Year." *The North Adams Transcript* 15 Nov 1897: 1. *Genealogy, Family Trees & Family History Records at Ancestry.com.* Web. 07 Apr 2013. <http://www.ancestry.com/>.

"James E. Hunter A Candidate." *The North Adams Transcript* 17 Nov 1897: 2. *Genealogy, Family Trees & Family History Records at Ancestry.com.* Web. 01 Aug 2013. <http://www.ancestry.com/>.

"One False Howl. The Statement the Citizens Should Have of Public Affairs is Coming." *The North Adams Transcript* 06 Dec 1897: 1. *Genealogy, Family Trees & Family History Records at Ancestry.com.* Web. 08 Aug 2013. <http://www.ancestry.com/>.

"More Hamer Mistakes." *The North Adams Transcript* 08 Dec 1897: 2. *Genealogy, Family Trees & Family History Records at Ancestry.com.* Web. 07 Apr 2013. <http://www.ancestry.com/>.

"The Inauguration." *The North Adams Transcript* 03 Jan 1898: 2. *Genealogy, Family Trees & Family History Records at Ancestry.com.* Web. 01 Aug 2013. <http://www.ancestry.com/>.

"Loss to the State. Shrinkage in the Value of Cotton Industry." *Boston Globe* 08 Apr 1898: 9. *Boston Globe Archives* Web. 03 Apr 2013. <https://secure.pqarchiver.com/boston/advancedsearch.html>.

"Sails for Europe. Ex-Mayor Houghton Sails on the Teutonic Tomorrow." *The North Adams Transcript* 25 Apr 1898: 8. *Genealogy, Family Trees & Family History Records at Ancestry.com.* Web. 16 Apr 2013. <http://www.ancestry.com/>.

"Mr. Houghton Reaches New York." *The North Adams Transcript* 28 Apr 1898: 2. *Genealogy, Family Trees & Family History Records at Ancestry.com.* Web. 24 Oct 2012. <http://www.ancestry.com/>.

"Charged with Forgery. Charles T. Ralston Forges Names of Foster E. Swift and A. C. Houghton." *The North Adams Transcript* 14 Oct 1898: 5. *Genealogy, Family Trees & Family History Records at Ancestry.com.* Web. 19 Apr 2013. <http://www.ancestry.com/>.

"Former Editor a Fugitive." *The New York Times* 15 Oct 1898. *The New York Times.* Web. 19 Apr 2013. <http://www.nytimes.com/>.

"Missing from North Adams. Warrant for Charles T. Ralston, Charging Forgery." *Boston Globe* 15 Oct 1898: 12. *Boston Globe Archives* Web. 19 Apr 2013. <https://secure.pqarchiver.com/boston/advancedsearch.html>.

292 | Sources

"He Gave Himself Up. Charles T. Ralston Gave Himself Up to the Police This Morning." *The North Adams Transcript* 15 Oct 1898: 5. *Genealogy, Family Trees & Family History Records at Ancestry.com.* Web. 19 Apr 2013. <http://www.ancestry.com/>.

"James Royal Houghton." *The North Adams Evening Transcript* 01 Dec 1898: 2. *Genealogy, Family Trees & Family History Records at Ancestry.com.* Web. 24 Oct 2011. <http://www.ancestry.com/>.

"Mrs. Ralston Very Ill." *The North Adams Transcript* 05 Jan 1899: 5. *Genealogy, Family Trees & Family History Records at Ancestry.com.* Web. 19 Apr 2013. <http://www.ancestry.com/>.

"C. T. Ralston's Case. Will Acknowledge His Forgeries Before the Grand Jury This Week." *The North Adams Transcript* 09 Jan 1899: 5. *Genealogy, Family Trees & Family History Records at Ancestry.com.* Web. 19 Apr 2013. <http://www.ancestry.com/>.

"Grand Jury's Report." *The North Adams Transcript* 12 Jan 1899: 5. *Genealogy, Family Trees & Family History Records at Ancestry.com.* Web. 19 Apr 2013. <http://www.ancestry.com/>.

"A View of the Ralston Case. Other Forgeries on Which He Got Money, Says a Local Writer." *The North Adams Transcript* 30 Jan 1899: 5. *Genealogy, Family Trees & Family History Records at Ancestry.com.* Web. 19 Apr 2013. <http://www.ancestry.com/>.

"Death of Mrs. Charles T. Ralston." *Boston Globe* 29 May 1899: 12. *Boston Globe Archives* Web. 19 Apr 2013. <https://secure.pqarchiver.com/boston/advancedsearch.html>.

"Death of Mrs. Ralston." *The North Adams Transcript* 29 May 1899: 2. *Genealogy, Family Trees & Family History Records at Ancestry.com.* Web. 19 Apr 2013. <http://www.ancestry.com/>.

"President M'Kinley Visits North Adams." *The North Adams Transcript* 26 Jun 1899: 8. *Genealogy, Family Trees & Family History Records at Ancestry.com.* Web. 10 Apr 2013. <http://www.ancestry.com/>.

"Rattle Snake Brook Bought." *The North Adams Transcript* 09 Nov 1899: 4. *Genealogy, Family Trees & Family History Records at Ancestry.com.* Web. 10 Apr 2013. <http://www.ancestry.com/>.

"The labor unions of North Adams propose to boycott Houghton's beer…" *Boston Evening Transcript* 01 Aug 1900: 1. *Google News Archives.* Web. 01 Aug 2013. <http://www.news.google.com >.

"Looms Idle. Cotton Plants Await Better Times." *Boston Globe* 03 Jun 1904: 8. *Boston Globe Archives* Web. 30 Mar 2013. <https://secure.pqarchiver.com/boston/advancedsearch.html>.

"Berkshires to Greet the President." *The New York Times* 18 Jun 1905. *The New York Times.* Web. 17 Feb 2013. <http://www.nytimes.com/>.

"Pres. Roosevelt to Present Diplomas." *Boston Globe* 18 Jun 1905: 34. *Boston Globe Archives* Web. 01 Apr 2013. <https://secure.pqarchiver.com/boston/advancedsearch.html>.

"President Has Rain All Day." *Boston Globe* 22 Jun 1905: 1. *Boston Globe Archives* Web. 01 Apr 2013. <https://secure.pqarchiver.com/boston/advancedsearch.html>.

"Ford by 635. Mayor of North Adams is Reelected." *Boston Globe* 20 Dec 1905: 2. *Boston Globe Archives* Web. 01 Apr 2013. <https://secure.pqarchiver.com/boston/advancedsearch.html>.

"Obituary – Edward H. Houghton." *The North Adams Transcript* 11 Feb 1907: 5. *Explore Historical Newspaper Archives Online.* Web. 10 Oct 2013. <http://newspaperarchive.com/>.

"Receiver for Print Works." *The New York Times* 07 Nov 1907. *The New York Times.* Web. 10 Sep 2011. <http://www.nytimes.com/>.

"Bank Asks a Receiver. North Pownal Plant is Embarrassed. Troubles Come From Failure of Arnold Print Works." *Boston Globe* 08 Nov 1907: 6. *Boston Globe Archives* Web. 30 Mar 2013. <https://secure.pqarchiver.com/boston/advancedsearch.html>.

"In Financial Trouble. Receiver Appointed for Arnold Print Works of North Adams, a Concern with 3000 Operatives." *The Vermont Phoenix* 08 Nov 1907: 5. *Library of Congress, Chronicling America, Historic American Newspapers.* Web. 09 Aug 2013. <http://chroniclingamerica.loc.gov/>.

"On Arnold Print Works. Receivers Submit Report." *Boston Globe* 07 Dec 1907: 12. *Boston Globe Archives* Web. 30 Mar 2013. <https://secure.pqarchiver.com/boston/advancedsearch.html>.

"Reorganization Planned." *Boston Globe* 31 Jul 1908: 10. *Boston Globe Archives* Web. 30 Mar 2013. <https://secure.pqarchiver.com/boston/advancedsearch.html>.

"Arnold Works to Resume." *The New York Times* 31 Jul 1908. *The New York Times.* Web. 26 Mar 2013. <http://www.nytimes.com/>.

"Arnold Print Works. First Report of Receivers Filed in U.S. Circuit Court – Principal Items in Claims." *Boston Globe* 16 Oct 1908: 13. *Boston Globe Archives* Web. 30 Mar 2013. <https://secure.pqarchiver.com/boston/advancedsearch.html>.

"Arnold Print Works. Sale of its Assets at Public Auction is Ordered." *Boston Globe* 20 Oct 1908: 3. *Boston Globe Archives* Web. 30 Mar 2013. <https://secure.pqarchiver.com/boston/advancedsearch.html>.

"Orders Arnold Print Works Sold." *The New York Times* 24 Oct 1908. *The New York Times.* Web. 10 Sep 2011. <http://www.nytimes.com/>.

"Eclipse and Beaver Sold. Syndicate Takes Big Arnold Plants." *Boston Globe* 22 Oct 1910: 3. *Boston Globe Archives* Web. 30 Mar 2013. <https://secure.pqarchiver.com/boston/advancedsearch.html>.

"Plunketts Take Two Arnold Mills." *Boston Globe* 25 Oct 1910: 4. *Boston Globe Archives* Web. 30 Mar 2013. <https://secure.pqarchiver.com/boston/advancedsearch.html>.

"Arnold Print Works." *Boston Globe* 15 Nov 1910: 16. *Boston Globe Archives* Web. 30 Mar 2013. <https://secure.pqarchiver.com/boston/advancedsearch.html>.

"Progress Encouraging. A.C. Houghton, North Adams Manufacturer, Ill in New York, Slowly, But Steadily Improving." *Boston Globe* 02 Mar 1911: 10. *Boston Globe Archives* Web. 01 Apr 2013. <https://secure.pqarchiver.com/boston/advancedsearch.html>.

"Houghton's Condition." *The Evening Union* 18 Mar 1911: 1. *The Republican Archives.* Web. 08 Oct 2012. <http://www.newslibrary.com/sites/un/>.

"Arnold Print Works Permits Assessors to See Their Books." *The North Adams Transcript* 05 Jul 1911: 1. *Explore Historical Newspaper Archives Online.* Web. 21 Oct 2013. <http://newspaperarchive.com/>.

"A. C. Houghton Dead." *The Springfield Daily Republican* 12 Aug 1914: 15. *The Republican Archives.* Web. 26 Oct 2011. <http://www.newslibrary.com/sites/un/>.

"Insurance Payments in 1914 Biggest Ever Made in U.S." *El Paso Herald* 12-13 Jun 1915: 3A. *Genealogy, Family Trees & Family History Records at Ancestry.com.* Web. 09 Aug 2013. <http://www.ancestry.com/>.

"Arnold Print Works Seeks to Reorganize." *The Lewiston Daily Sun* 03 Sep 1935. *Google News Archives.* Web. 11 Feb 2013. <http://www.news.google.com/news.advanced_news_search?as_drrb=a>.

"Stiff Political Battle to Get Teacher's College." *The North Adams Transcript* 23 May 1938: 7. *Genealogy, Family Trees & Family History Records at Ancestry.com.* Web. 24 Oct 2012. <http://www.ancestry.com/>.

"Arnold Print Works Liquidation is Voted." *Boston Globe* 02 May 1942: 6. *Boston Globe Archives* Web. 30 Mar 2013. <https://secure.pqarchiver.com/boston/advancedsearch.html>.

"Arnold Print Works Auction Under Way." *The Springfield Republican* 17 Nov 1943: 22. *The Republican Archives.* Web. 27 Oct 2011. <http://www.newslibrary.com/sites/un/>.

Richards, Victor. "Blackington Mansion Has Been City's Library for 75 Years. " *The North Adams Transcript* 15 Apr 1971: 5. *Explore Historical Newspaper Archives Online.* Web. 08 Oct 2013. <http://newspaperarchive.com/>.

"Move to Save Old City Hall Gets Little Initial Support." *The Springfield Union* 16 Apr 1974: 4. *The Republican Archives.* Web. 08 Nov 2011. <http://www.newslibrary.com/sites/un/>.

Walsh, James V. "Old City Hall Crumbles as Anniversaries Abound. " *The North Adams Transcript* 28 Mar 1978: 1, 10. *Explore Historical Newspaper Archives Online.* Web. 07 Oct 2013. <http://newspaperarchive.com/>.

"Move to Save Old City Hall Gets Little Initial Support." *The Springfield Union* 25 Mar 1986: 12. *The Republican Archives.* Web. 08 Oct 2012. <http://www.newslibrary.com/sites/un/>.

"Vermont, Vital Records, 1760-1954," index and images, FamilySearch (https://familysearch.org/pal:/MM9.1.1/XFVV-NZK : accessed 13 Nov 2012), Jennie C Houghton, 1861.

"Massachusetts, Deaths, 1841-1915," index and images, *FamilySearch* (https://familysearch.org/pal:/MM9.1.1/N4H4-GSQ : accessed 10 Dec 2013), Albert C Houghton, 1914.

Chapter 3 (Cordelia Houghton)

"Kappa Phi Alpha. A Brilliant Reception to be Given at Columbia Opera House." *The North Adams Transcript* 02 Jul 1895: 2. *Genealogy, Family Trees & Family History Records at Ancestry.com.* Web. 06 Apr 2013. <http://www.ancestry.com/>.

"Death of Albert R. Smith." *The Springfield Republican* 09 May 1913: 18. *The Republican Archives.* Web. 13 Nov 2011. <http://www.newslibrary.com/sites/un/>.

"Mrs. Houghton Dead." *The Springfield Republican* 27 Feb 1918: 11. *The Republican Archives.* Web. 26 Oct 2011. <http://www.newslibrary.com/sites/un/>.

Chapter 5 (Florence Houghton Gallup: Her Life and Family)

"Mr. Gallup Thrown from His Horse." *The New York Times* 03 Jul 1892. *The New York Times.* Web. 10 Sep 2011. <http://www.nytimes.com/>.

"Congregationalists Home from Northfield." *The North Adams Transcript* 17 Jul 1919: 5. *Explore Historical Newspaper Archives Online.* Web. 17 Oct 2013. <http://newspaperarchive.com/>.

"Would Reclaim all Waste Land." *The North Adams Transcript* 28 Jul 1919: 2. *Genealogy, Family Trees & Family History Records at Ancestry.com.* Web. 05 Aug 2013. <http://www.ancestry.com/>.

"Completes Fifty Years at Arnold Print Works." *The North Adams Transcript* 20 Dec 1919: 2. *Genealogy, Family Trees & Family History Records at Ancestry.com.* Web. 14 Mar 2013. <http://www.ancestry.com/>.

"List of Honorary Members Increases. Girls' Club Membership Campaign Meeting With Success." *The North Adams Transcript* 24 Nov 1920: 5. *Explore Historical Newspaper Archives Online.* Web. 17 Oct 2013. <http://newspaperarchive.com/>.

"Miss Pollard Bride of W. A. Gallup." *The Springfield Republican* 06 Jun 1921: 4. *The Republican Archives.* Web. 26 Oct 2011. <http://www.newslibrary.com/sites/un/>.

"Mutual Benefit of A. P. W. Gathers." *The North Adams Transcript* 11 May 1926: 5. *Genealogy, Family Trees & Family History Records at Ancestry.com.* Web. 13 Aug 2013. <http://www.ancestry.com/>.

"Gallup Purchases Residence in Hub." *The North Adams Transcript* 15 Jul 1927: 3. *Genealogy, Family Trees & Family History Records at Ancestry.com.* Web. 24 Oct 2012. <http://www.ancestry.com/>.

"Woman Killed, Son Hurt in Lanesboro Mishap." *Boston Globe* 28 Oct 1928: A18. *Boston Globe Archives* Web. 21 Apr 2013. <https://secure.pqarchiver.com/boston/advancedsearch.html>.

"80 Acres of Land Presented to City by Mrs. W. A. Gallup and Mrs. Andrew P. McKean." *The North Adams Transcript* 19 Mar 1929: 20. *Explore Historical Newspaper Archives Online.* Web. 21 Oct 2013. <http://newspaperarchive.com/>.

"Gift of $2,500 for Methodist Church." *The North Adams Transcript* 18 Feb 1930: 16. *Explore Historical Newspaper Archives Online.* Web. 09 Mar 2013. <http://newspaperarchive.com/>.

"Hospital's New Maternity Wing Up to the Minute." *The North Adams Transcript* 29 Mar 1930: 2. *Explore Historical Newspaper Archives Online.* Web. 16 Oct 2013. <http://newspaperarchive.com/>.

"North Adams Mill Closes in Respect for W. A. Gallup." *The Springfield Republican* 12 Aug 1930: 2. *The Republican Archives.* Web. 27 Oct 2011. <http://www.newslibrary.com/sites/un/>.

"William A. Gallup." *The Boston Globe* 12 Aug 1930: 4. *Boston Globe Archives.* Web. 30 Mar 2013. <https://secure.pqarchiver.com/boston/advancedsearch.html>.

"Memorial Services for William Arthur Gallup." *The Boston Globe* 29 Oct 1930: 14. *Boston Globe Archives.* Web. 11 Apr 2013. <https://secure.pqarchiver.com/boston/advancedsearch.html>.

"W. A. Gallup's Estate Listed at $1,425,549." *The Springfield Republican* 18 Feb 1931: 2. *The Republican Archives.* Web. 08 Nov 2011. <http://www.newslibrary.com/sites/un/>.

"Mrs. Wm. Arthur Gallup Dies in Her 70th Year." *The North Adams Transcript* 13 May 1939: 3. *Genealogy, Family Trees & Family History Records at Ancestry.com.* Web. 11 Feb 2013. <http://www.ancestry.com/>.

"Mrs William Gallup Dies at West Newton." *The Springfield Sunday Union* and Republican 14 May 1939: 12A. *The Republican Archives.* Web. 26 Oct 2011. <http://www.newslibrary.com/sites/un/>.

"Mrs William Gallup Dies at West Newton." *The Springfield Sunday Union* and Republican 14 May 1939: 12A. *The Republican Archives.* Web. 26 Oct 2011. <http://www.newslibrary.com/sites/un/>.

"Private Rites for Mrs. Gallup. Held at Her Home in West Newton." *The North Adams Transcript* 15 May 1939: 3. *Explore Historical Newspaper Archives Online.* Web. 17 Oct 2013. <http://newspaperarchive.com/>.

"$25,000 Bequeathed Unborn Grandchild." *Boston Globe* 23 May 1939: 8. *Boston Globe Archives* Web. 11 Apr 2013. <https://secure.pqarchiver.com/boston/advancedsearch.html>.

"Flood Home Reported Sold to Physicians for Medical Center." *The North Adams Transcript* 27 Mar 1954: 5. *Explore Historical Newspaper Archives Online.* Web. 21 Oct 2013. <http://newspaperarchive.com/>.

"Mr. and Mrs. W. L. Bolt Buy Former Parsonage." *The North Adams Transcript* 20 Aug 1954: 3. *Explore Historical Newspaper Archives Online.* Web. 28 Oct 2013. <http://newspaperarchive.com/>.

"George B. Flood Dies; Retired Industrialist, Civic Affairs Leader." *The North Adams Transcript* 22 Nov 1954: 2. *Explore Historical Newspaper Archives Online.* Web. 28 Oct 2013. <http://newspaperarchive.com/>.

"Funeral. Dr. William Albert Gallup." *The North Adams Transcript* 15 Jan 1957: 3. *Genealogy, Family Trees & Family History Records at Ancestry.com*. Web. 14 Mar 2011. <http://www.ancestry.com/>.

"William A. Gallup, Investment Councilor, Episcopal Churchman." *The Boston Globe* 15 Jan 1957: 32. *Boston Globe Archives*. Web. 30 Mar 2013. https://secure.pqarchiver.com/boston/advancedsearch.html>.

"Library, St. John's Church to Receive $10,000 Bequests." *The North Adams Transcript* 10 Jul 1957: 4. *Genealogy, Family Trees & Family History Records at Ancestry.com*. Web. 10 Nov 2011. <http://www.ancestry.com/>.

"Gallup Beacon Hill House Reported Sold." *The North Adams Transcript* 14 Oct 1957: 5. *Genealogy, Family Trees & Family History Records at Ancestry.com*. Web. 12 Feb 2013. <http://www.ancestry.com/>.

"Mrs. Samuel Jones, APW President's Widow, Dies at 75." *The North Adams Transcript* 03 Dec 1963: 3. *Genealogy, Family Trees & Family History Records at Ancestry.com*. Web. 03 Mar 2013. <http://www.ancestry.com/>.

"History of Area YMCA spans 85 Years." *The North Adams Transcript* 23 Oct 1971: 9, 10. *Explore Historical Newspaper Archives Online*. Web. 21 Oct 2013. <http://newspaperarchive.com/>.

"Deaths. Marion E. Flood." *The North Adams Transcript* 26 Dec 1975: 20. *Explore Historical Newspaper Archives Online*. Web. 28 Oct 2013. <http://newspaperarchive.com/>.

"Glimpse Given of Home for Retarded Citizens." *The North Adams Transcript* 23 Sep 1976: 15, 28. *Explore Historical Newspaper Archives Online*. Web. 28 Oct 2013. <http://newspaperarchive.com/>.

National Archives and Records Administration (NARA); Washington D.C.; Passport Applications, 1795-1905; Collection Number: ARC Identifier 566612 / MLR Number A1 508; NARA Series: M1372; Roll #: 369. Florence Houghton.

Chapter 6 (Susan Houghton McKean: Her Life and Family)

"Houghton-McKean Wedding." *The North Adams Transcript* 23 Mar 1899: 8. *Genealogy, Family Trees & Family History Records at Ancestry.com*. Web. 14 Sep 2011. <http://www.ancestry.com/>.

"Gives Memorial for Her Sisters. Mrs. Andrew P. McKean Creates Fund." *The North Adams Transcript* 14 Jan 1926: 9. *Explore Historical Newspaper Archives Online*. Web. 08 Oct 2013. <http://newspaperarchive.com/>.

"Stole $15,000 in Jewelry." *The Frederick Post* 12 Jul 1938: 10. *Explore Historical Newspaper Archives Online*. Web. 28 Oct 2013. <http://newspaperarchive.com/>.

"Trojan's Son Killed on Western Front." *The Troy Record* 14 Feb 1945: 2. *Genealogy, Family Trees & Family History Records at Ancestry.com*. Web. 27 Mar 2013. <http://www.ancestry.com/>.

"Funeral Rites Held for A. P. McKean." *The Troy Record* 10 Jul 1954: 3. *Genealogy, Family Trees & Family History Records at Ancestry.com*. Web. 24 Oct 2012. <http://www.ancestry.com/>.

"Mrs. McKean, Former Trojan, Dies." *The Times Record* 14 Sep 1955: 1. *Genealogy, Family Trees & Family History Records at Ancestry.com*. Web. 24 Oct 2012. <http://www.ancestry.com/>.

"Mrs. McKean Dies; Daughter of First No. Adams Mayor." *The North Adams Transcript* 17 Sep 1955: 3. *Genealogy, Family Trees & Family History Records at Ancestry.com*. Web. 08 Oct 2013. <http://www.ancestry.com/>.

National Archives and Records Administration (NARA); Washington D.C.; *Passport Applications, 1795-1905*; Collection Number: *ARC Identifier 566612 / MLR Number A1 508*; NARA Series: *M1372*; Roll #: *369*, Susie Houghton.

Chapter 7 (Alice Houghton Wilkinson: Her Life and Family)

"Houghton-Wilkinson Wedding." *The North Adams Transcript* 20 Apr 1899. *Genealogy, Family Trees & Family History Records at Ancestry.com.* Web. 14 Sep 2011. <http://www.ancestry.com/>.

"Edward S. Wilkinson." *The Troy Northern Budget* 28 Dec 1902. *Google News Archives.* Web. 26 Mar 2013. <http://www.news.google.com/news.advanced_news_search?as_drrb=a>.

"E. S. Wilkinson Leaves the Arnold Print Works." *The North Adams Transcript* 02 Jan 1908: 5. *Explore Historical Newspaper Archives Online.* Web. 08 Oct 2013. <http://newspaperarchive.com/>.

"Philadelphia Personnel Board of Y. M. C. A. War Work Council, Called Most Efficient in Country, With Local Man as Secretary." *The North Adams Transcript* 11 Feb 1919: 2. *Genealogy, Family Trees & Family History Records at Ancestry.com.* Web. 11 Feb 2013. <http://www.ancestry.com/>.

"E. S. Wilkinson Arrives Home." *The North Adams Transcript* 06 Aug 1919: 3. *Genealogy, Family Trees & Family History Records at Ancestry.com.* Web. 17 Mar 2013. <http://www.ancestry.com/>.

"Campaign Closes; Result Awaited." *The North Adams Transcript* 08 Dec 1924: 5. *Explore Historical Newspaper Archives Online.* Web. 27 Oct 2013. <http://newspaperarchive.com/>.

"Wilkinson Follows His Wife in Death." *The North Adams Transcript* 21 Apr 1926: 3. *Genealogy, Family Trees & Family History Records at Ancestry.com.* Web. 11 Feb 2013. <http://www.ancestry.com/>.

"Att. J. B. Boland to Run for Mayor." *The North Adams Transcript* 06 Aug 1926: 18. *Genealogy, Family Trees & Family History Records at Ancestry.com.* Web. 11 Feb 2013. <http://www.ancestry.com/>.

"Vote for Mayor in Former Years." *The North Adams Transcript* 16 Dec 1926: 2. *Explore Historical Newspaper Archives Online.* Web. 27 Oct 2013. <http://newspaperarchive.com/>.

"Donates Car for Visiting Nurse." *The North Adams Transcript* 10 Jan 1934: 2. *Explore Historical Newspaper Archives Online.* Web. 27 Oct 2013. <http://newspaperarchive.com/>.

"Community Chest Annual Meeting. Edward S. Wilkinson is Re-Elected President." *The North Adams Transcript* 29 Apr 1936: 2. *Genealogy, Family Trees & Family History Records at Ancestry.com.* Web. 17 Mar 2013. <http://www.ancestry.com/>.

"Edw. S. Wilkinson Dies; End Comes as He Sleeps." *The North Adams Transcript* 12 Jun 1939: 3. *Genealogy, Family Trees & Family History Records at Ancestry.com.* Web. 22 Sep 2011. <http://www.ancestry.com/>.

"Chamber Elects New Directors. Edward S. Wilkinson Whose Death Occurred Last Night Among 12." *The North Adams Transcript* 12 Jun 1939: 9. *Genealogy, Family Trees & Family History Records at Ancestry.com.* Web. 17 Mar 2013. <http://www.ancestry.com/>.

"E. S. Wilkinson Dies; Lauded as Civic Benefactor." *The Springfield Republican* 13 Jun 1939. 4. *The Republican Archives.* Web. 08 Oct 2012. <http://www.newslibrary.com/sites/un/>.

"Edw. S. Wilkinson is Laid to Rest." *The North Adams Transcript* 14 Jun 1939: 3. *Genealogy, Family Trees & Family History Records at Ancestry.com.* Web. 17 Mar 2013. <http://www.ancestry.com/>.

"Sand Springs Corp. Makes Assignment; Hope to Sell Plant." *The North Adams Transcript* 25 Apr 1953: 5. *Genealogy, Family Trees & Family History Records at Ancestry.com.* Web. 27 Oct 2013. <http://www.ancestry.com/>.

"Six Realty Sales Reported in Area." *The North Adams Transcript* 05 Jun 1971: 12. *Explore Historical Newspaper Archives Online.* Web. 27 Oct 2013. <http://newspaperarchive.com/>.

Chapter 8 (Mary Cordelia Houghton)

"Historical Society Annual. Executive Committee to Plan Something in Nature of Public Gathering." *The North Adams Transcript* 03 Nov 1903: 8. *Explore Historical Newspaper Archives Online*. Web. 08 Oct 2013. <http://newspaperarchive.com/>.

"Funerals of Tragic Automobile Accident Victims." *The Springfield Republican* 05 Aug 1914: 14. *The Republican Archives*. Web. 27 Oct 2011. <http://www.newslibrary.com/sites/un/>.

"Administrators Named. Will Handle Estate of Miss Mary C. Houghton – One Will on a Sheet of Writing Paper." *The Springfield Republican* 18 Nov 1914: 12. *The Republican Archives*. Web. 08 Oct 2012. <http://www.newslibrary.com/sites/un/>.

"Inventory of Houghton Estate." *The Springfield Republican* 09 Dec 1914: 14. *The Republican Archives*. Web. 27 Oct 2011. <http://www.newslibrary.com/sites/un/>.

Chapter 9 (The Man Known as John Widders)

"Bank Crumbled Under Load and Big Boiler Topples." *The North Adams Evening Transcript* 4 Jun 1903: 8. *Explore Historical Newspaper Archives Online*. Web. 08 Oct 2013. <http://newspaperarchive.com/>.

"Auto Tragedy Sequel. Chauffeur is a Suicide. John Widders Shoots Self." *The Springfield Republican* 03 Aug 1914: 16. *The Republican Archives*. Web. 26 Oct 2011. <http://www.newslibrary.com/sites/un/>.

"Vermont Notes- Chauffeur Who Drove Death Car Commits Suicide." *The Burlington Free Press and Times* 06 Aug 1914: 7. *Explore Historical Newspaper Archives Online*. Web. 08 Oct 2013. <http://newspaperarchive.com/>.

"Commonwealth May Get Estate." *The Springfield Republican* 15 Aug 1914: 14. *The Republican Archives*. Web. 08 Nov 2011. <http://www.newslibrary.com/sites/un/>.

"Lays Claim to Estate. Mrs. Henrietta Ostrander Believes She is Mother of the Late John Widders." *The Springfield Republican* 25 Sep 1914: 16. *The Republican Archives*. Web. 26 Oct 2011. <http://www.newslibrary.com/sites/un/>.

"Relatives of Winters Tell of Early History." *The North Adams Transcript* 23 Dec 1914: 3. *Explore Historical Newspaper Archives Online*. Web. 07 Oct 2013. <http://newspaperarchive.com/>.

"Winters Case Heard Today." *The North Adams Transcript* 29 Dec 1914: 2. *Explore Historical Newspaper Archives Online*. Web. 07 Oct 2013. <http://newspaperarchive.com/>.

"Hearing on Winters Will. Testimony Taken Regarding Estate of Former Houghton Coachman." *The Springfield Republican* 12 Mar 1915: 16. *The Republican Archives*. Web. 26 Oct 2011. <http://www.newslibrary.com/sites/un/>.

"United States Census, 1860," index, FamilySearch (https://familysearch.org/pal:/MM9.1.1/MC7S-KKM : accessed 27 Oct 2011), John Winters, , Rensselaer, New York; citing "1860 U.S. Federal Census - Population," Fold3.com; p. 34, family 738, NARA microfilm publication M653; FHL microfilm 803848.

Chapter 10 (Sybil Cady Hutton)

"A New Candidate. Henry A. Cady Will Take the Field on Nomination Papers." *The North Adams Transcript* 08 Oct 1896: 1. *Explore Historical Newspaper Archives Online*. Web. 17 Oct 2013. <http://newspaperarchive.com/>.

"Henry A. Cady Found Dead." *The North Adams Transcript* 30 Nov 1897: 1. *Genealogy, Family Trees & Family History Records at Ancestry.com*. Web. 25 Apr 2013. < http://www.ancestry.com/>.

"Henry A. Cady." *The North Adams Transcript* 01 Dec 1897: 1. *Genealogy, Family Trees & Family History Records at Ancestry.com.* Web. 24 Apr 2013. < http://www.ancestry.com/>.

"Furman-Cady. Marriage Service Performed at the Universalist Church of North Adams – Reception Followed." *Boston Globe* 17 Apr 1901: 2. *Boston Globe Archives* Web. 02 Apr 2013. <https://secure.pqarchiver.com/boston/advancedsearch.html>.

"Doctor's Wife Killed in Crash. Mrs. Robert L. Hutton Meet Death When Auto Goes Over Embankment." *New York Tribune* 02 Aug 1914: 10. *Genealogy, Family Trees & Family History Records at Ancestry.com.* Web. 12 Oct 2012. <http://www.ancestry.com/>.

"Funeral of Mrs. Hutton." *The Springfield Republican* 04 Aug 1914: 16. *The Republican Archives.* Web. 08 Nov 2011. <http://www.newslibrary.com/sites/un/>.

"Mrs. Cady's Funeral Saturday at 3 P.M. Body Will Arrive Here This Afternoon." *The North Adams Transcript* 13 Apr 1923: 20. *Explore Historical Newspaper Archives Online.* Web. 23 Oct 2013. <http://newspaperarchive.com/>.

"Miss Mary R. Cady Dies at Age 92." *The North Adams Transcript* 28 Dec 1948: 3. *Genealogy, Family Trees & Family History Records at Ancestry.com.* Web. 14 Apr 2013. <http://www.ancestry.com/>.

Chapter 11 (Houghton Mansion)

"Inquest on the Death of Ringwood." *The North Adams Transcript* 28 May 1895: 2. *Genealogy, Family Trees & Family History Records at Ancestry.com.* Web. 14 Sep 2011. <http://www.ancestry.com/>.

"Will Live in New York This Winter." *The North Adams Transcript* 15 Nov 1898: 5. *Genealogy, Family Trees & Family History Records at Ancestry.com.* Web. 10 Apr 2013. <http://www.ancestry.com/>.

"Houghton Residence Opened." *The North Adams Transcript* 22 Apr 1899: 1. *Genealogy, Family Trees & Family History Records at Ancestry.com.* Web. 16 Apr 2013. <http://www.ancestry.com/>.

"Stubborn Fire in Old Blackinton House." *The North Adams Transcript* 06 Jul 1906: 8. *Explore Historical Newspaper Archives Online.* Web. 07 Oct 2013. <http://newspaperarchive.com/>.

"North Adams Masons Complete Plans for Purchase of Houghton Mansion for Temple." *The Springfield Republican* 03 Aug 1927: 8. *The Republican Archives.* Web. 26 Oct 2011. <http://www.newslibrary.com/sites/un/>.

"Transfer is Made of Houghton Home." *The North Adams Transcript* 04 Aug 1927: 5. *Genealogy, Family Trees & Family History Records at Ancestry.com.* Web. 14 Mar 2013. <http://www.ancestry.com/>.

"Real Estate Deals May Begin 1928 Boom." *The Springfield Republican* 18 Jan 1928: 12. *The Republican Archives.* Web. 18 Jan 2011. <http://www.newslibrary.com/sites/un/>.

"Open House Observed at Proposed Temple. More than 1200 Masons and Families Visit Recently Acquired Mansion." *The Springfield Republican* 02 Feb 1928: 4. *The Republican Archives.* Web. 26 Oct 2011. <http://www.newslibrary.com/sites/un/>.

"Masonic Campaign Making Progress." *The North Adams Transcript* 14 Feb 1928: 14. *Explore Historical Newspaper Archives Online.* Web. 26 Oct 2013. <http://newspaperarchive.com/>.

"Permit to Construct $75,000 House Refused. Morris Gold Would Build 12-Family Apartment and Nine-Car Garage." *The Springfield Republican* 02 Mar 1928: 4. *The Republican Archives.* Web. 08 Oct 2011. <http://www.newslibrary.com/sites/un/>.

"Building Permits Granted." *The Springfield Republican* 31 Mar 1928: 4. *The Republican Archives.* Web. 27 Oct 2011. <http://www.newslibrary.com/sites/un/>.

"Installing Organ in Masonic Temple. Gift of J.D. Hunter as Memorial to Father." *The North Adams Transcript* 20 Jan 1929: 16. *Explore Historical Newspaper Archives Online*. Web. 23 Oct 2013. <http://newspaperarchive.com/>.

"Masonic Event April 5. Entire State Grand Lodge Expected at Temple Dedication." *The Springfield Republican* 08 Mar 1929: 14. *The Republican Archives*. Web. 26 Oct 2011. <http://www.newslibrary.com/sites/un/>.

"Lodge Hall in New Masonic Temple at North Adams Which Will be Dedicated This Week." *The Springfield* Sunday Union and Republican 31 Mar 1929: 4B. *The Republican Archives*. Web. 27 Oct 2011. <http://www.newslibrary.com/sites/un/>.

"Hundreds of Masons Gather for Dedication of Temple." *The North Adams Transcript* 06 Apr 1929: 7. *Genealogy, Family Trees & Family History Records at Ancestry.com*. Web. 14 Sep 2011. <http://www.ancestry.com/>.

"Oil Portrait of Houghton Hung." *The North Adams Transcript* 06 Apr 1929: 7. *Genealogy, Family Trees & Family History Records at Ancestry.com*. Web. 14 Sep 2011. <http://www.ancestry.com/>.

"Masonic Temple Damage is $2000. Fire Not a Serious One But Difficult for Firemen to Get Out." *The North Adams Transcript* 26 May 1934: 3. *Explore Historical Newspaper Archives Online*. Web. 24 Oct 2013. <http://newspaperarchive.com/>.

"Fire Damages Masonic Temple." *The North Adams Transcript* 20 Apr 1960: 1. *Explore Historical Newspaper Archives Online*. Web. 24 Oct 2013. <http://newspaperarchive.com/>.

"Long-Smoldering Fire Damages Masonic Temple." *The North Adams Transcript* 20 Apr 1960: 3. *Explore Historical Newspaper Archives Online*. Web. 24 Oct 2013. <http://newspaperarchive.com/>.

"Masonic Temple Blaze is Labeled as Spontaneous." *The Springfield* Republican 21 Apr 1960: 41. *The Republican Archives*. Web. 26 Oct 2011. <http://www.newslibrary.com/sites/un/>.

"Masonic Temple Fire Said Worst of 42 This Year." *The North Adams Transcript* 14 Jun 1960: 4. *Explore Historical Newspaper Archives Online*. Web. 24 Oct 2013. <http://newspaperarchive.com/>.

"Greylock Lodge Names Millberry its New Master." *The North Adams Transcript* 14 Sep 1960: 2. *Explore Historical Newspaper Archives Online*. Web. 24 Oct 2013. <http://newspaperarchive.com/>.

"Historic Nomination." *The Springfield* Union 01 Dec 1982: 11. *The Republican Archives*. Web. 08 Nov 2011. <http://www.newslibrary.com/sites/un/>

About the Author

David Raby founded a paranormal investigation group based in Connecticut. He serves as Lead Investigator, Case Manager and Technical Manager. He is the author of dozens of online articles that deal with the paranormal.

A native of Meriden, Connecticut, he graduated from Central Connecticut State University. He received his degree in environmental science with a concentration in biology. Although it was history, especially the stories of fellow human beings, that has a special place in his heart.

A Roman Catholic, David refuses to apologize for his personal faith in God and an afterlife. He is adamant that science has not and could not disprove God and spirits.

David works in a marketing department overseeing the production of television, radio, online and print media as well as the development of websites.

He currently resides in Manchester, Connecticut with his wife and two children.